CYBERPUNK TREK!

WITH ROBOTMAN® AND HIS EVIL TWIN, BRUCE

BY JIM MEDDICK

TOPPER BOOKS

AN IMPRINT OF PHAROS BOOKS • A SCRIPPS HOWARD COMPANY

NEW YORK

FIRST PUBLISHED IN 1990.

ROBOTMAN COMIC STRIPS: © 1987, 1988, 1989 UNITED FEATURE SYNDICATE, INC.

LIBRARY OF CONGRESS CARD CATALOG NUMBER 89-043710

PHAROS ISBN: 0-88687-485-8

PRINTED IN THE UNITED STATES OF AMERICA

TOPPER BOOKS
AN IMPRINT OF PHAROS BOOKS
A SCRIPPS HOWARD COMPANY
200 PARK AVENUE
NEW YORK, NY 10166
10 9 8 7 6 5 4 3 2 1

COVER & INTERIOR DESIGN: JIM MEDDICK

CONTENTS

INTRODUCTION

AS A VULCAN, I CANNOT LIE. I WAS PRESENTED WITH THE FOLLOWING COMPILATION OF SEQUENTIAL COMIC PANELS AND WAS ASKED TO COMPOSE A SUITABLE INTRODUCTION. I READ THEM. I REREAD THEM. I EVEN WENT SO FAR AS TO RUN A TRICORDER CHECK ON THEM. AS OF THIS WRITING, I CANNOT UNDERSTAND A SINGLE PANEL.

DURING MY INVESTIGATIONS, I PRESENTED SOME OF THE MATERIAL TO DR. LEONARD McCOY. HE STUDIED IT, THEN INDICATED IT HAD HUMOROUS CONTENT. AT FIRST, I INTERPRETED THIS POSITIVELY, THEN I RECALLED THAT THE DOCTOR HAS BEEN KNOWN TO LAUGH CONVULSIVELY WHILE READING "ZIGGY." (IF MEMORY SERVES, ONE SUCH EPISODE ENDED WITH LIQUID DAIRY PRODUCTS BEING EJECTED FROM McCOY'S NOSE.)

HERE I MIGHT OFFER ONE ADDITIONAL ANECDOTE (WHILE NOT DIRECTLY RELEVANT, IT MAY, NEVERTHELESS, SHED LIGHT ON THE TOPIC). THROUGH MY EXPERIENCE IN WRITING THIS INTRODUCTION, I HAD THE OPPORTUNITY TO MEET WITH THE BOOK'S AUTHOR AND AFTER A SERIES OF EVENTS TOO DETAILED TO OUTLINE HERE,* I ENTERED INTO A VULCAN MIND MELD WITH HIM. WITHOUT LAUNCHING INTO A LENGTHY FREUDIAN ANALYSIS, LET IT SUFFICE TO SAY THE AUTHOR OF THIS BOOK DEMONSTRATES A MENTAL FUNCTIONING THAT, BY COMPARISON, MAKES DR. McCOY'S MIND LOOK AS STABLE AS A DESKTOP PC.

FINALLY, GIVEN THIS COLLECTIVE DATA, I MUST COME TO THE REGRETTABLE CONCLUSION THAT THE MATERIAL CONTAINED HEREIN, IS, WITHOUT EXCEPTION, ILLOGICAL, NON-LINEAR, AND UNIQUELY DEVOID OF INTELLECTUAL VALIDITY. IN SHORT, IT EXHIBITS ALL THE QUALITIES NECESSARY FOR HUMAN CONSUMPTION.

LIVE LONG AND PROSPER,

Mr. Spock

MR. SPOCK

---

*VERY BRIEFLY, IT INVOLVED AN EXCESSIVELY COMPETITIVE GAME OF TWENTY QUESTIONS.

THE ORIGIN

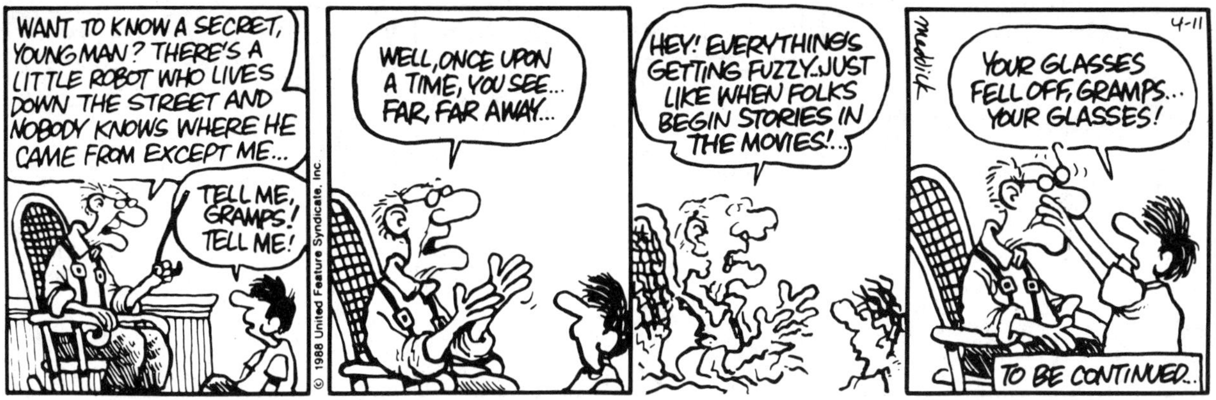
WANT TO KNOW A SECRET, YOUNG MAN? THERE'S A LITTLE ROBOT WHO LIVES DOWN THE STREET AND NOBODY KNOWS WHERE HE CAME FROM EXCEPT ME...
TELL ME, GRAMPS! TELL ME!
© 1988 United Feature Syndicate, Inc.
WELL, ONCE UPON A TIME, YOU SEE... FAR, FAR AWAY...
HEY! EVERYTHING'S GETTING FUZZY..JUST LIKE WHEN FOLKS BEGIN STORIES IN THE MOVIES!...
meddick
4-11
YOUR GLASSES FELL OFF, GRAMPS... YOUR GLASSES!
TO BE CONTINUED...

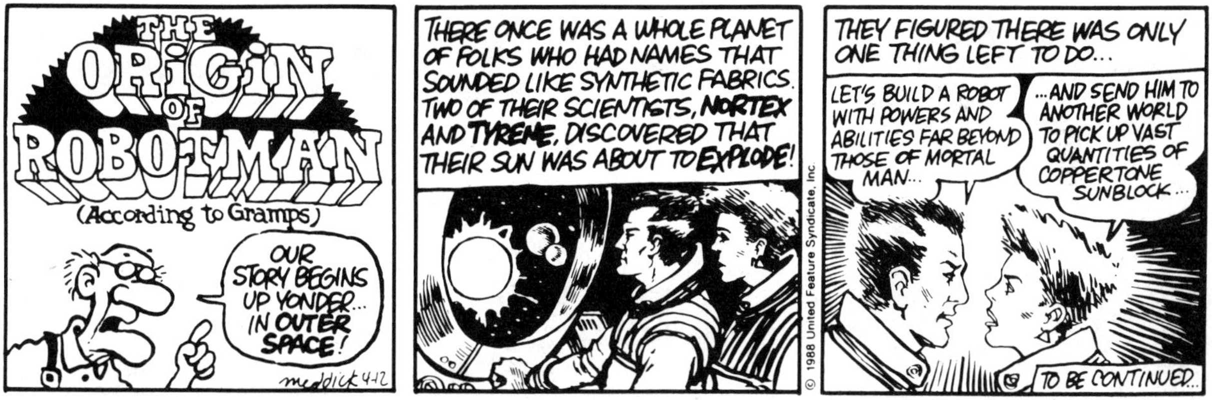
THE ORIGIN OF ROBOTMAN
(According to Gramps)
OUR STORY BEGINS UP YONDER... IN OUTER SPACE!
meddick 4-12
THERE ONCE WAS A WHOLE PLANET OF FOLKS WHO HAD NAMES THAT SOUNDED LIKE SYNTHETIC FABRICS. TWO OF THEIR SCIENTISTS, NORTEX AND TYRENE, DISCOVERED THAT THEIR SUN WAS ABOUT TO EXPLODE!
© 1988 United Feature Syndicate, Inc.
THEY FIGURED THERE WAS ONLY ONE THING LEFT TO DO...
LET'S BUILD A ROBOT WITH POWERS AND ABILITIES FAR BEYOND THOSE OF MORTAL MAN...
...AND SEND HIM TO ANOTHER WORLD TO PICK UP VAST QUANTITIES OF COPPERTONE SUNBLOCK...
TO BE CONTINUED...

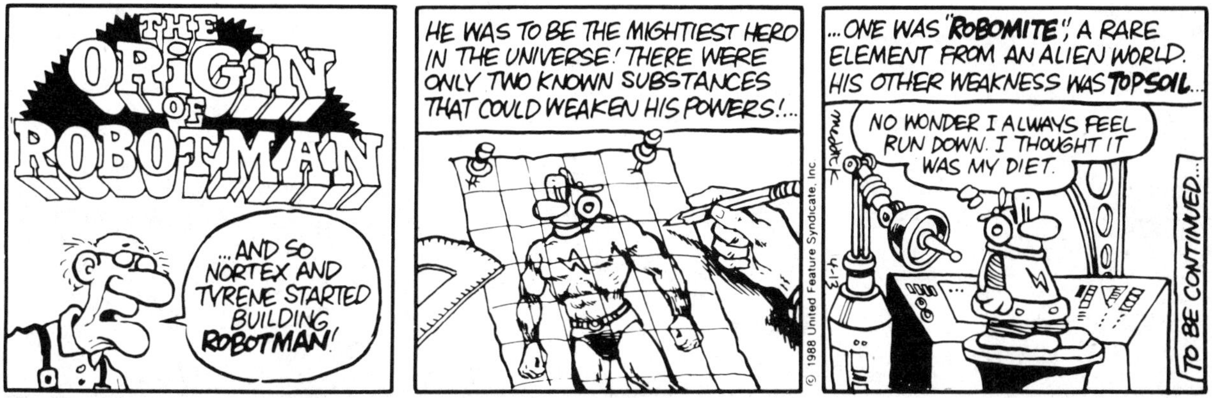
THE ORIGIN OF ROBOTMAN
...AND SO NORTEX AND TYRENE STARTED BUILDING ROBOTMAN!
HE WAS TO BE THE MIGHTIEST HERO IN THE UNIVERSE! THERE WERE ONLY TWO KNOWN SUBSTANCES THAT COULD WEAKEN HIS POWERS!...
© 1988 United Feature Syndicate, Inc.
...ONE WAS "ROBOMITE", A RARE ELEMENT FROM AN ALIEN WORLD. HIS OTHER WEAKNESS WAS TOPSOIL...
meddick
4-13
NO WONDER I ALWAYS FEEL RUN DOWN. I THOUGHT IT WAS MY DIET.
TO BE CONTINUED...

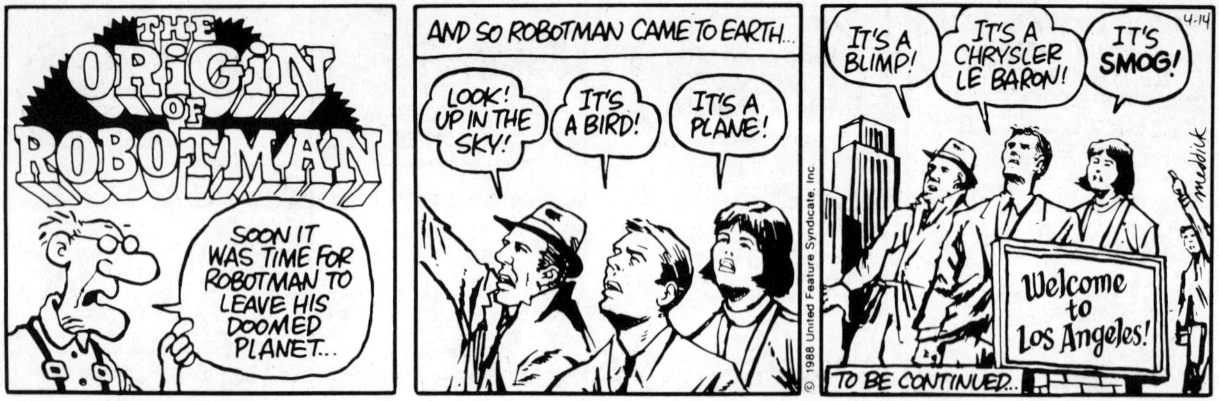
THE ORIGIN OF ROBOTMAN
SOON IT WAS TIME FOR ROBOTMAN TO LEAVE HIS DOOMED PLANET...
AND SO ROBOTMAN CAME TO EARTH...
LOOK! UP IN THE SKY!
IT'S A BIRD!
IT'S A PLANE!
© 1988 United Feature Syndicate, Inc
4-14
IT'S A BLIMP!
IT'S A CHRYSLER LE BARON!
IT'S SMOG!
Welcome to Los Angeles!
meddick
TO BE CONTINUED...

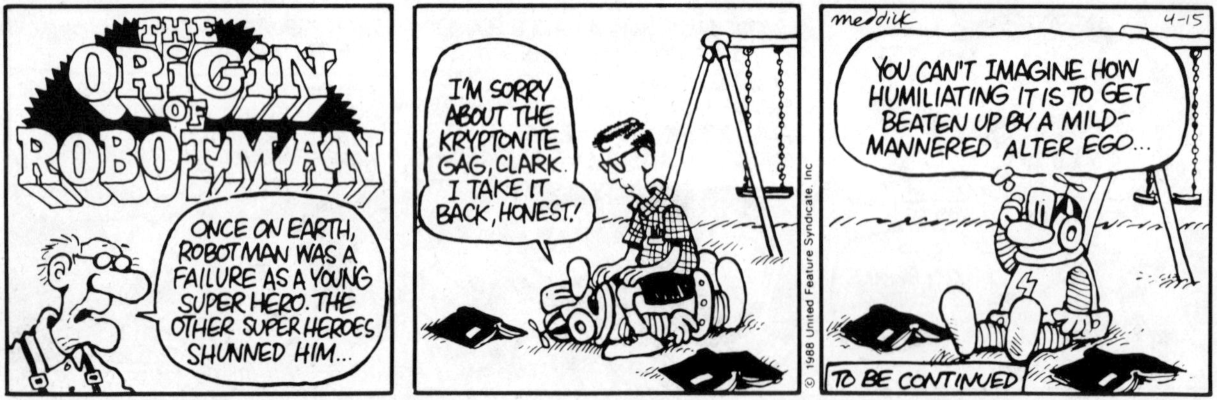
THE ORIGIN OF ROBOTMAN
ONCE ON EARTH, ROBOTMAN WAS A FAILURE AS A YOUNG SUPER HERO. THE OTHER SUPER HEROES SHUNNED HIM...
I'M SORRY ABOUT THE KRYPTONITE GAG, CLARK. I TAKE IT BACK, HONEST!
© 1988 United Feature Syndicate, Inc
meddick
4-15
YOU CAN'T IMAGINE HOW HUMILIATING IT IS TO GET BEATEN UP BY A MILD-MANNERED ALTER EGO...
TO BE CONTINUED

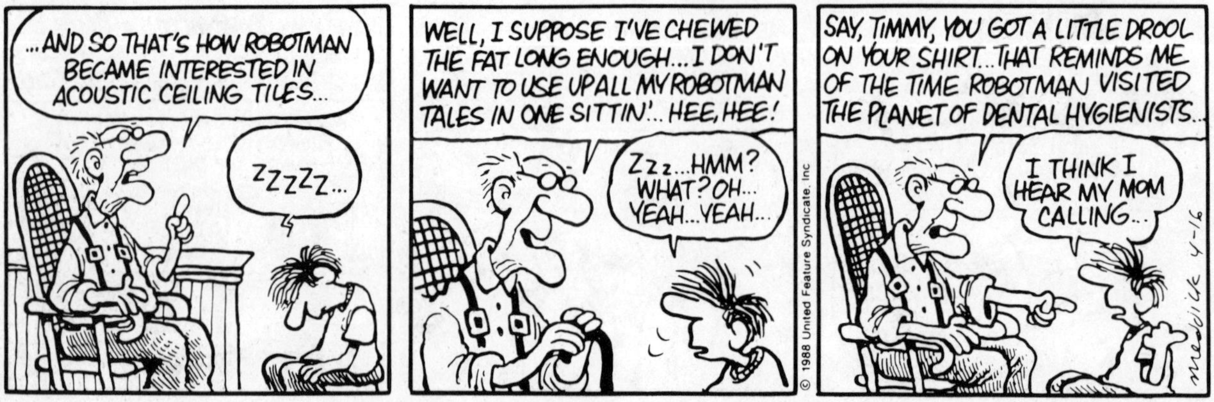
...AND SO THAT'S HOW ROBOTMAN BECAME INTERESTED IN ACOUSTIC CEILING TILES...
ZZZZZ...
WELL, I SUPPOSE I'VE CHEWED THE FAT LONG ENOUGH... I DON'T WANT TO USE UP ALL MY ROBOTMAN TALES IN ONE SITTIN'... HEE, HEE!
Zzz...HMM? WHAT? OH... YEAH... YEAH...
© 1988 United Feature Syndicate, Inc
SAY, TIMMY, YOU GOT A LITTLE DROOL ON YOUR SHIRT... THAT REMINDS ME OF THE TIME ROBOTMAN VISITED THE PLANET OF DENTAL HYGIENISTS...
I THINK I HEAR MY MOM CALLING...
meddick 4-16

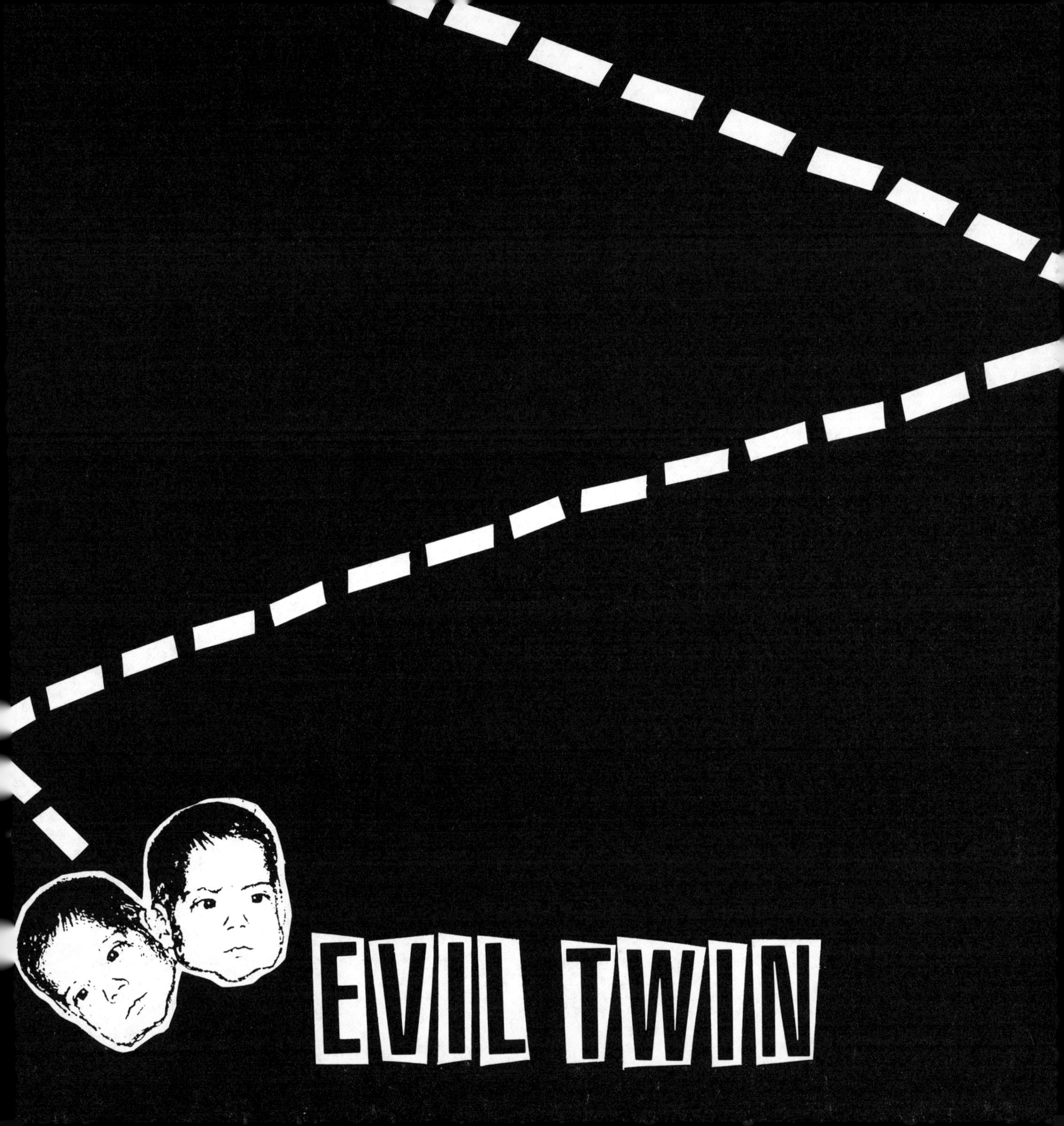
EVIL TWIN

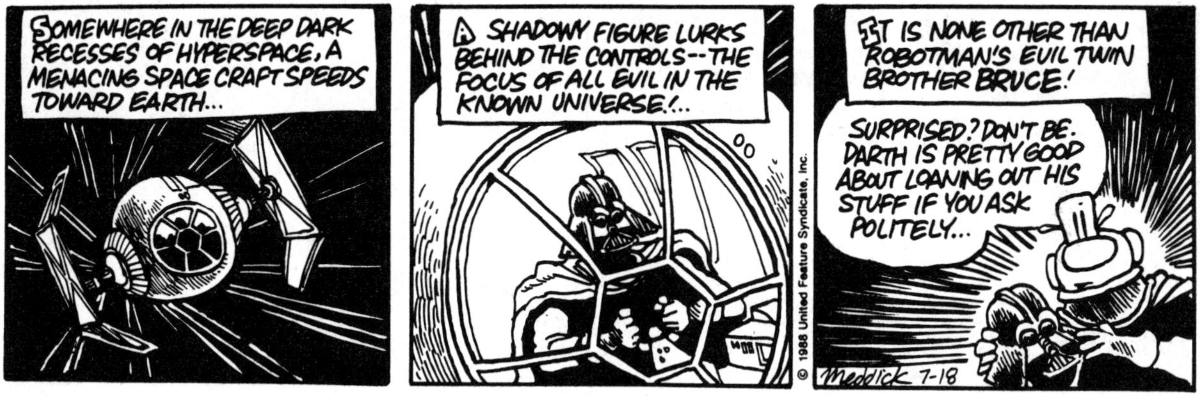
SOMEWHERE IN THE DEEP DARK RECESSES OF HYPERSPACE, A MENACING SPACE CRAFT SPEEDS TOWARD EARTH...
A SHADOWY FIGURE LURKS BEHIND THE CONTROLS--THE FOCUS OF ALL EVIL IN THE KNOWN UNIVERSE!...
IT IS NONE OTHER THAN ROBOTMAN'S EVIL TWIN BROTHER BRUCE!
SURPRISED? DON'T BE. DARTH IS PRETTY GOOD ABOUT LOANING OUT HIS STUFF IF YOU ASK POLITELY...
© 1988 United Feature Syndicate, Inc.
Meddick 7-18

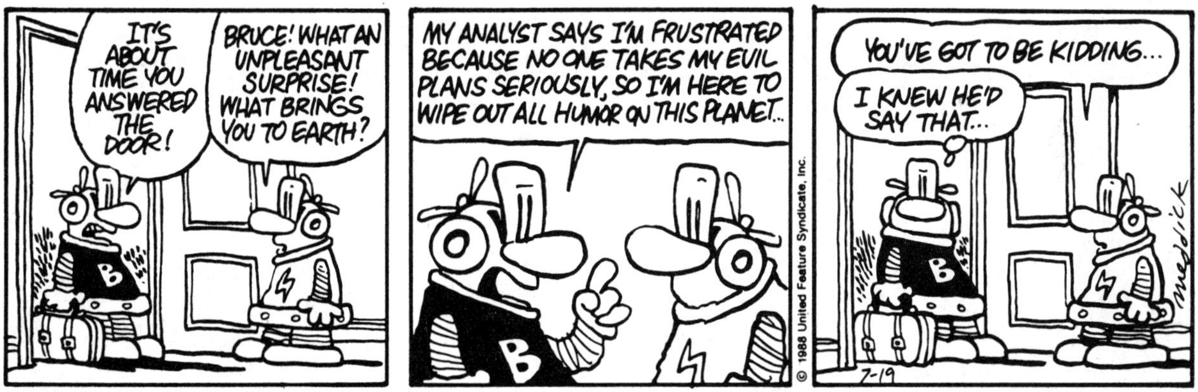
IT'S ABOUT TIME YOU ANSWERED THE DOOR!
BRUCE! WHAT AN UNPLEASANT SURPRISE! WHAT BRINGS YOU TO EARTH?
MY ANALYST SAYS I'M FRUSTRATED BECAUSE NO ONE TAKES MY EVIL PLANS SERIOUSLY, SO I'M HERE TO WIPE OUT ALL HUMOR ON THIS PLANET...
© 1988 United Feature Syndicate, Inc.
YOU'VE GOT TO BE KIDDING...
I KNEW HE'D SAY THAT...
Meddick
7-19

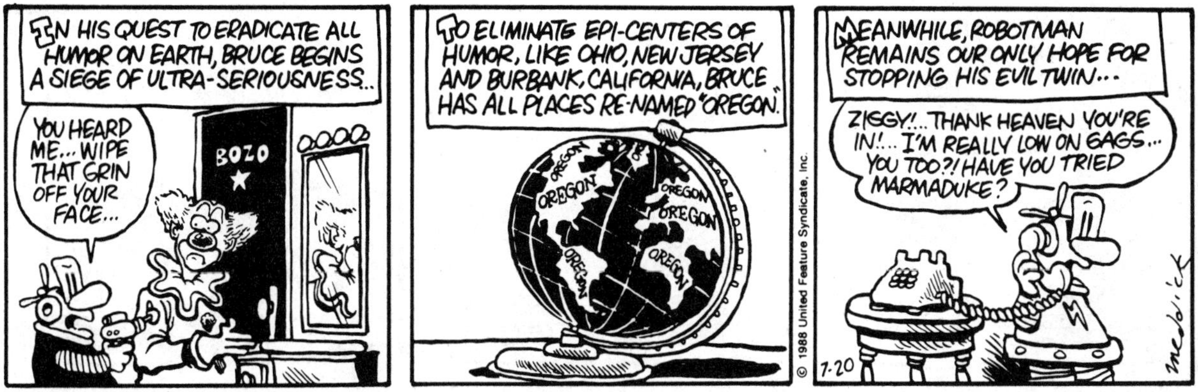
IN HIS QUEST TO ERADICATE ALL HUMOR ON EARTH, BRUCE BEGINS A SIEGE OF ULTRA-SERIOUSNESS...
YOU HEARD ME... WIPE THAT GRIN OFF YOUR FACE...
BOZO
TO ELIMINATE EPI-CENTERS OF HUMOR, LIKE OHIO, NEW JERSEY AND BURBANK, CALIFORNIA, BRUCE HAS ALL PLACES RE-NAMED "OREGON."
OREGON
OREGON
OREGON
OREGON
OREGON
OREGON
© 1988 United Feature Syndicate, Inc.
MEANWHILE, ROBOTMAN REMAINS OUR ONLY HOPE FOR STOPPING HIS EVIL TWIN...
ZIGGY!... THANK HEAVEN YOU'RE IN!... I'M REALLY LOW ON GAGS... YOU TOO?! HAVE YOU TRIED MARMADUKE?
Meddick
7-20

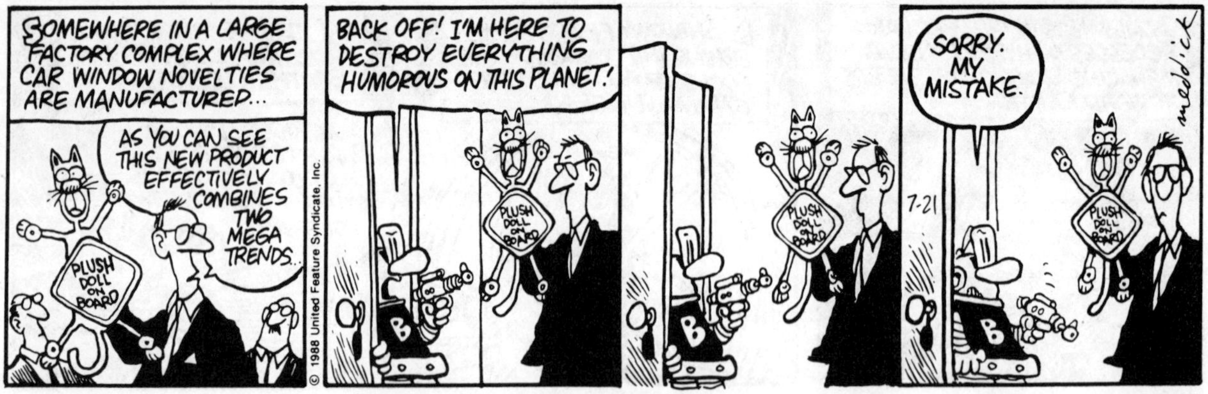
SOMEWHERE IN A LARGE FACTORY COMPLEX WHERE CAR WINDOW NOVELTIES ARE MANUFACTURED...
AS YOU CAN SEE THIS NEW PRODUCT EFFECTIVELY COMBINES TWO MEGA TRENDS...
PLUSH DOLL ON BOARD
© 1988 United Feature Syndicate, Inc.
BACK OFF! I'M HERE TO DESTROY EVERYTHING HUMOROUS ON THIS PLANET!
7-21
SORRY. MY MISTAKE.

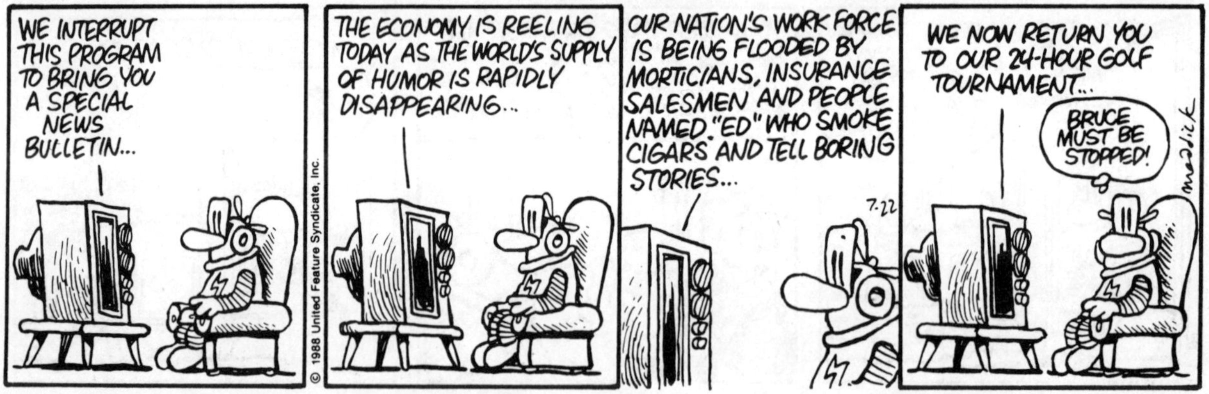
WE INTERRUPT THIS PROGRAM TO BRING YOU A SPECIAL NEWS BULLETIN...
© 1988 United Feature Syndicate, Inc.
THE ECONOMY IS REELING TODAY AS THE WORLD'S SUPPLY OF HUMOR IS RAPIDLY DISAPPEARING...
OUR NATION'S WORK FORCE IS BEING FLOODED BY MORTICIANS, INSURANCE SALESMEN AND PEOPLE NAMED "ED" WHO SMOKE CIGARS AND TELL BORING STORIES...
7-22
WE NOW RETURN YOU TO OUR 24-HOUR GOLF TOURNAMENT...
BRUCE MUST BE STOPPED!

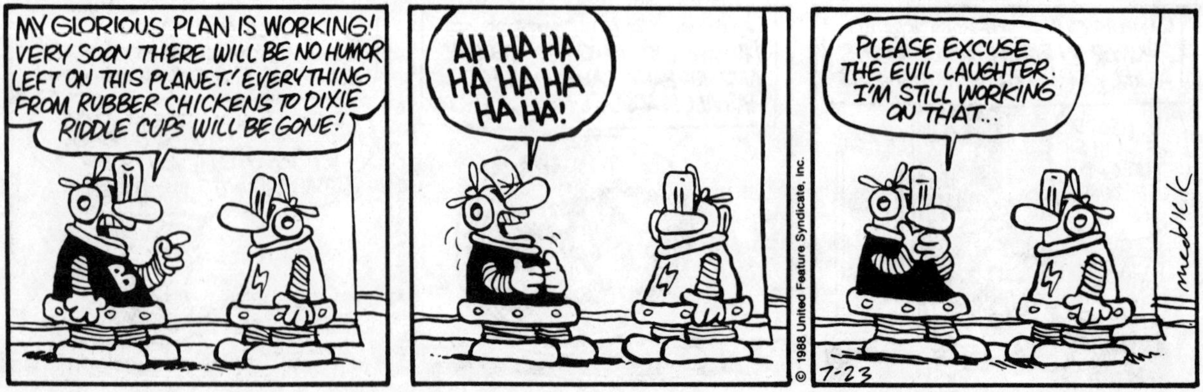
MY GLORIOUS PLAN IS WORKING! VERY SOON THERE WILL BE NO HUMOR LEFT ON THIS PLANET! EVERYTHING FROM RUBBER CHICKENS TO DIXIE RIDDLE CUPS WILL BE GONE!
AH HA HA HA HA HA HA HA!
© 1988 United Feature Syndicate, Inc.
PLEASE EXCUSE THE EVIL LAUGHTER. I'M STILL WORKING ON THAT...
7-23

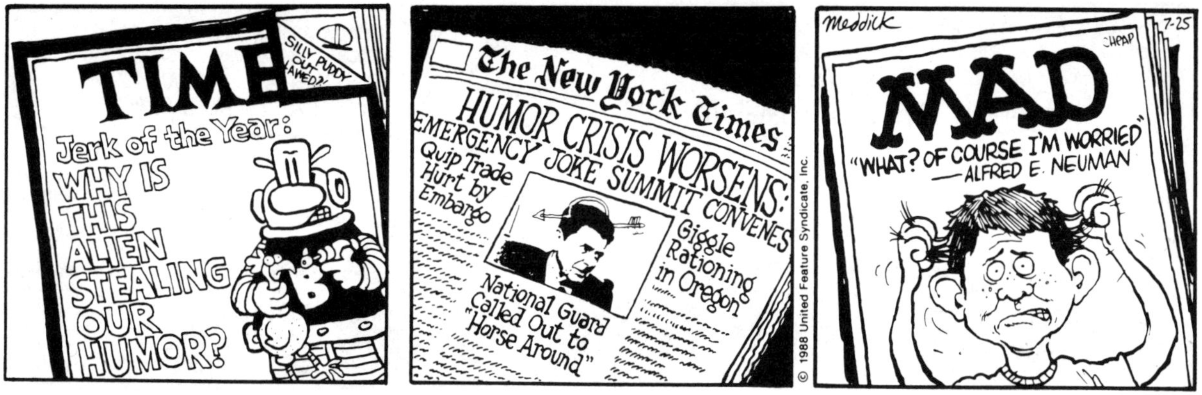
TIME
SILLY PUDDY OUTLAWED?!
Jerk of the Year:
WHY IS THIS ALIEN STEALING OUR HUMOR?
The New York Times
HUMOR CRISIS WORSENS: EMERGENCY JOKE SUMMIT CONVENES
Quip Trade Hurt by Embargo
Giggle Rationing in Oregon
National Guard Called Out to "Horse Around"
© 1988 United Feature Syndicate, Inc.
Meddick 7-25
MAD
CHEAP
"WHAT? OF COURSE I'M WORRIED"
—ALFRED E. NEUMAN

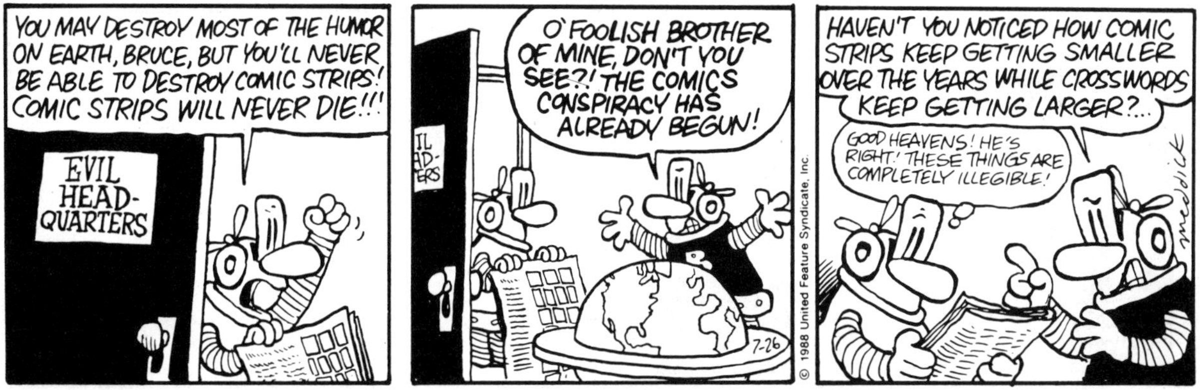
YOU MAY DESTROY MOST OF THE HUMOR ON EARTH, BRUCE, BUT YOU'LL NEVER BE ABLE TO DESTROY COMIC STRIPS! COMIC STRIPS WILL NEVER DIE!!!
EVIL HEAD-QUARTERS
O' FOOLISH BROTHER OF MINE, DON'T YOU SEE?! THE COMICS CONSPIRACY HAS ALREADY BEGUN!
7-26
© 1988 United Feature Syndicate, Inc.
HAVEN'T YOU NOTICED HOW COMIC STRIPS KEEP GETTING SMALLER OVER THE YEARS WHILE CROSSWORDS KEEP GETTING LARGER?...
GOOD HEAVENS! HE'S RIGHT! THESE THINGS ARE COMPLETELY ILLEGIBLE!
meddick

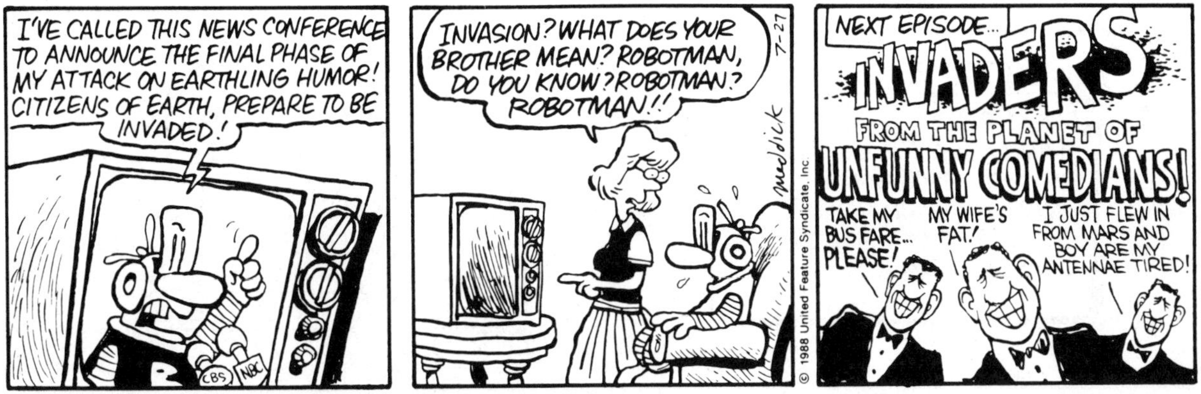
I'VE CALLED THIS NEWS CONFERENCE TO ANNOUNCE THE FINAL PHASE OF MY ATTACK ON EARTHLING HUMOR! CITIZENS OF EARTH, PREPARE TO BE INVADED!
CBS
NBC
INVASION? WHAT DOES YOUR BROTHER MEAN? ROBOTMAN, DO YOU KNOW? ROBOTMAN? ROBOTMAN!!
7-27
meddick
© 1988 United Feature Syndicate, Inc.
NEXT EPISODE...
INVADERS
FROM THE PLANET OF
UNFUNNY COMEDIANS!
TAKE MY BUS FARE... PLEASE!
MY WIFE'S FAT!
I JUST FLEW IN FROM MARS AND BOY ARE MY ANTENNAE TIRED!

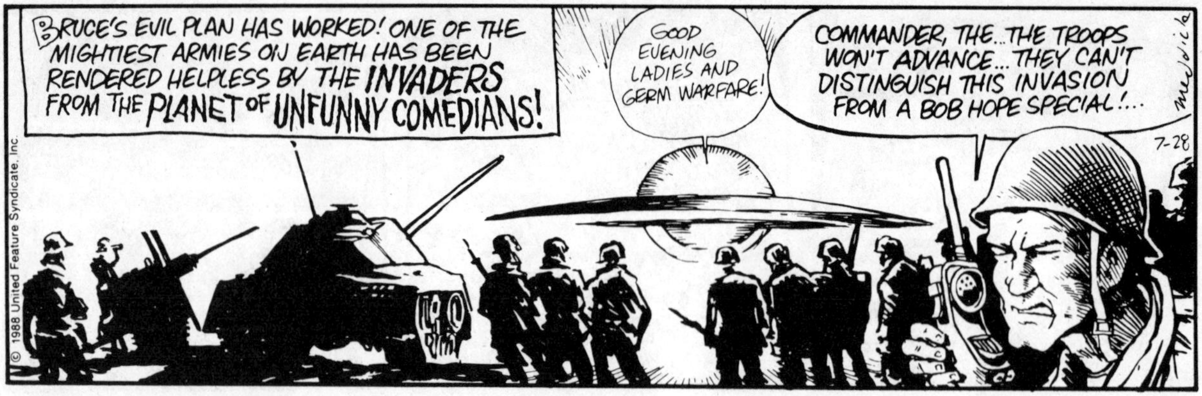
BRUCE'S EVIL PLAN HAS WORKED! ONE OF THE MIGHTIEST ARMIES ON EARTH HAS BEEN RENDERED HELPLESS BY THE INVADERS FROM THE PLANET OF UNFUNNY COMEDIANS!
GOOD EVENING LADIES AND GERM WARFARE!
COMMANDER, THE... THE TROOPS WON'T ADVANCE... THEY CAN'T DISTINGUISH THIS INVASION FROM A BOB HOPE SPECIAL!...
meddick
7-28
© 1988 United Feature Syndicate, Inc.

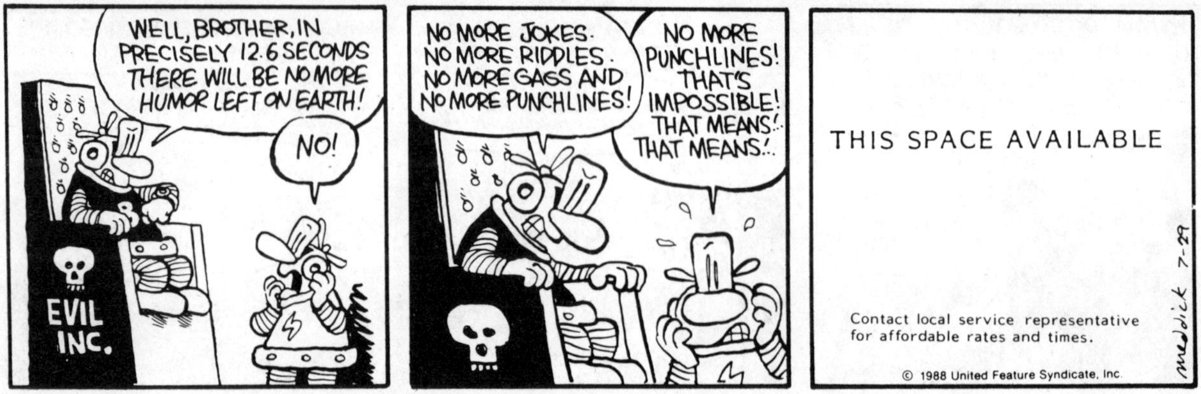
WELL, BROTHER, IN PRECISELY 12.6 SECONDS THERE WILL BE NO MORE HUMOR LEFT ON EARTH!
NO!
EVIL INC.
NO MORE JOKES. NO MORE RIDDLES. NO MORE GAGS AND NO MORE PUNCHLINES!
NO MORE PUNCHLINES! THAT'S IMPOSSIBLE! THAT MEANS!.. THAT MEANS!..
THIS SPACE AVAILABLE
Contact local service representative for affordable rates and times.
© 1988 United Feature Syndicate, Inc.
meddick 7-29

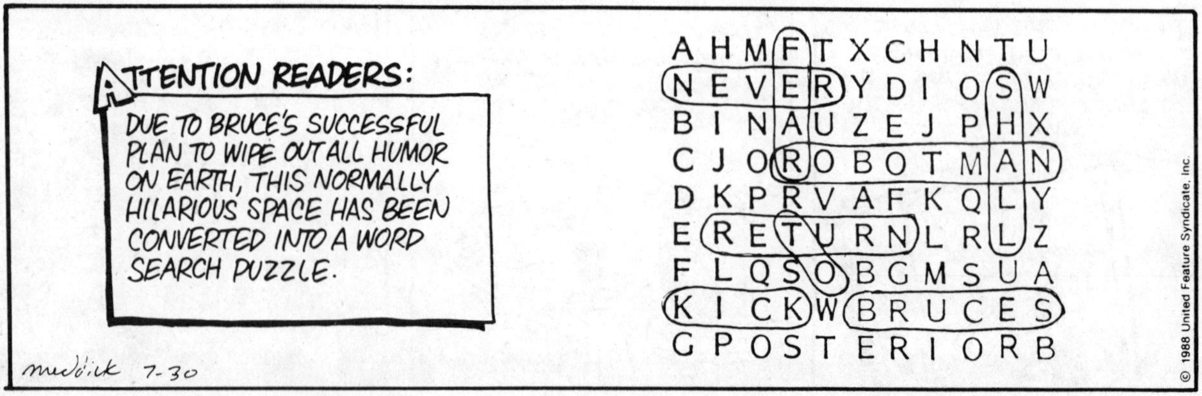
ATTENTION READERS:
DUE TO BRUCE'S SUCCESSFUL PLAN TO WIPE OUT ALL HUMOR ON EARTH, THIS NORMALLY HILARIOUS SPACE HAS BEEN CONVERTED INTO A WORD SEARCH PUZZLE.
A H M F T X C H N T U
N E V E R Y D I O S W
B I N A U Z E J P H X
C J O R O B O T M A N
D K P R V A F K Q L Y
E R E T U R N L R L Z
F L Q S O B G M S U A
K I C K W B R U C E S
G P O S T E R I O R B
meddick 7-30
© 1988 United Feature Syndicate, Inc.

STAR TREK

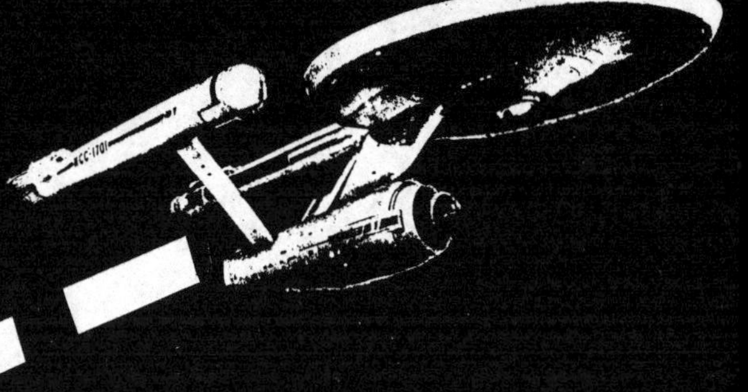

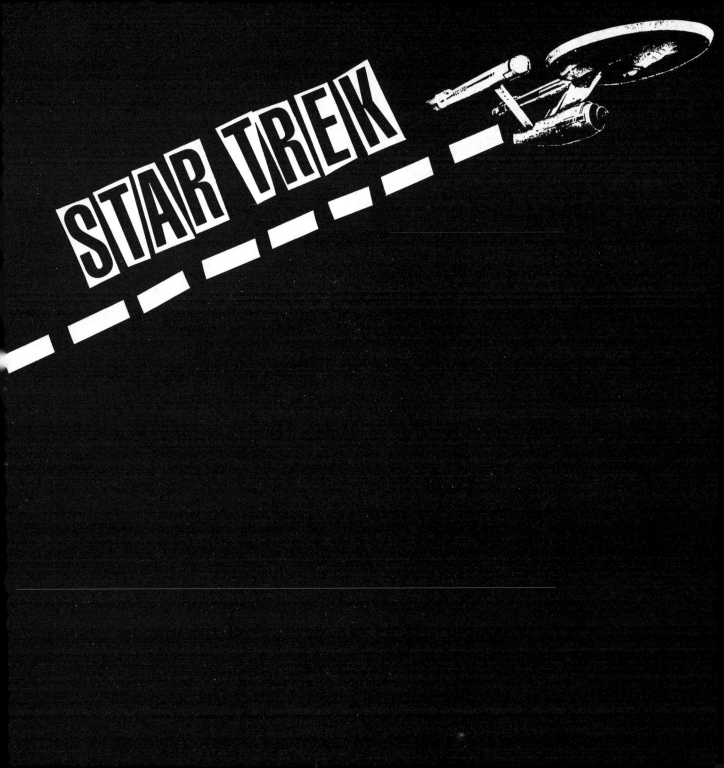

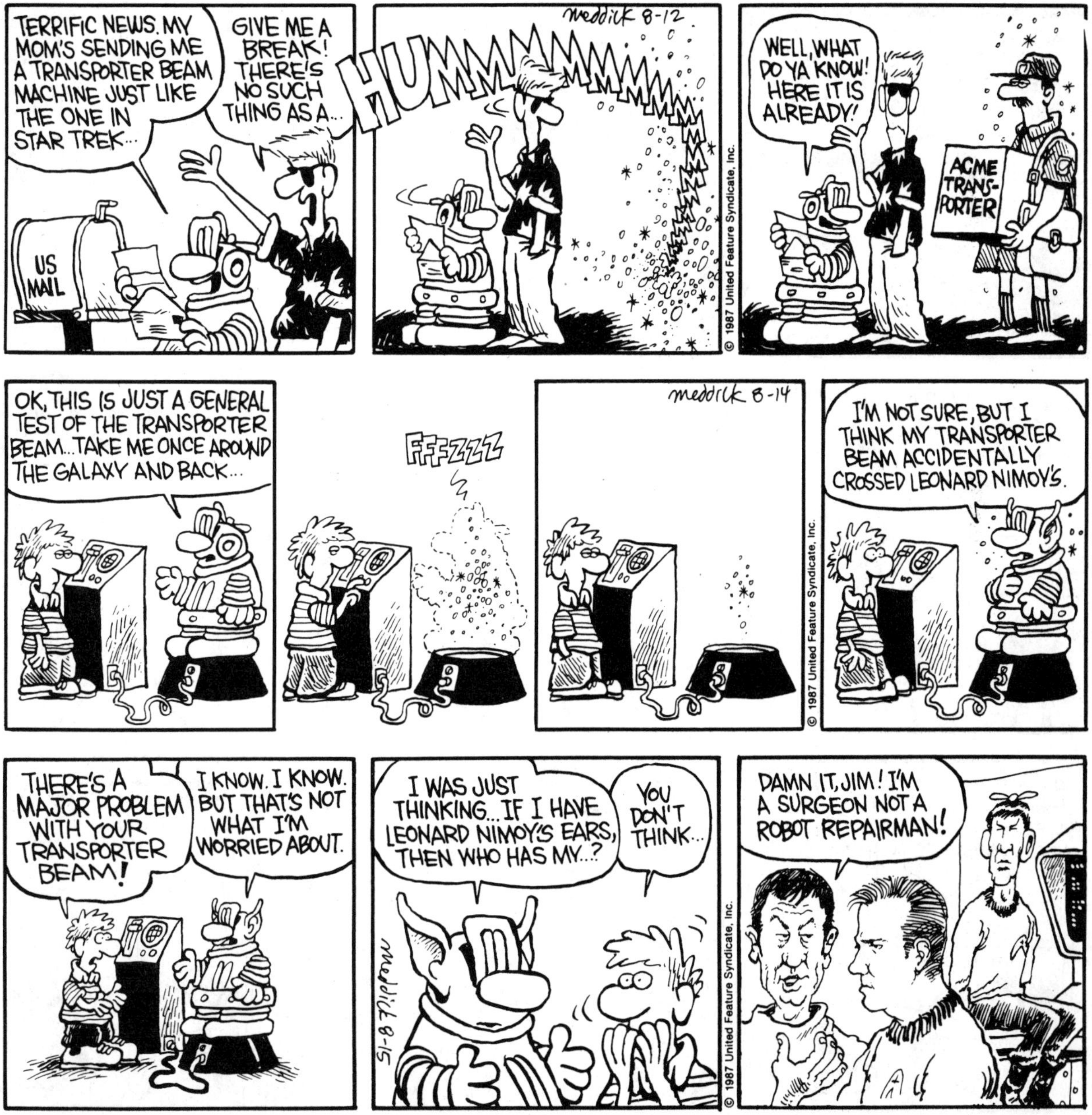
TERRIFIC NEWS. MY MOM'S SENDING ME A TRANSPORTER BEAM MACHINE JUST LIKE THE ONE IN STAR TREK...
GIVE ME A BREAK! THERE'S NO SUCH THING AS A...
US MAIL
meddick 8-12
HUMMMMMMMMMMMMMM
© 1987 United Feature Syndicate, Inc.
WELL, WHAT DO YA KNOW! HERE IT IS ALREADY!
ACME TRANSPORTER
OK, THIS IS JUST A GENERAL TEST OF THE TRANSPORTER BEAM... TAKE ME ONCE AROUND THE GALAXY AND BACK...
FFFZZZZ
meddick 8-14
© 1987 United Feature Syndicate, Inc.
I'M NOT SURE, BUT I THINK MY TRANSPORTER BEAM ACCIDENTALLY CROSSED LEONARD NIMOY'S.
THERE'S A MAJOR PROBLEM WITH YOUR TRANSPORTER BEAM!
I KNOW. I KNOW. BUT THAT'S NOT WHAT I'M WORRIED ABOUT.
meddick 8-15
I WAS JUST THINKING... IF I HAVE LEONARD NIMOY'S EARS, THEN WHO HAS MY...?
YOU DON'T THINK...
© 1987 United Feature Syndicate, Inc.
DAMN IT, JIM! I'M A SURGEON NOT A ROBOT REPAIRMAN!

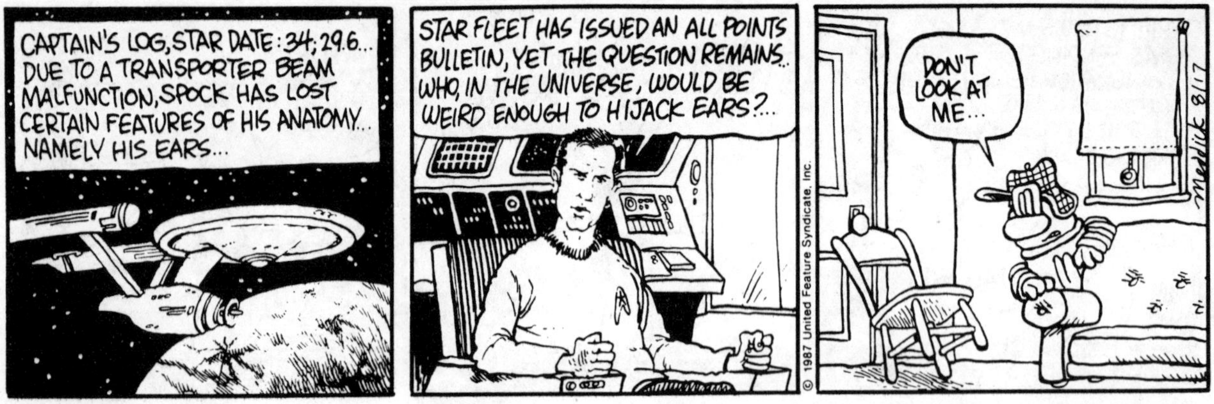
CAPTAIN'S LOG, STAR DATE: 34; 29.6... DUE TO A TRANSPORTER BEAM MALFUNCTION, SPOCK HAS LOST CERTAIN FEATURES OF HIS ANATOMY... NAMELY HIS EARS...
STAR FLEET HAS ISSUED AN ALL POINTS BULLETIN, YET THE QUESTION REMAINS... WHO, IN THE UNIVERSE, WOULD BE WEIRD ENOUGH TO HIJACK EARS?...
© 1987 United Feature Syndicate, Inc.
DON'T LOOK AT ME...
meddick 8/17

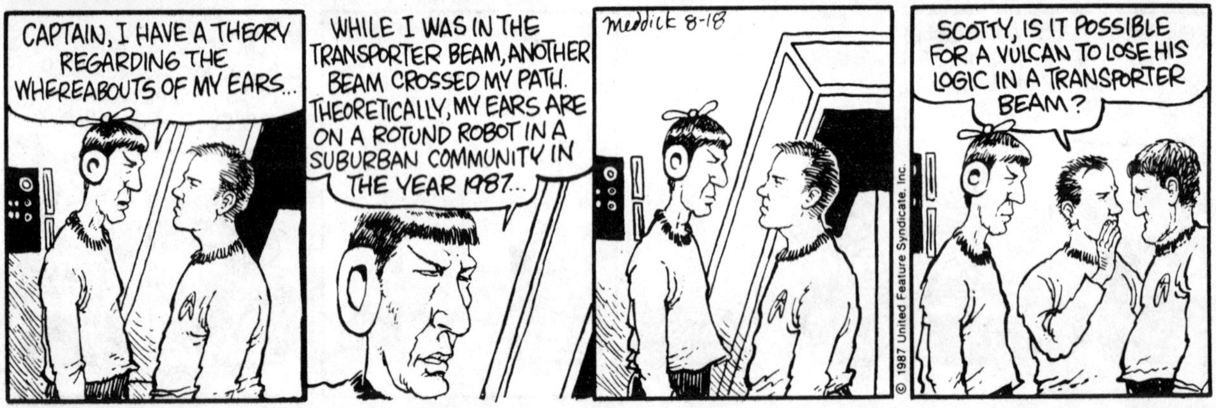
CAPTAIN, I HAVE A THEORY REGARDING THE WHEREABOUTS OF MY EARS...
WHILE I WAS IN THE TRANSPORTER BEAM, ANOTHER BEAM CROSSED MY PATH. THEORETICALLY, MY EARS ARE ON A ROTUND ROBOT IN A SUBURBAN COMMUNITY IN THE YEAR 1987...
meddick 8-18
© 1987 United Feature Syndicate, Inc.
SCOTTY, IS IT POSSIBLE FOR A VULCAN TO LOSE HIS LOGIC IN A TRANSPORTER BEAM?

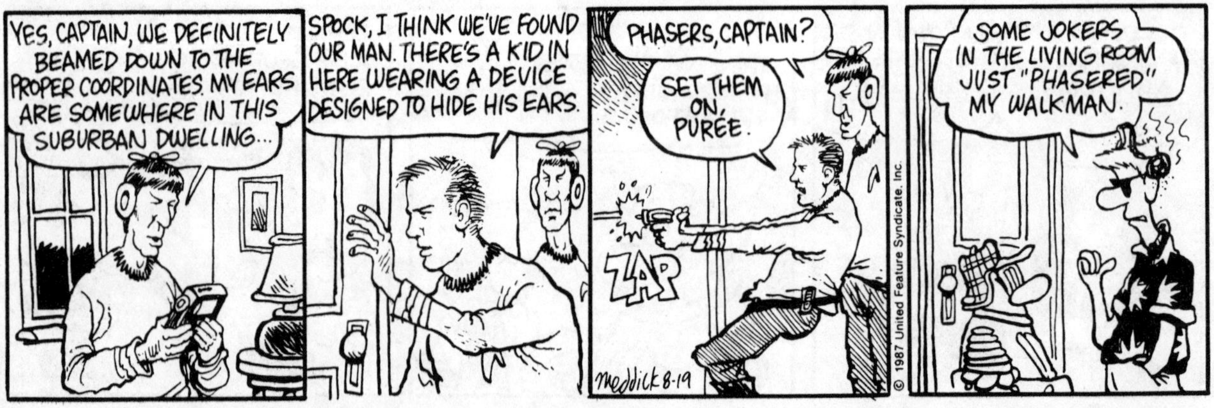
YES, CAPTAIN, WE DEFINITELY BEAMED DOWN TO THE PROPER COORDINATES. MY EARS ARE SOMEWHERE IN THIS SUBURBAN DWELLING...
SPOCK, I THINK WE'VE FOUND OUR MAN. THERE'S A KID IN HERE WEARING A DEVICE DESIGNED TO HIDE HIS EARS.
PHASERS, CAPTAIN?
SET THEM ON, PURÉE.
ZAP
meddick 8-19
© 1987 United Feature Syndicate, Inc.
SOME JOKERS IN THE LIVING ROOM JUST "PHASERED" MY WALKMAN.

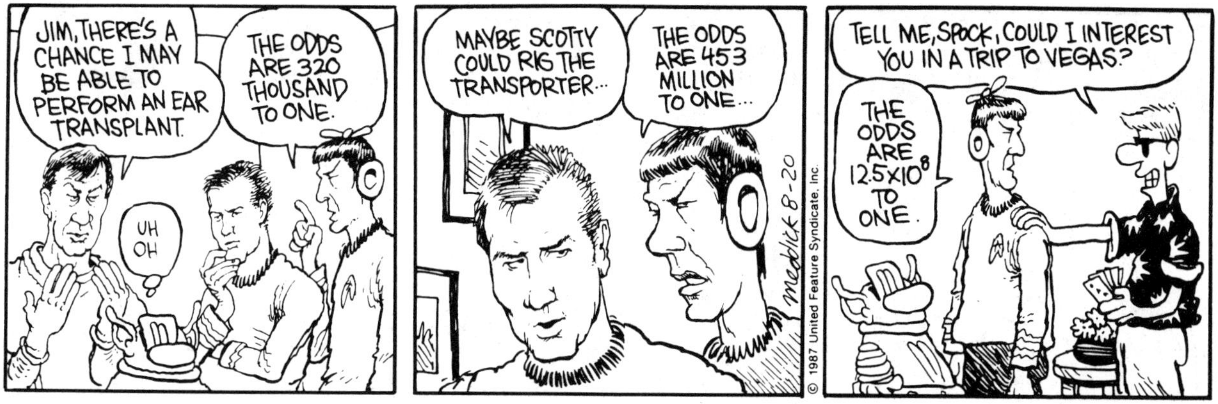
JIM, THERE'S A CHANCE I MAY BE ABLE TO PERFORM AN EAR TRANSPLANT.
THE ODDS ARE 320 THOUSAND TO ONE.
UH OH
MAYBE SCOTTY COULD RIG THE TRANSPORTER...
THE ODDS ARE 453 MILLION TO ONE...
meddick 8-20
© 1987 United Feature Syndicate, Inc.
TELL ME, SPOCK, COULD I INTEREST YOU IN A TRIP TO VEGAS?
THE ODDS ARE 12.5×10^8 TO ONE.

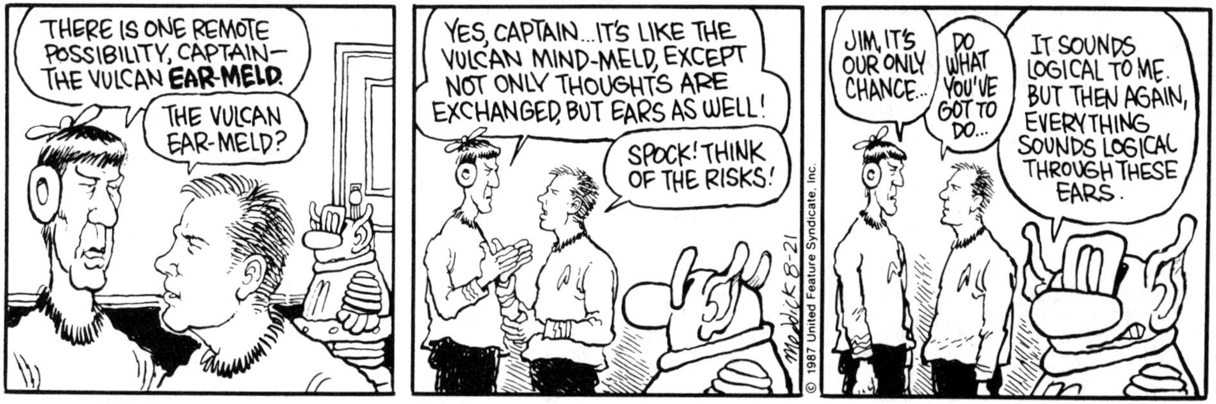
THERE IS ONE REMOTE POSSIBILITY, CAPTAIN— THE VULCAN **EAR-MELD**.
THE VULCAN EAR-MELD?
YES, CAPTAIN... IT'S LIKE THE VULCAN MIND-MELD, EXCEPT NOT ONLY THOUGHTS ARE EXCHANGED, BUT EARS AS WELL!
SPOCK! THINK OF THE RISKS!
meddick 8-21
© 1987 United Feature Syndicate, Inc.
JIM, IT'S OUR ONLY CHANCE...
DO WHAT YOU'VE GOT TO DO...
IT SOUNDS LOGICAL TO ME. BUT THEN AGAIN, EVERYTHING SOUNDS LOGICAL THROUGH THESE EARS.

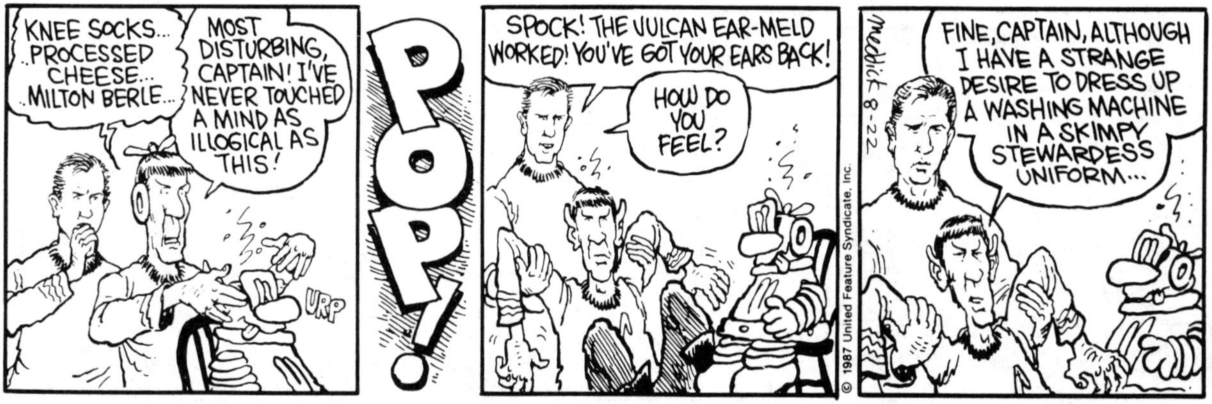
KNEE SOCKS... ..PROCESSED CHEESE... ..MILTON BERLE...
MOST DISTURBING, CAPTAIN! I'VE NEVER TOUCHED A MIND AS ILLOGICAL AS THIS!
URP
POP!
SPOCK! THE VULCAN EAR-MELD WORKED! YOU'VE GOT YOUR EARS BACK!
HOW DO YOU FEEL?
© 1987 United Feature Syndicate, Inc.
meddick 8-22
FINE, CAPTAIN, ALTHOUGH I HAVE A STRANGE DESIRE TO DRESS UP A WASHING MACHINE IN A SKIMPY STEWARDESS UNIFORM...

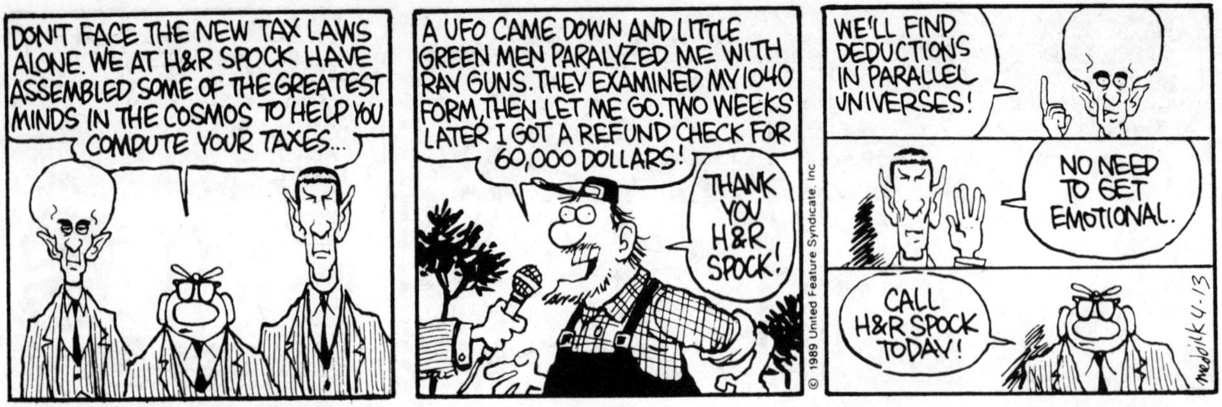
DON'T FACE THE NEW TAX LAWS ALONE. WE AT H&R SPOCK HAVE ASSEMBLED SOME OF THE GREATEST MINDS IN THE COSMOS TO HELP YOU COMPUTE YOUR TAXES...
A UFO CAME DOWN AND LITTLE GREEN MEN PARALYZED ME WITH RAY GUNS. THEY EXAMINED MY 1040 FORM, THEN LET ME GO. TWO WEEKS LATER I GOT A REFUND CHECK FOR 60,000 DOLLARS!
THANK YOU H&R SPOCK!
© 1989 United Feature Syndicate, Inc
WE'LL FIND DEDUCTIONS IN PARALLEL UNIVERSES!
NO NEED TO GET EMOTIONAL.
CALL H&R SPOCK TODAY!

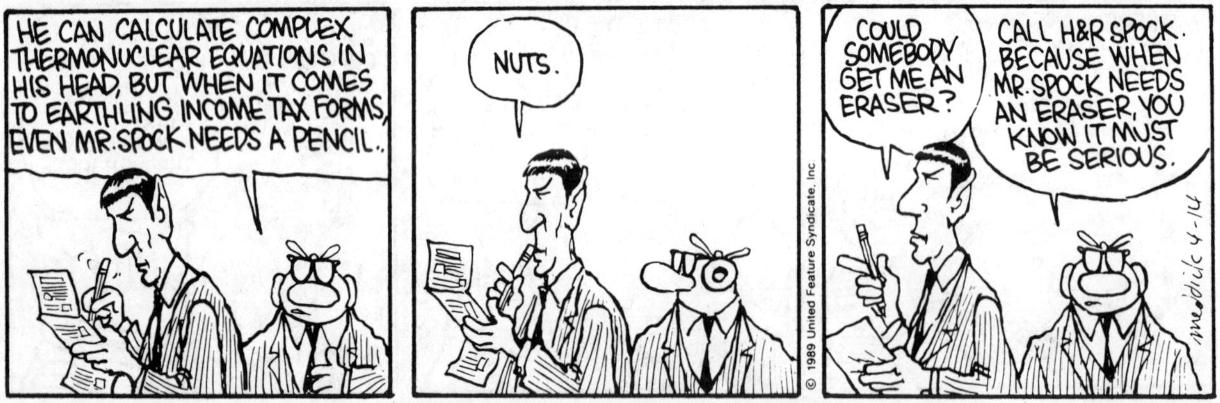
HE CAN CALCULATE COMPLEX THERMONUCLEAR EQUATIONS IN HIS HEAD, BUT WHEN IT COMES TO EARTHLING INCOME TAX FORMS, EVEN MR. SPOCK NEEDS A PENCIL..
NUTS.
© 1989 United Feature Syndicate, Inc.
COULD SOMEBODY GET ME AN ERASER?
CALL H&R SPOCK. BECAUSE WHEN MR. SPOCK NEEDS AN ERASER, YOU KNOW IT MUST BE SERIOUS.

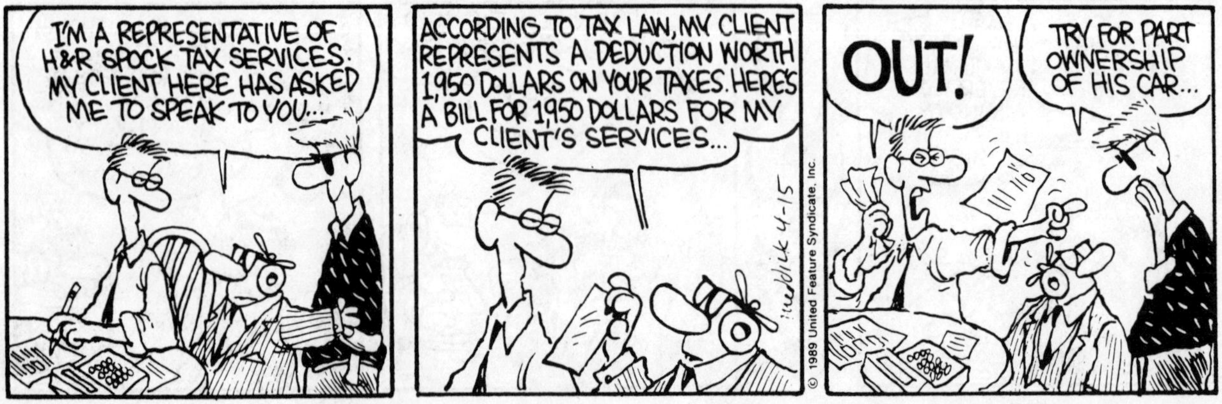
I'M A REPRESENTATIVE OF H&R SPOCK TAX SERVICES. MY CLIENT HERE HAS ASKED ME TO SPEAK TO YOU...
ACCORDING TO TAX LAW, MY CLIENT REPRESENTS A DEDUCTION WORTH 1,950 DOLLARS ON YOUR TAXES. HERE'S A BILL FOR 1,950 DOLLARS FOR MY CLIENT'S SERVICES...
© 1989 United Feature Syndicate, Inc.
OUT!
TRY FOR PART OWNERSHIP OF HIS CAR...

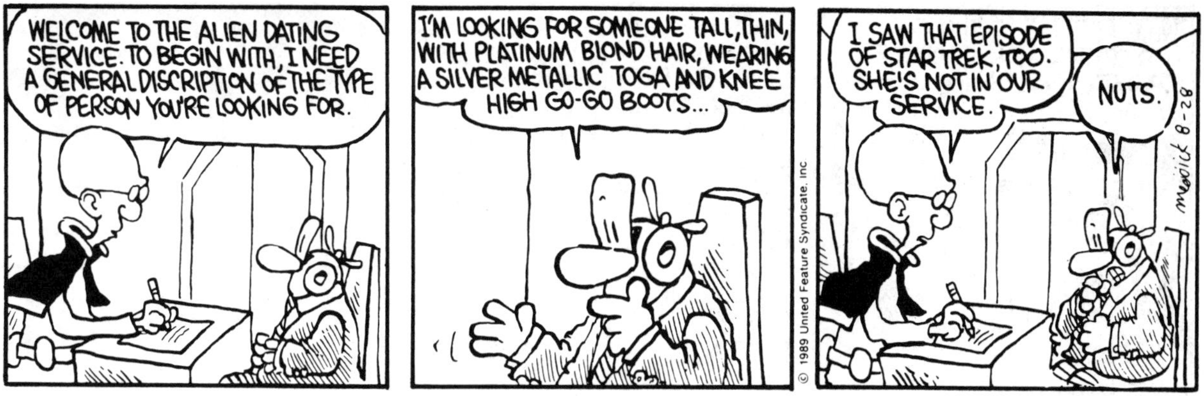
WELCOME TO THE ALIEN DATING SERVICE. TO BEGIN WITH, I NEED A GENERAL DISCRIPTION OF THE TYPE OF PERSON YOU'RE LOOKING FOR.
I'M LOOKING FOR SOMEONE TALL, THIN, WITH PLATINUM BLOND HAIR, WEARING A SILVER METALLIC TOGA AND KNEE HIGH GO-GO BOOTS...
I SAW THAT EPISODE OF STAR TREK, TOO. SHE'S NOT IN OUR SERVICE.
NUTS.
meddick 8-28

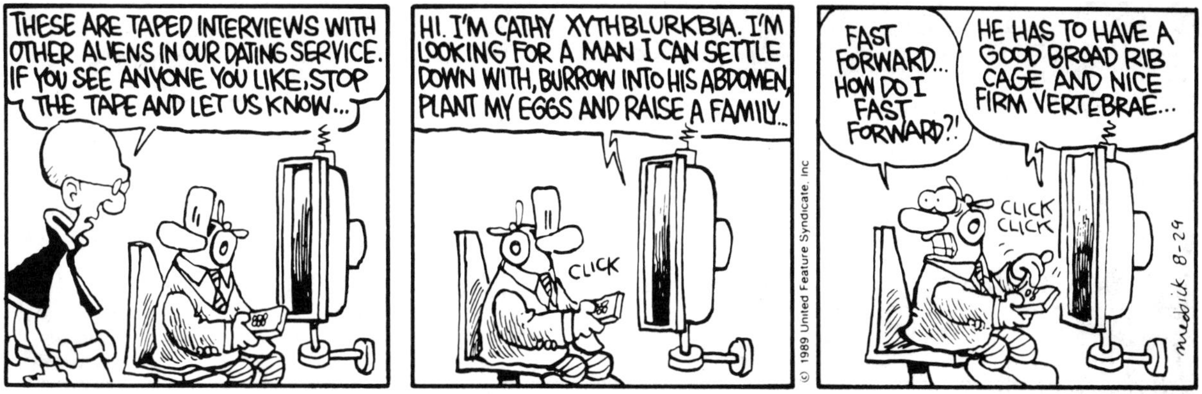
THESE ARE TAPED INTERVIEWS WITH OTHER ALIENS IN OUR DATING SERVICE. IF YOU SEE ANYONE YOU LIKE, STOP THE TAPE AND LET US KNOW...
HI. I'M CATHY XYTHBLURKBIA. I'M LOOKING FOR A MAN I CAN SETTLE DOWN WITH, BURROW INTO HIS ABDOMEN, PLANT MY EGGS AND RAISE A FAMILY...
CLICK
FAST FORWARD... HOW DO I FAST FORWARD?!
HE HAS TO HAVE A GOOD BROAD RIB CAGE AND NICE FIRM VERTEBRAE...
CLICK CLICK
meddick 8-29

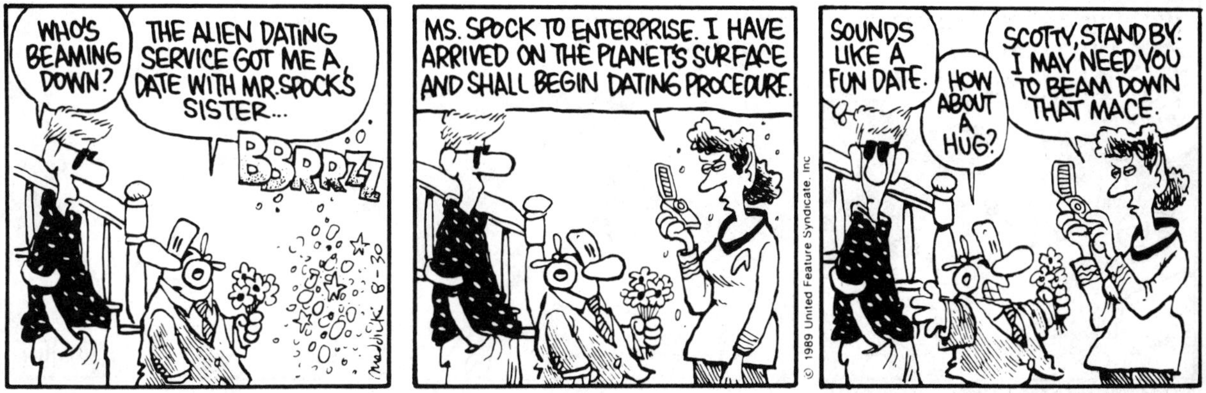
WHO'S BEAMING DOWN?
THE ALIEN DATING SERVICE GOT ME A DATE WITH MR. SPOCK'S SISTER...
BBRRZZ
meddick 8-30
MS. SPOCK TO ENTERPRISE. I HAVE ARRIVED ON THE PLANET'S SURFACE AND SHALL BEGIN DATING PROCEDURE.
SOUNDS LIKE A FUN DATE.
HOW ABOUT A HUG?
SCOTTY, STAND BY. I MAY NEED YOU TO BEAM DOWN THAT MACE.

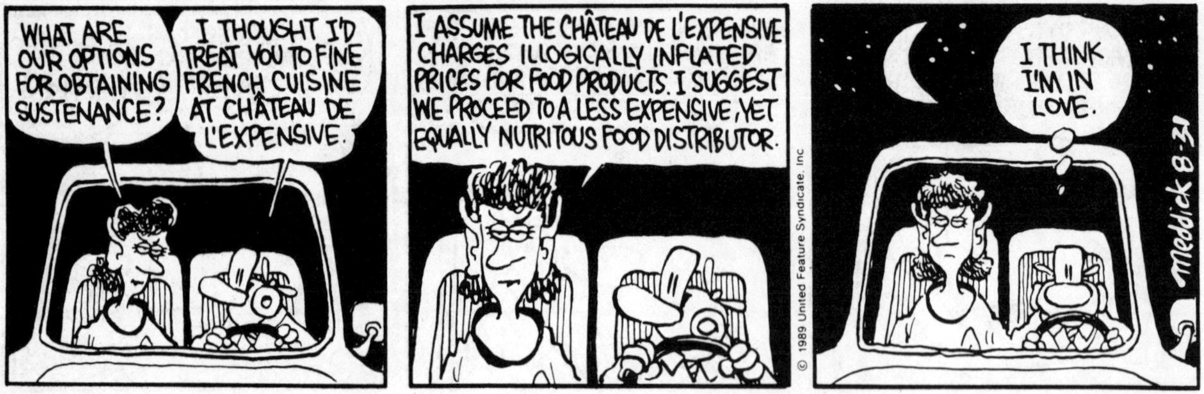
WHAT ARE OUR OPTIONS FOR OBTAINING SUSTENANCE?
I THOUGHT I'D TREAT YOU TO FINE FRENCH CUISINE AT CHÂTEAU DE L'EXPENSIVE.
I ASSUME THE CHÂTEAU DE L'EXPENSIVE CHARGES ILLOGICALLY INFLATED PRICES FOR FOOD PRODUCTS. I SUGGEST WE PROCEED TO A LESS EXPENSIVE, YET EQUALLY NUTRITOUS FOOD DISTRIBUTOR.
© 1989 United Feature Syndicate, Inc
I THINK I'M IN LOVE.
Meddick 8-31

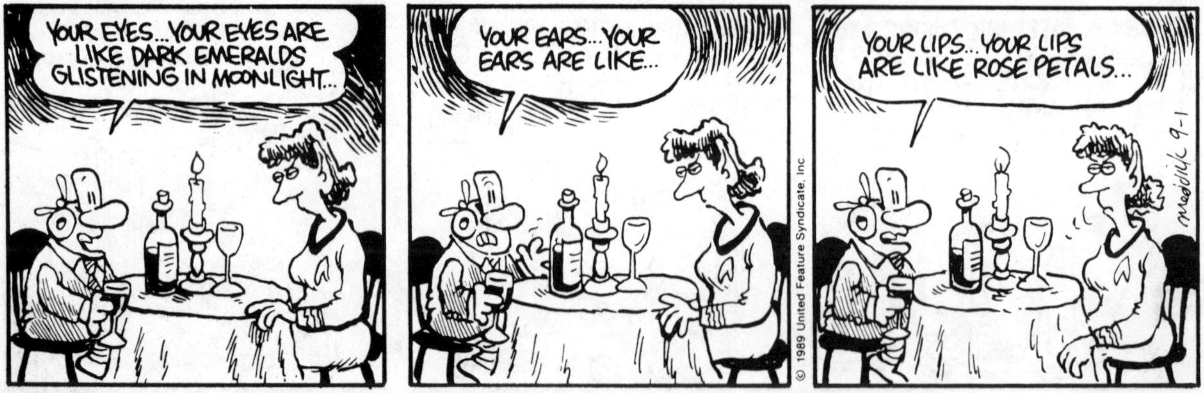
YOUR EYES... YOUR EYES ARE LIKE DARK EMERALDS GLISTENING IN MOONLIGHT...
YOUR EARS... YOUR EARS ARE LIKE...
© 1989 United Feature Syndicate, Inc
YOUR LIPS... YOUR LIPS ARE LIKE ROSE PETALS...
Meddick 9-1

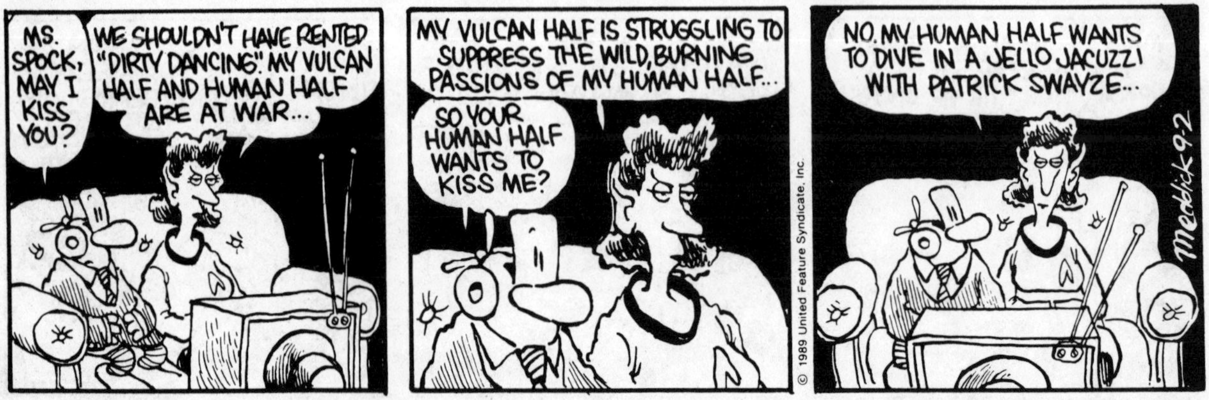
MS. SPOCK, MAY I KISS YOU?
WE SHOULDN'T HAVE RENTED "DIRTY DANCING." MY VULCAN HALF AND HUMAN HALF ARE AT WAR...
MY VULCAN HALF IS STRUGGLING TO SUPPRESS THE WILD, BURNING PASSIONS OF MY HUMAN HALF...
SO YOUR HUMAN HALF WANTS TO KISS ME?
© 1989 United Feature Syndicate, Inc
NO. MY HUMAN HALF WANTS TO DIVE IN A JELLO JACUZZI WITH PATRICK SWAYZE...
Meddick 9-2

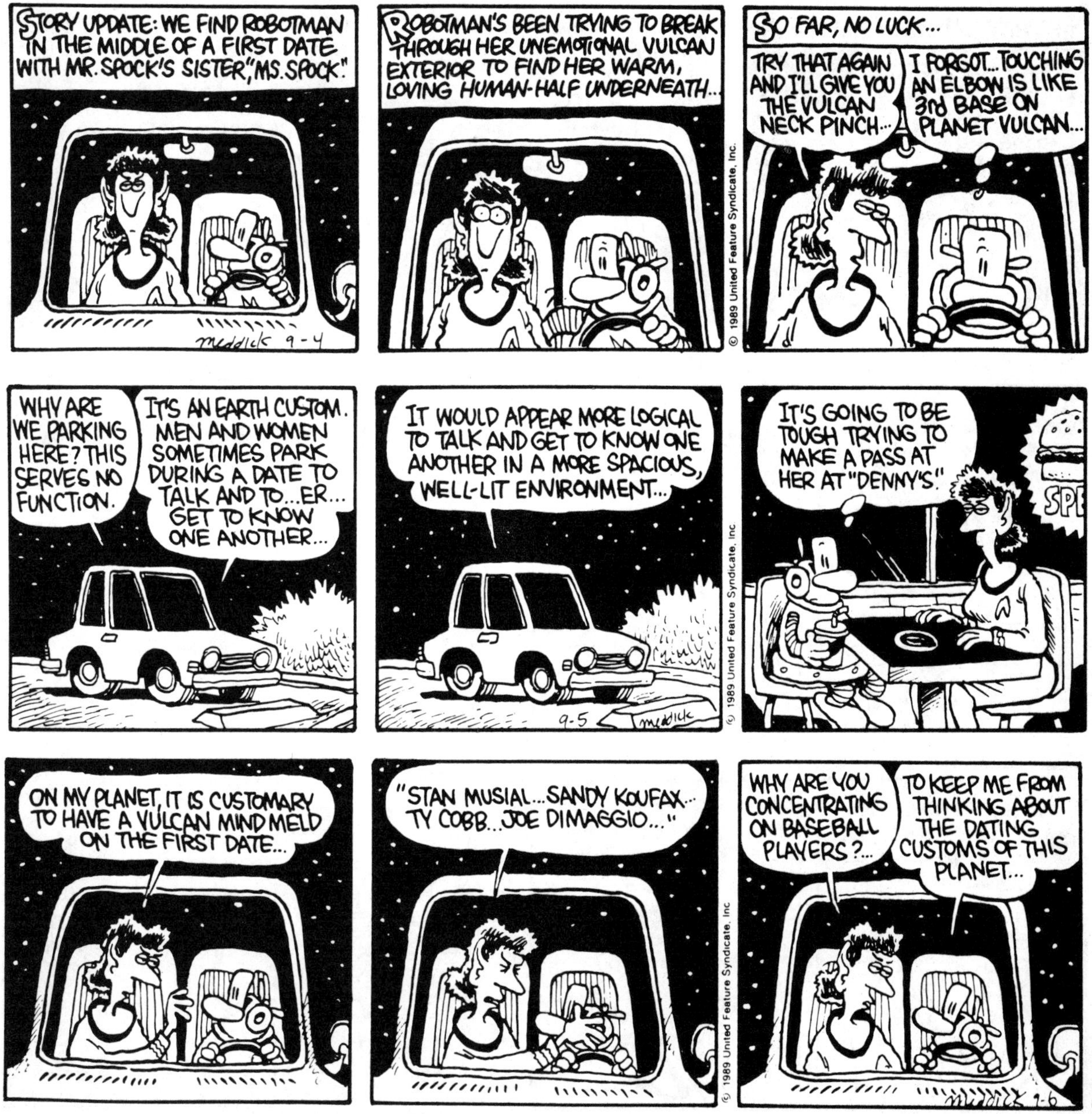
STORY UPDATE: WE FIND ROBOTMAN IN THE MIDDLE OF A FIRST DATE WITH MR. SPOCK'S SISTER, "MS. SPOCK."
ROBOTMAN'S BEEN TRYING TO BREAK THROUGH HER UNEMOTIONAL VULCAN EXTERIOR TO FIND HER WARM, LOVING HUMAN-HALF UNDERNEATH...
SO FAR, NO LUCK...
TRY THAT AGAIN AND I'LL GIVE YOU THE VULCAN NECK PINCH...
I FORGOT...TOUCHING AN ELBOW IS LIKE 3rd BASE ON PLANET VULCAN...
© 1989 United Feature Syndicate, Inc.
WHY ARE WE PARKING HERE? THIS SERVES NO FUNCTION.
IT'S AN EARTH CUSTOM. MEN AND WOMEN SOMETIMES PARK DURING A DATE TO TALK AND TO...ER... GET TO KNOW ONE ANOTHER...
IT WOULD APPEAR MORE LOGICAL TO TALK AND GET TO KNOW ONE ANOTHER IN A MORE SPACIOUS, WELL-LIT ENVIRONMENT...
© 1989 United Feature Syndicate, Inc.
IT'S GOING TO BE TOUGH TRYING TO MAKE A PASS AT HER AT "DENNY'S."
ON MY PLANET, IT IS CUSTOMARY TO HAVE A VULCAN MIND MELD ON THE FIRST DATE...
"STAN MUSIAL...SANDY KOUFAX... TY COBB...JOE DIMAGGIO..."
© 1989 United Feature Syndicate, Inc.
WHY ARE YOU CONCENTRATING ON BASEBALL PLAYERS?...
TO KEEP ME FROM THINKING ABOUT THE DATING CUSTOMS OF THIS PLANET...

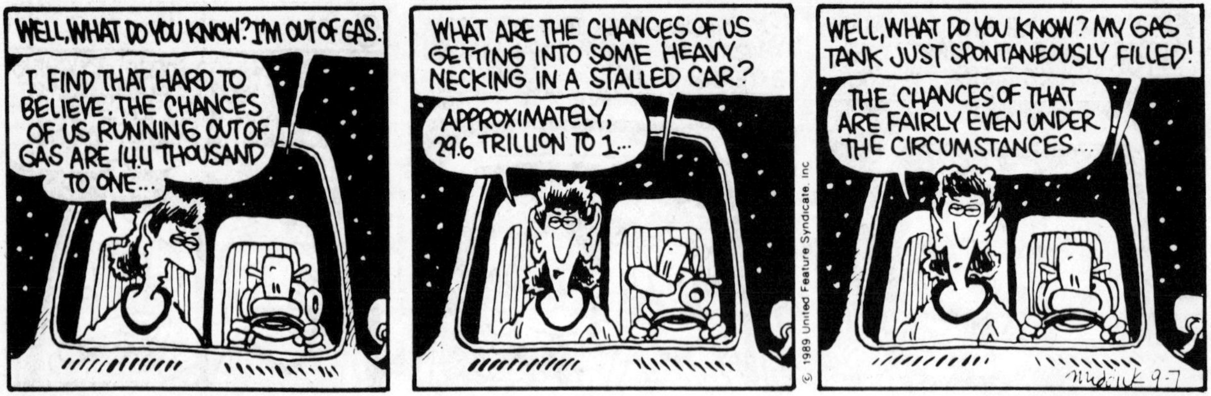
WELL, WHAT DO YOU KNOW? I'M OUT OF GAS.
I FIND THAT HARD TO BELIEVE. THE CHANCES OF US RUNNING OUT OF GAS ARE 14.4 THOUSAND TO ONE...
WHAT ARE THE CHANCES OF US GETTING INTO SOME HEAVY NECKING IN A STALLED CAR?
APPROXIMATELY, 29.6 TRILLION TO 1...
WELL, WHAT DO YOU KNOW? MY GAS TANK JUST SPONTANEOUSLY FILLED!
THE CHANCES OF THAT ARE FAIRLY EVEN UNDER THE CIRCUMSTANCES...
© 1989 United Feature Syndicate, Inc.

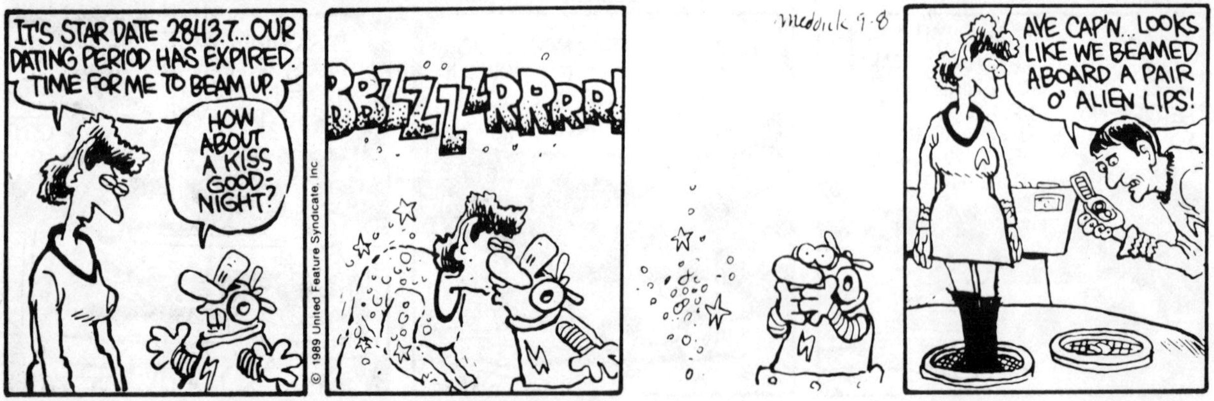
IT'S STAR DATE 2843.7... OUR DATING PERIOD HAS EXPIRED. TIME FOR ME TO BEAM UP.
HOW ABOUT A KISS GOOD-NIGHT?
© 1989 United Feature Syndicate, Inc.
BBZZZZZRRRRR!
AYE CAP'N... LOOKS LIKE WE BEAMED ABOARD A PAIR O' ALIEN LIPS!

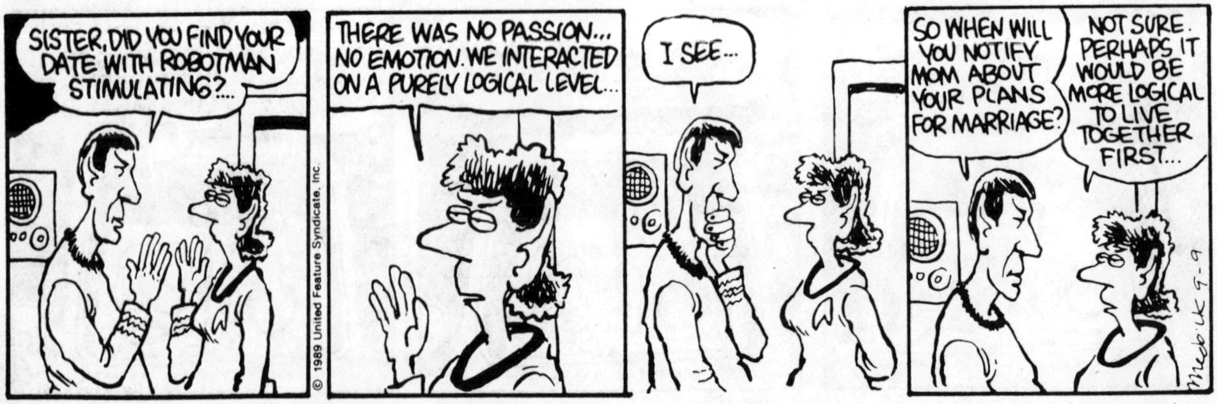
SISTER, DID YOU FIND YOUR DATE WITH ROBOTMAN STIMULATING?...
© 1989 United Feature Syndicate, Inc.
THERE WAS NO PASSION... NO EMOTION. WE INTERACTED ON A PURELY LOGICAL LEVEL...
I SEE...
SO WHEN WILL YOU NOTIFY MOM ABOUT YOUR PLANS FOR MARRIAGE?
NOT SURE. PERHAPS IT WOULD BE MORE LOGICAL TO LIVE TOGETHER FIRST...

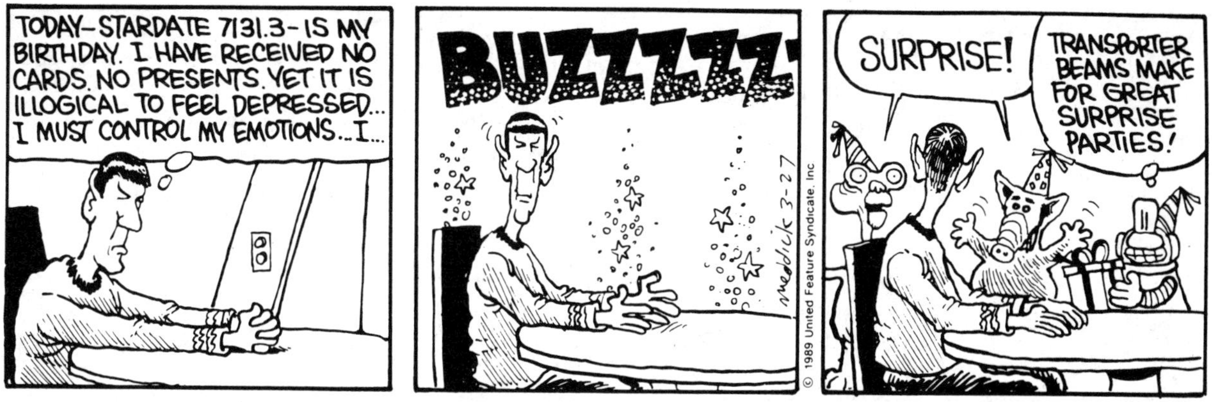
TODAY–STARDATE 7131.3–IS MY BIRTHDAY. I HAVE RECEIVED NO CARDS. NO PRESENTS. YET IT IS ILLOGICAL TO FEEL DEPRESSED... I MUST CONTROL MY EMOTIONS... I...
BUZZZZZZ
SURPRISE!
TRANSPORTER BEAMS MAKE FOR GREAT SURPRISE PARTIES!
© 1989 United Feature Syndicate, Inc

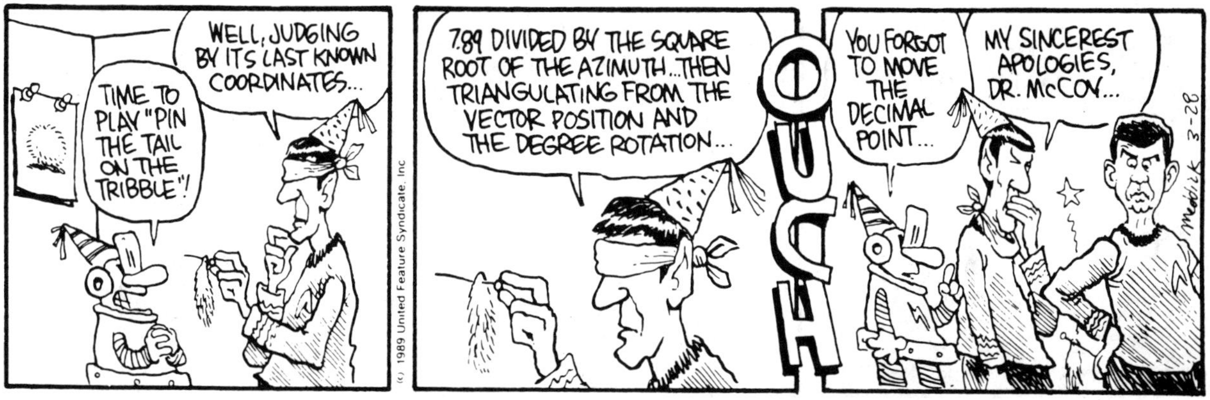
TIME TO PLAY "PIN THE TAIL ON THE TRIBBLE"!
WELL, JUDGING BY ITS LAST KNOWN COORDINATES...
7.89 DIVIDED BY THE SQUARE ROOT OF THE AZIMUTH...THEN TRIANGULATING FROM THE VECTOR POSITION AND THE DEGREE ROTATION...
OUCH
YOU FORGOT TO MOVE THE DECIMAL POINT...
MY SINCEREST APOLOGIES, DR. McCOY...
(c) 1989 United Feature Syndicate, Inc

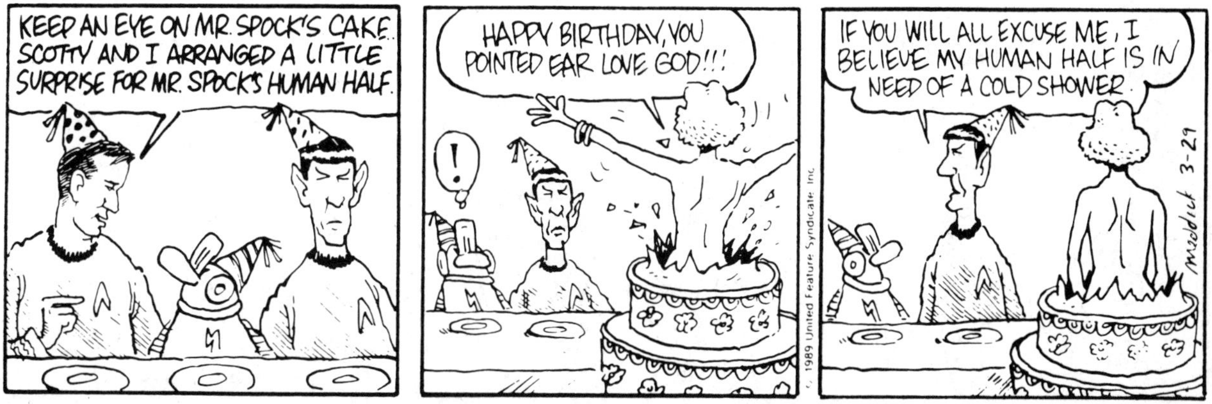
KEEP AN EYE ON MR. SPOCK'S CAKE. SCOTTY AND I ARRANGED A LITTLE SURPRISE FOR MR. SPOCK'S HUMAN HALF.
!
HAPPY BIRTHDAY, YOU POINTED EAR LOVE GOD!!!
IF YOU WILL ALL EXCUSE ME, I BELIEVE MY HUMAN HALF IS IN NEED OF A COLD SHOWER.
© 1989 United Feature Syndicate, Inc

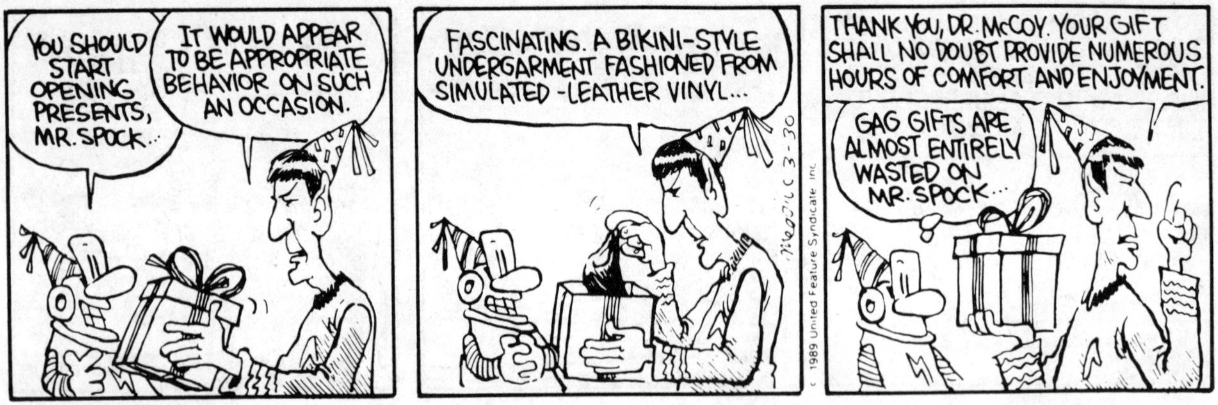
YOU SHOULD START OPENING PRESENTS, MR. SPOCK...
IT WOULD APPEAR TO BE APPROPRIATE BEHAVIOR ON SUCH AN OCCASION.
FASCINATING. A BIKINI-STYLE UNDERGARMENT FASHIONED FROM SIMULATED-LEATHER VINYL...
THANK YOU, DR. McCOY. YOUR GIFT SHALL NO DOUBT PROVIDE NUMEROUS HOURS OF COMFORT AND ENJOYMENT.
GAG GIFTS ARE ALMOST ENTIRELY WASTED ON MR. SPOCK...

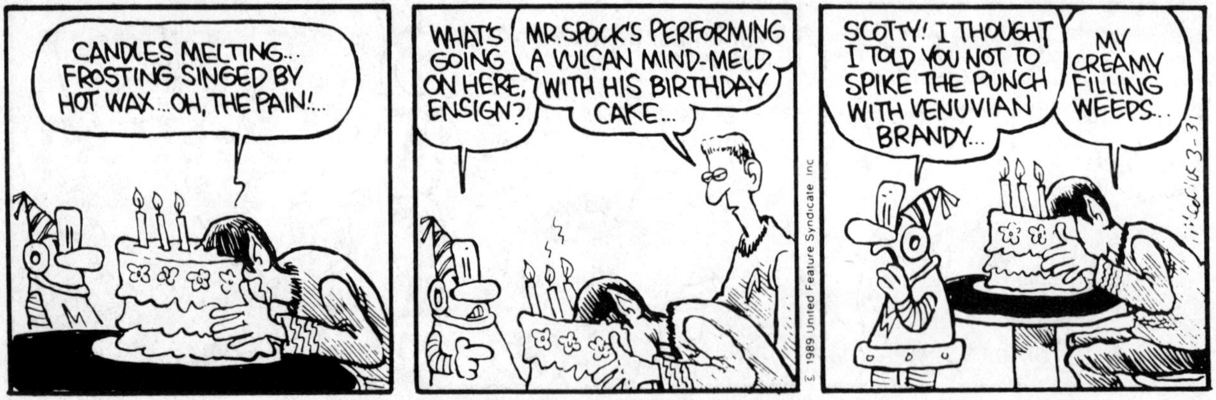
CANDLES MELTING... FROSTING SINGED BY HOT WAX... OH, THE PAIN!...
WHAT'S GOING ON HERE, ENSIGN?
MR. SPOCK'S PERFORMING A VULCAN MIND-MELD WITH HIS BIRTHDAY CAKE...
SCOTTY! I THOUGHT I TOLD YOU NOT TO SPIKE THE PUNCH WITH VENUVIAN BRANDY...
MY CREAMY FILLING WEEPS...

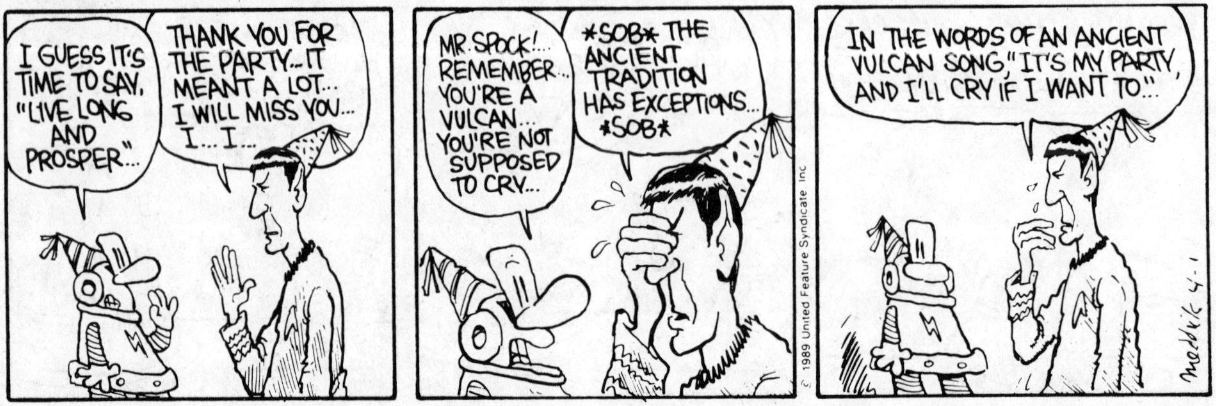
I GUESS IT'S TIME TO SAY, "LIVE LONG AND PROSPER"...
THANK YOU FOR THE PARTY... IT MEANT A LOT... I WILL MISS YOU... I... I...
MR. SPOCK!... REMEMBER... YOU'RE A VULCAN... YOU'RE NOT SUPPOSED TO CRY...
SOB THE ANCIENT TRADITION HAS EXCEPTIONS... *SOB*
IN THE WORDS OF AN ANCIENT VULCAN SONG, "IT'S MY PARTY, AND I'LL CRY IF I WANT TO."

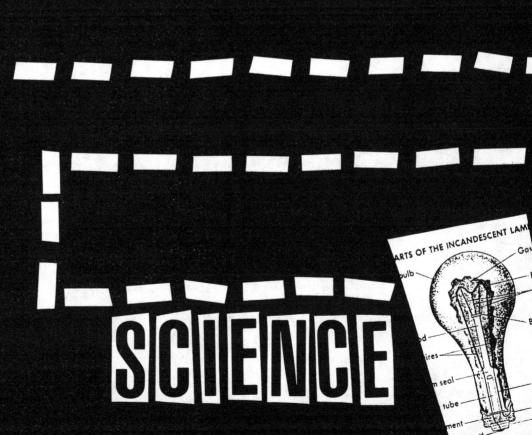

SCIENCE

PARTS OF THE INCANDESCENT LAMP

Gas

Fi

S

Button

Fuse

Scre

Glas

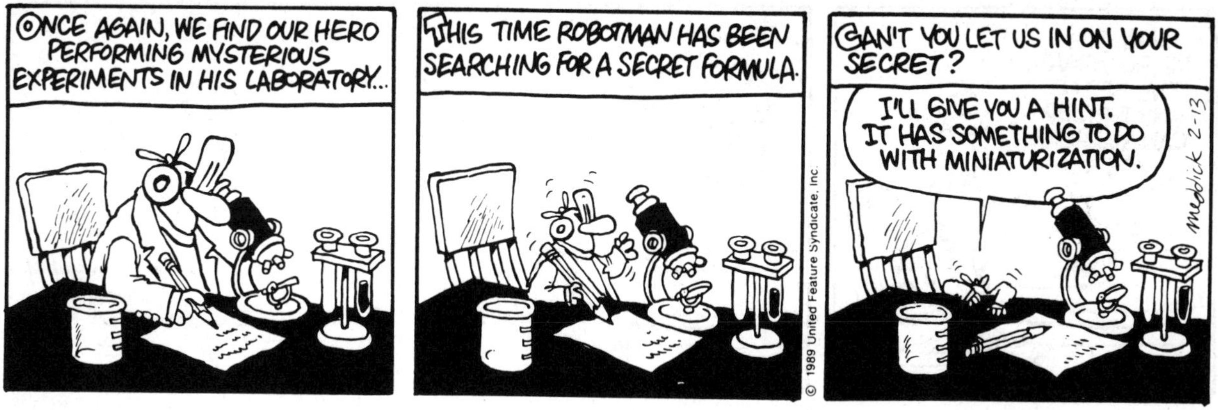
ONCE AGAIN, WE FIND OUR HERO PERFORMING MYSTERIOUS EXPERIMENTS IN HIS LABORATORY...
THIS TIME ROBOTMAN HAS BEEN SEARCHING FOR A SECRET FORMULA.
© 1989 United Feature Syndicate, Inc.
CAN'T YOU LET US IN ON YOUR SECRET?
I'LL GIVE YOU A HINT. IT HAS SOMETHING TO DO WITH MINIATURIZATION.
meddick 2-13

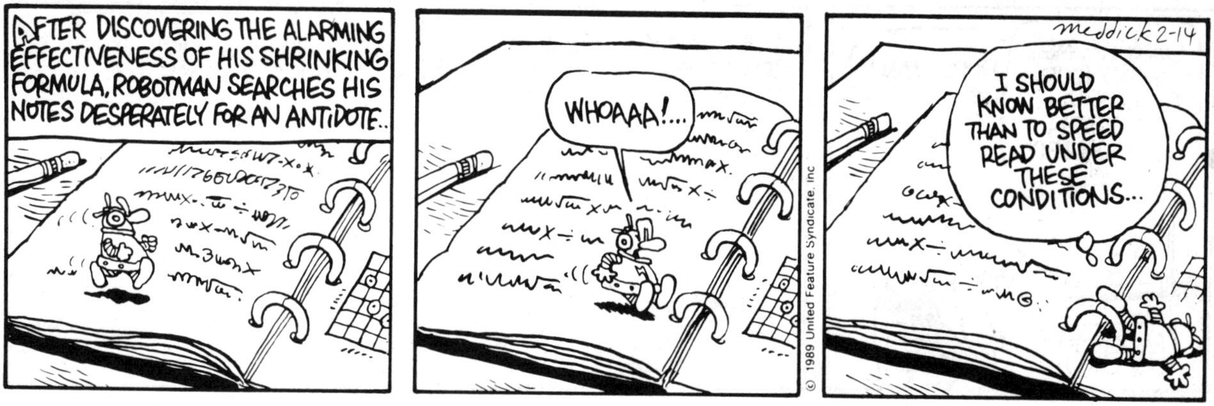
AFTER DISCOVERING THE ALARMING EFFECTIVENESS OF HIS SHRINKING FORMULA, ROBOTMAN SEARCHES HIS NOTES DESPERATELY FOR AN ANTIDOTE...
WHOAAA!...
© 1989 United Feature Syndicate, Inc.
meddick 2-14
I SHOULD KNOW BETTER THAN TO SPEED READ UNDER THESE CONDITIONS...

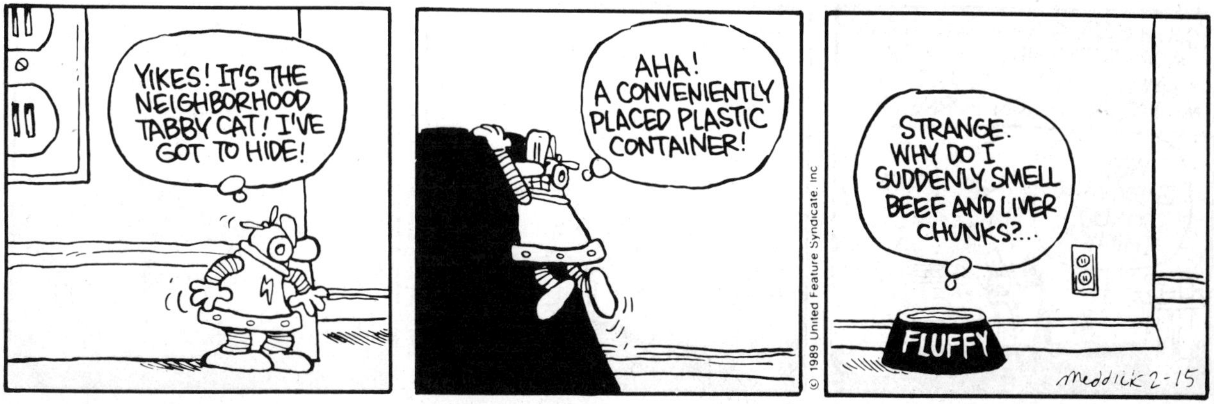
YIKES! IT'S THE NEIGHBORHOOD TABBY CAT! I'VE GOT TO HIDE!
AHA! A CONVENIENTLY PLACED PLASTIC CONTAINER!
© 1989 United Feature Syndicate, Inc.
STRANGE. WHY DO I SUDDENLY SMELL BEEF AND LIVER CHUNKS?...
FLUFFY
meddick 2-15

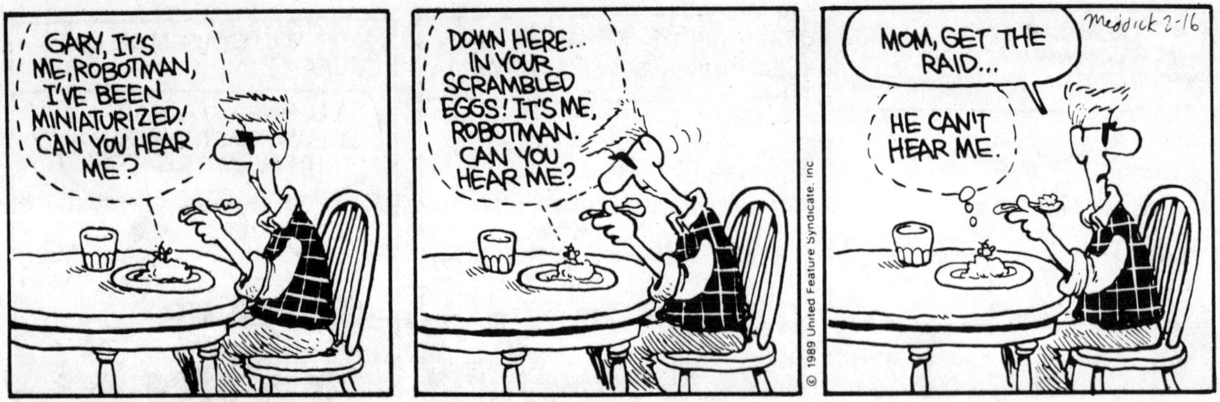
GARY, IT'S ME, ROBOTMAN, I'VE BEEN MINIATURIZED! CAN YOU HEAR ME?
DOWN HERE... IN YOUR SCRAMBLED EGGS! IT'S ME, ROBOTMAN. CAN YOU HEAR ME?
meddick 2-16
MOM, GET THE RAID...
HE CAN'T HEAR ME.
© 1989 United Feature Syndicate, Inc

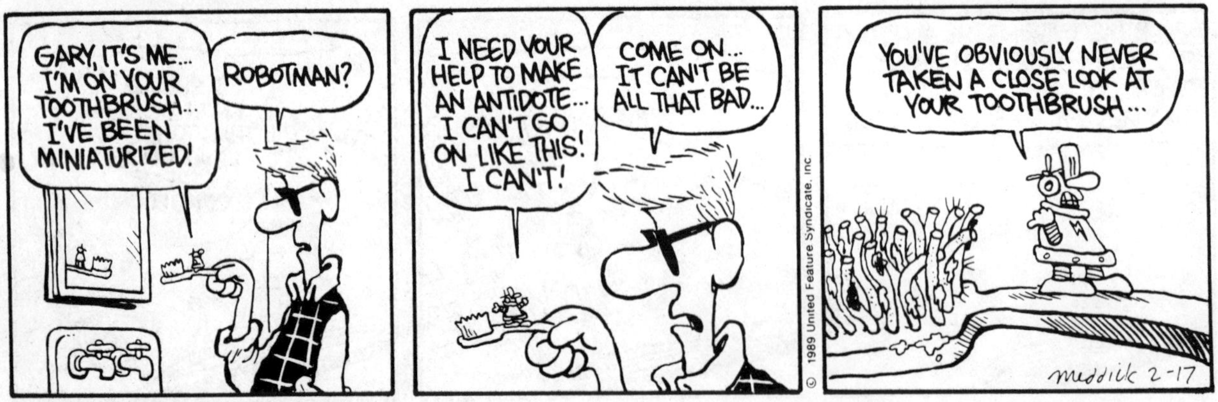
GARY, IT'S ME... I'M ON YOUR TOOTHBRUSH... I'VE BEEN MINIATURIZED!
ROBOTMAN?
I NEED YOUR HELP TO MAKE AN ANTIDOTE... I CAN'T GO ON LIKE THIS! I CAN'T!
COME ON... IT CAN'T BE ALL THAT BAD...
YOU'VE OBVIOUSLY NEVER TAKEN A CLOSE LOOK AT YOUR TOOTHBRUSH...
meddick 2-17
© 1989 United Feature Syndicate, Inc

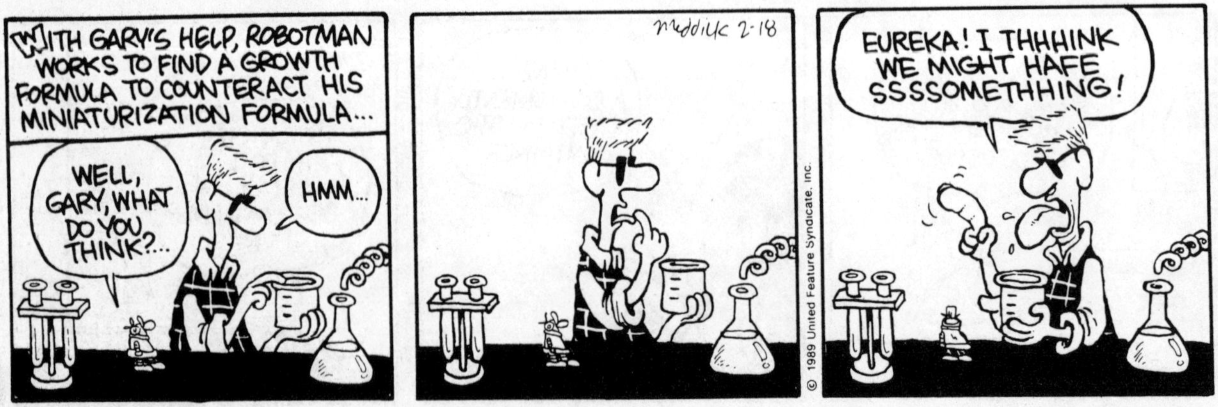
WITH GARY'S HELP, ROBOTMAN WORKS TO FIND A GROWTH FORMULA TO COUNTERACT HIS MINIATURIZATION FORMULA...
WELL, GARY, WHAT DO YOU THINK?...
HMM...
meddick 2-18
EUREKA! I THHHINK WE MIGHT HAFE SSSSOMETHHING!
© 1989 United Feature Syndicate, Inc

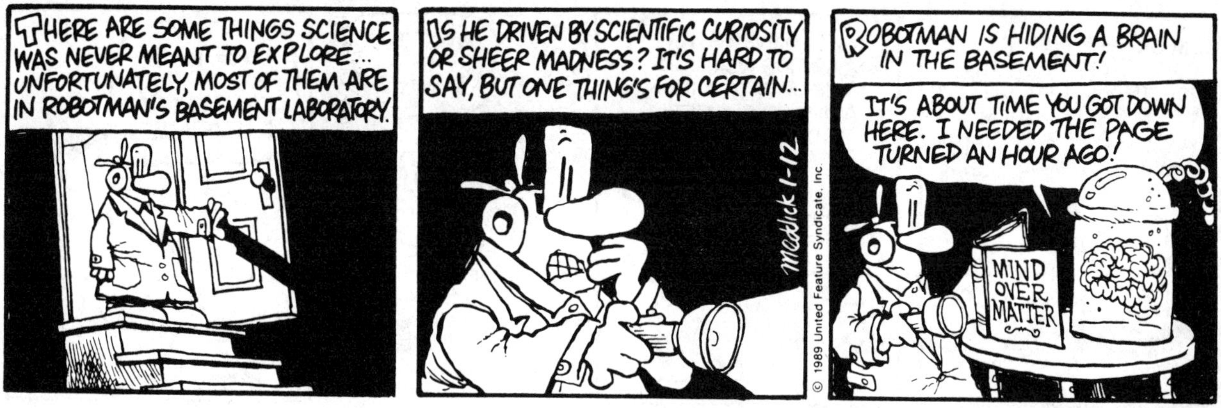
THERE ARE SOME THINGS SCIENCE WAS NEVER MEANT TO EXPLORE... UNFORTUNATELY, MOST OF THEM ARE IN ROBOTMAN'S BASEMENT LABORATORY.
IS HE DRIVEN BY SCIENTIFIC CURIOSITY OR SHEER MADNESS? IT'S HARD TO SAY, BUT ONE THING'S FOR CERTAIN...
© 1989 United Feature Syndicate, Inc.
ROBOTMAN IS HIDING A BRAIN IN THE BASEMENT!
IT'S ABOUT TIME YOU GOT DOWN HERE. I NEEDED THE PAGE TURNED AN HOUR AGO!
MIND OVER MATTER

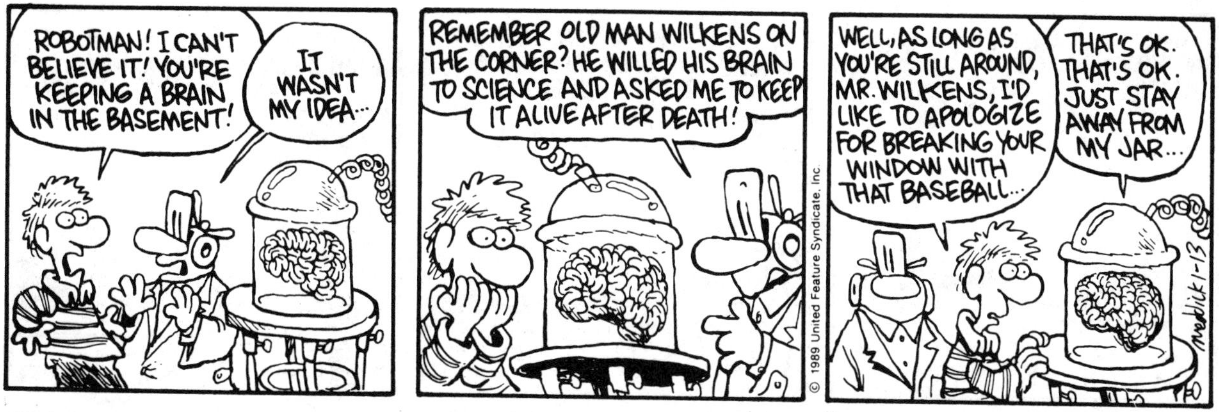
ROBOTMAN! I CAN'T BELIEVE IT! YOU'RE KEEPING A BRAIN IN THE BASEMENT!
IT WASN'T MY IDEA...
REMEMBER OLD MAN WILKENS ON THE CORNER? HE WILLED HIS BRAIN TO SCIENCE AND ASKED ME TO KEEP IT ALIVE AFTER DEATH!
© 1989 United Feature Syndicate, Inc.
WELL, AS LONG AS YOU'RE STILL AROUND, MR. WILKENS, I'D LIKE TO APOLOGIZE FOR BREAKING YOUR WINDOW WITH THAT BASEBALL...
THAT'S OK. THAT'S OK. JUST STAY AWAY FROM MY JAR...

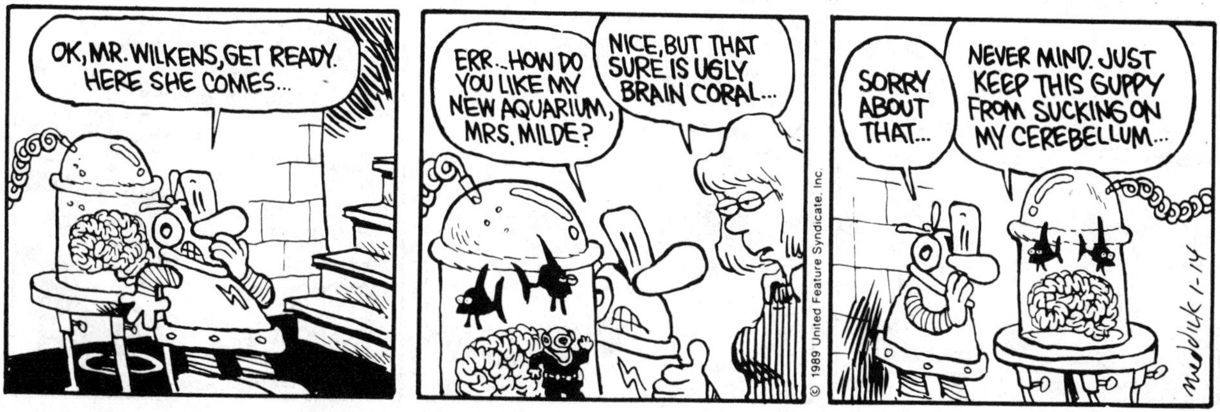
OK, MR. WILKENS, GET READY. HERE SHE COMES...
ERR...HOW DO YOU LIKE MY NEW AQUARIUM, MRS. MILDE?
NICE, BUT THAT SURE IS UGLY BRAIN CORAL...
© 1989 United Feature Syndicate, Inc.
SORRY ABOUT THAT...
NEVER MIND. JUST KEEP THIS GUPPY FROM SUCKING ON MY CEREBELLUM...

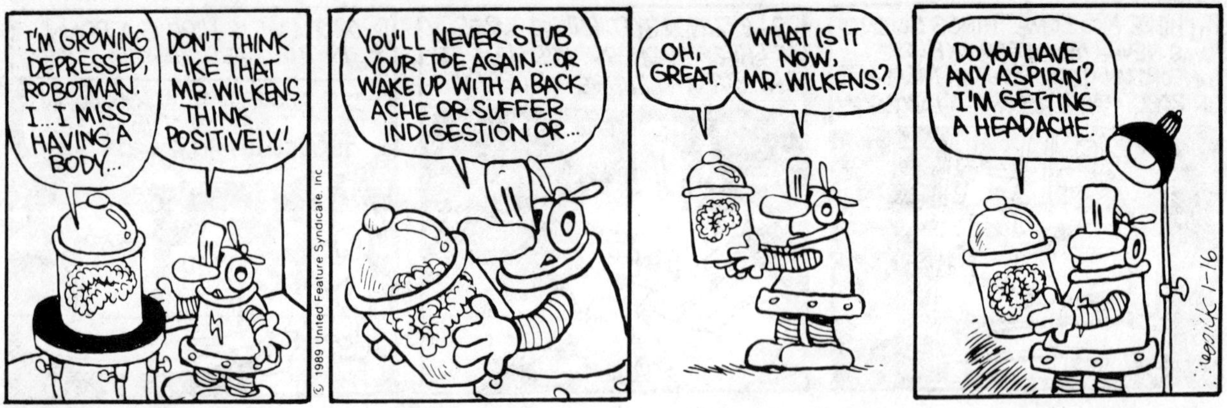
I'M GROWING DEPRESSED, ROBOTMAN. I...I MISS HAVING A BODY...
DON'T THINK LIKE THAT MR. WILKENS. THINK POSITIVELY!
© 1989 United Feature Syndicate, Inc
YOU'LL NEVER STUB YOUR TOE AGAIN...OR WAKE UP WITH A BACK ACHE OR SUFFER INDIGESTION OR...
OH, GREAT.
WHAT IS IT NOW, MR. WILKENS?
DO YOU HAVE ANY ASPIRIN? I'M GETTING A HEADACHE.

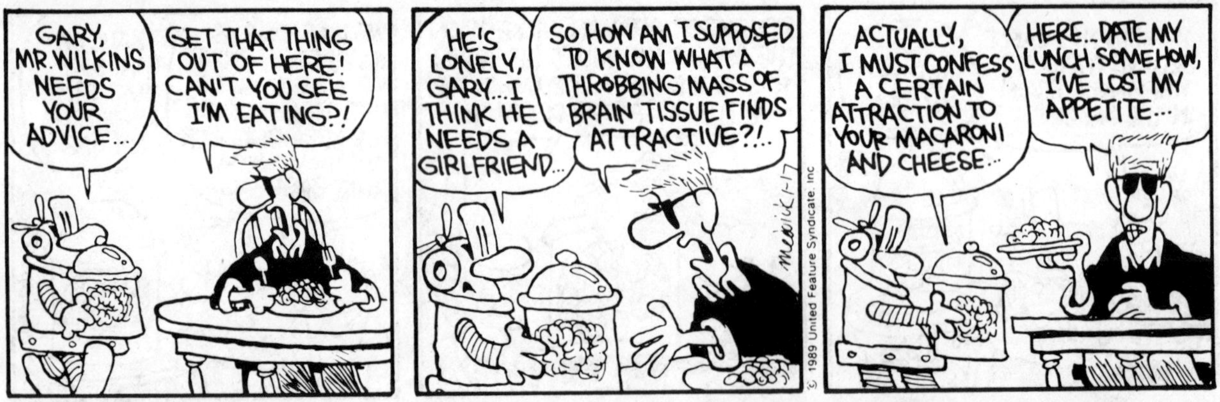
GARY, MR. WILKINS NEEDS YOUR ADVICE...
GET THAT THING OUT OF HERE! CAN'T YOU SEE I'M EATING?!
HE'S LONELY, GARY...I THINK HE NEEDS A GIRLFRIEND...
SO HOW AM I SUPPOSED TO KNOW WHAT A THROBBING MASS OF BRAIN TISSUE FINDS ATTRACTIVE?!..
© 1989 United Feature Syndicate, Inc
ACTUALLY, I MUST CONFESS A CERTAIN ATTRACTION TO YOUR MACARONI AND CHEESE...
HERE...DATE MY LUNCH. SOMEHOW, I'VE LOST MY APPETITE...

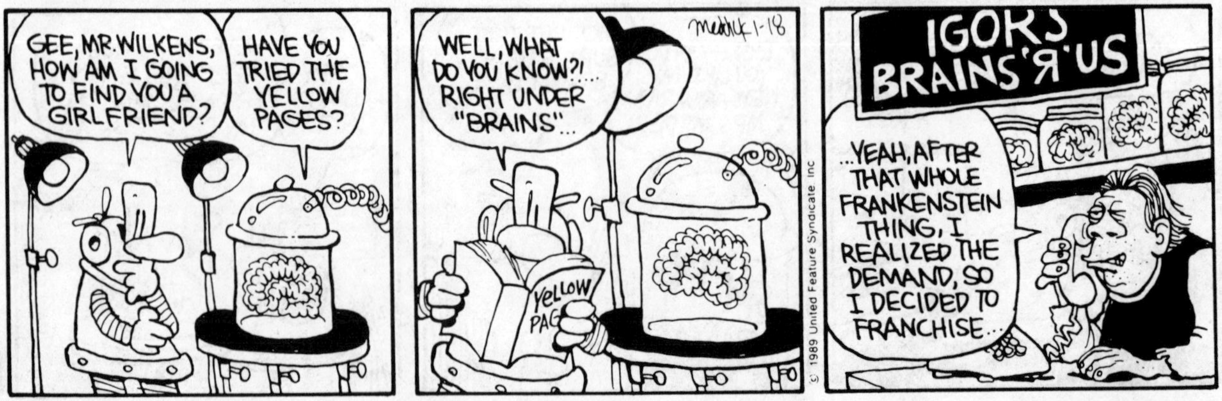
GEE, MR. WILKENS, HOW AM I GOING TO FIND YOU A GIRLFRIEND?
HAVE YOU TRIED THE YELLOW PAGES?
WELL, WHAT DO YOU KNOW?!... RIGHT UNDER "BRAINS"...
YELLOW PAG
© 1989 United Feature Syndicate, Inc
IGORS
BRAINS 'R' US
...YEAH, AFTER THAT WHOLE FRANKENSTEIN THING, I REALIZED THE DEMAND, SO I DECIDED TO FRANCHISE...

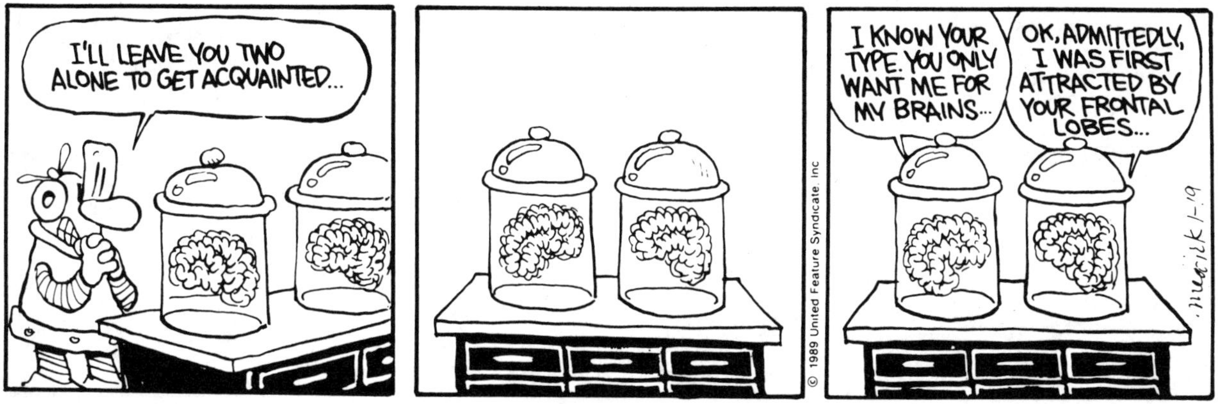
I'LL LEAVE YOU TWO ALONE TO GET ACQUAINTED...
I KNOW YOUR TYPE. YOU ONLY WANT ME FOR MY BRAINS...
OK, ADMITTEDLY, I WAS FIRST ATTRACTED BY YOUR FRONTAL LOBES...
© 1989 United Feature Syndicate, Inc.

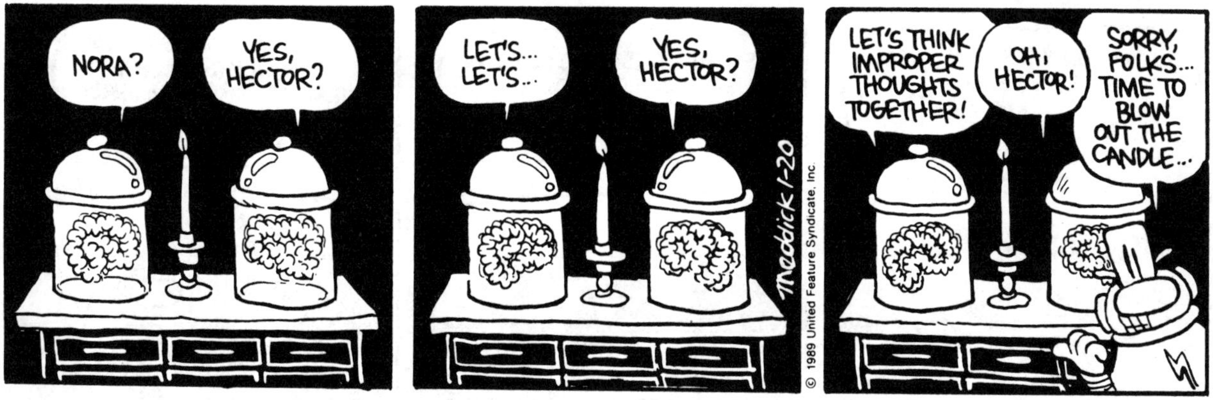
NORA?
YES, HECTOR?
LET'S... LET'S...
YES, HECTOR?
LET'S THINK IMPROPER THOUGHTS TOGETHER!
OH, HECTOR!
SORRY, FOLKS... TIME TO BLOW OUT THE CANDLE...
© 1989 United Feature Syndicate, Inc.

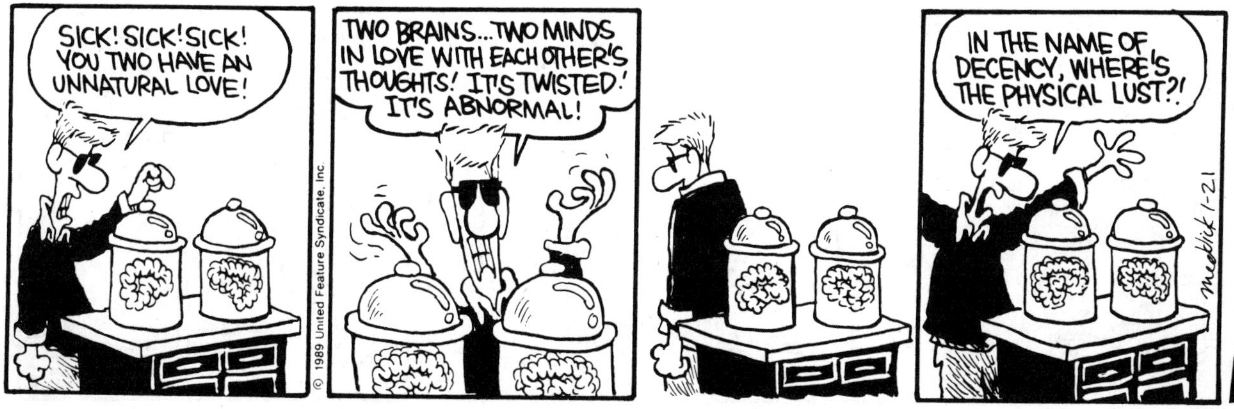
SICK! SICK! SICK! YOU TWO HAVE AN UNNATURAL LOVE!
TWO BRAINS...TWO MINDS IN LOVE WITH EACH OTHER'S THOUGHTS! IT'S TWISTED! IT'S ABNORMAL!
IN THE NAME OF DECENCY, WHERE'S THE PHYSICAL LUST?!
© 1989 United Feature Syndicate, Inc.

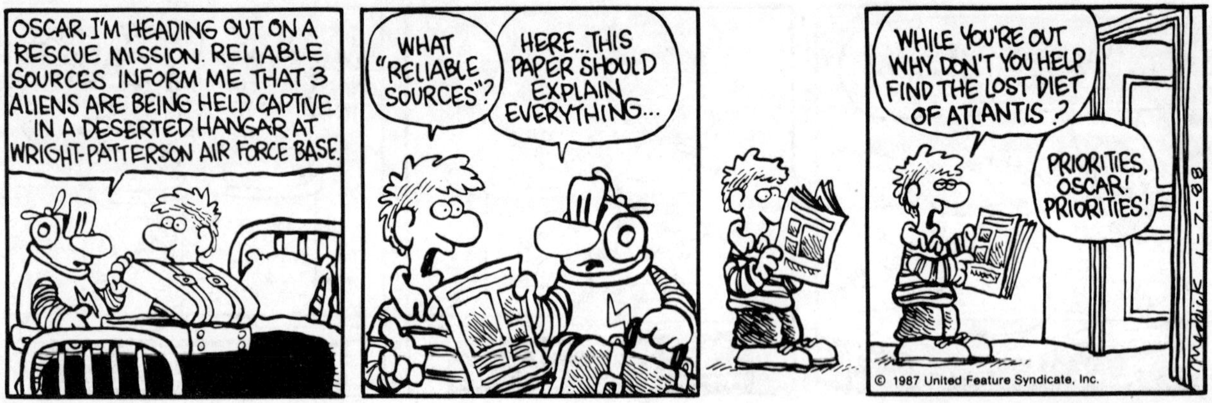
OSCAR, I'M HEADING OUT ON A RESCUE MISSION. RELIABLE SOURCES INFORM ME THAT 3 ALIENS ARE BEING HELD CAPTIVE IN A DESERTED HANGAR AT WRIGHT-PATTERSON AIR FORCE BASE.
WHAT "RELIABLE SOURCES"?
HERE...THIS PAPER SHOULD EXPLAIN EVERYTHING...
WHILE YOU'RE OUT WHY DON'T YOU HELP FIND THE LOST DIET OF ATLANTIS ?
PRIORITIES, OSCAR! PRIORITIES!
meddick 1-7-88
© 1987 United Feature Syndicate, Inc.

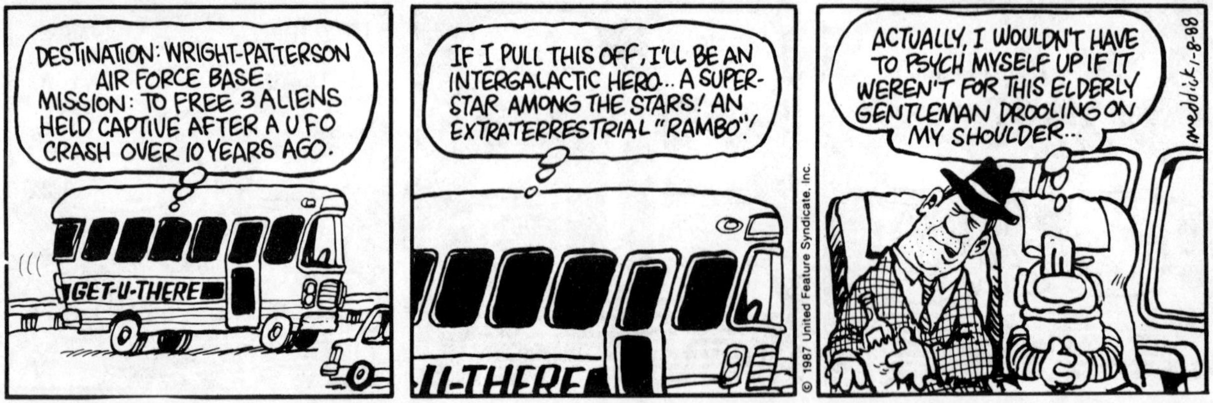
DESTINATION: WRIGHT-PATTERSON AIR FORCE BASE. MISSION: TO FREE 3 ALIENS HELD CAPTIVE AFTER A U F O CRASH OVER 10 YEARS AGO.
GET-U-THERE
IF I PULL THIS OFF, I'LL BE AN INTERGALACTIC HERO... A SUPER-STAR AMONG THE STARS! AN EXTRATERRESTRIAL "RAMBO"!
U-THERE
ACTUALLY, I WOULDN'T HAVE TO PSYCH MYSELF UP IF IT WEREN'T FOR THIS ELDERLY GENTLEMAN DROOLING ON MY SHOULDER...
© 1987 United Feature Syndicate, Inc.
meddick 1-8-88

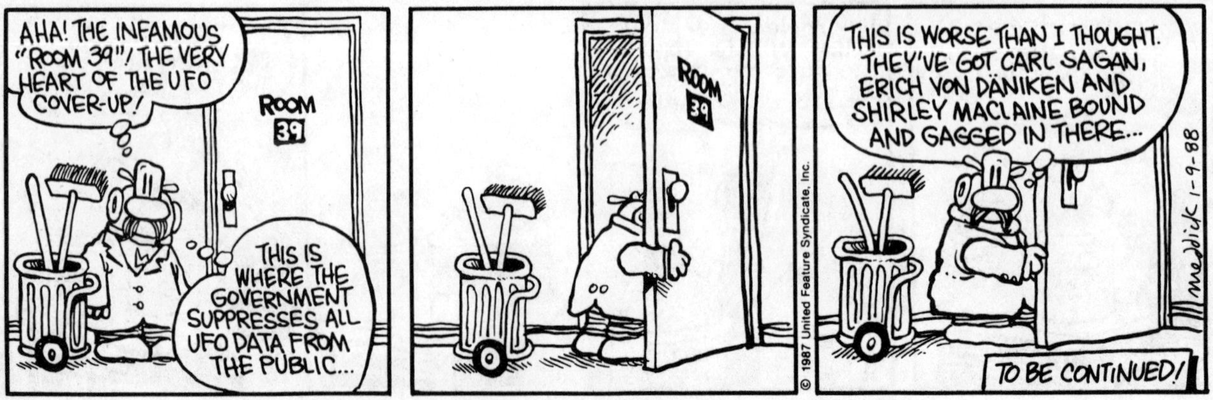
AHA! THE INFAMOUS "ROOM 39"! THE VERY HEART OF THE U F O COVER-UP!
ROOM 39
THIS IS WHERE THE GOVERNMENT SUPPRESSES ALL UFO DATA FROM THE PUBLIC...
ROOM 39
THIS IS WORSE THAN I THOUGHT. THEY'VE GOT CARL SAGAN, ERICH VON DÄNIKEN AND SHIRLEY MACLAINE BOUND AND GAGGED IN THERE...
TO BE CONTINUED!
© 1987 United Feature Syndicate, Inc.
meddick 1-9-88

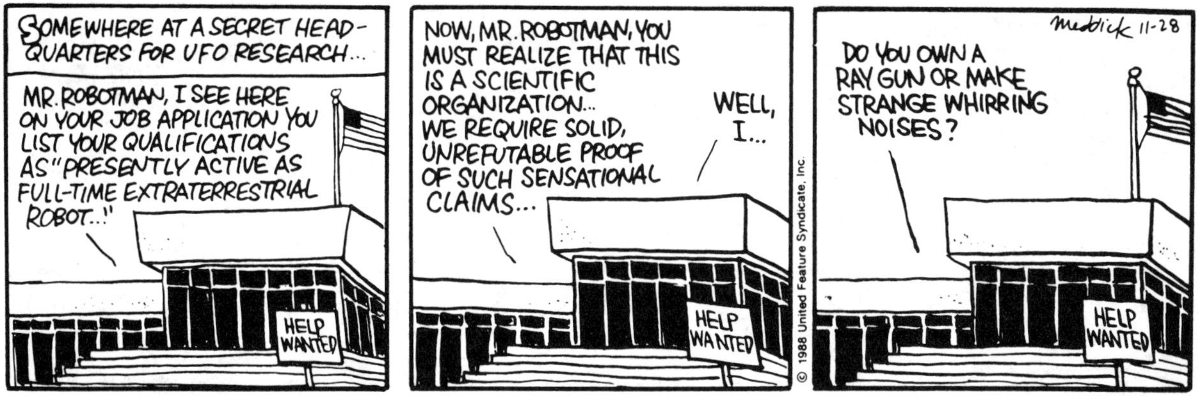
SOMEWHERE AT A SECRET HEADQUARTERS FOR UFO RESEARCH...
MR. ROBOTMAN, I SEE HERE ON YOUR JOB APPLICATION YOU LIST YOUR QUALIFICATIONS AS "PRESENTLY ACTIVE AS FULL-TIME EXTRATERRESTRIAL ROBOT..."
HELP WANTED
NOW, MR. ROBOTMAN, YOU MUST REALIZE THAT THIS IS A SCIENTIFIC ORGANIZATION... WE REQUIRE SOLID, UNREFUTABLE PROOF OF SUCH SENSATIONAL CLAIMS...
WELL, I...
HELP WANTED
© 1988 United Feature Syndicate, Inc.
meddick 11-28
DO YOU OWN A RAY GUN OR MAKE STRANGE WHIRRING NOISES?
HELP WANTED

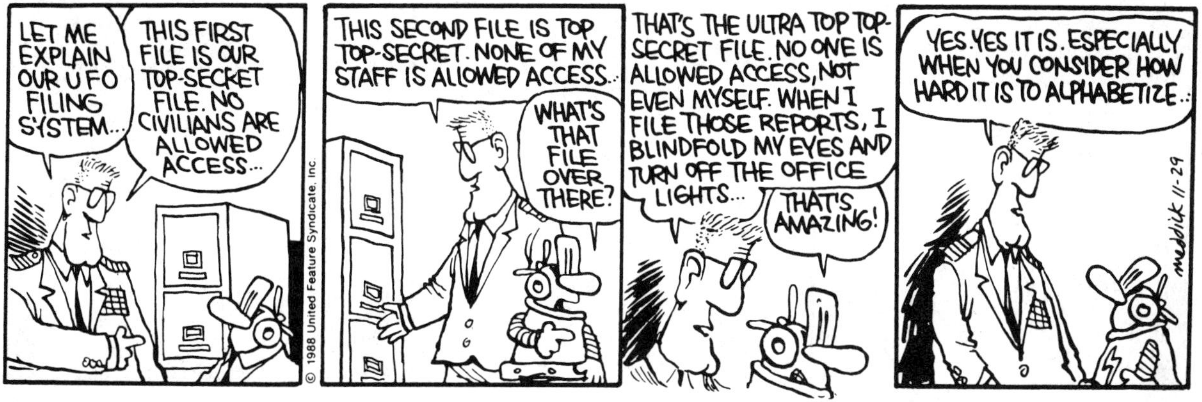
LET ME EXPLAIN OUR UFO FILING SYSTEM...
THIS FIRST FILE IS OUR TOP-SECRET FILE. NO CIVILIANS ARE ALLOWED ACCESS...
© 1988 United Feature Syndicate, Inc.
THIS SECOND FILE IS TOP TOP-SECRET. NONE OF MY STAFF IS ALLOWED ACCESS...
WHAT'S THAT FILE OVER THERE?
THAT'S THE ULTRA TOP TOP-SECRET FILE. NO ONE IS ALLOWED ACCESS, NOT EVEN MYSELF. WHEN I FILE THOSE REPORTS, I BLINDFOLD MY EYES AND TURN OFF THE OFFICE LIGHTS...
THAT'S AMAZING!
YES. YES IT IS. ESPECIALLY WHEN YOU CONSIDER HOW HARD IT IS TO ALPHABETIZE...
meddick 11-29

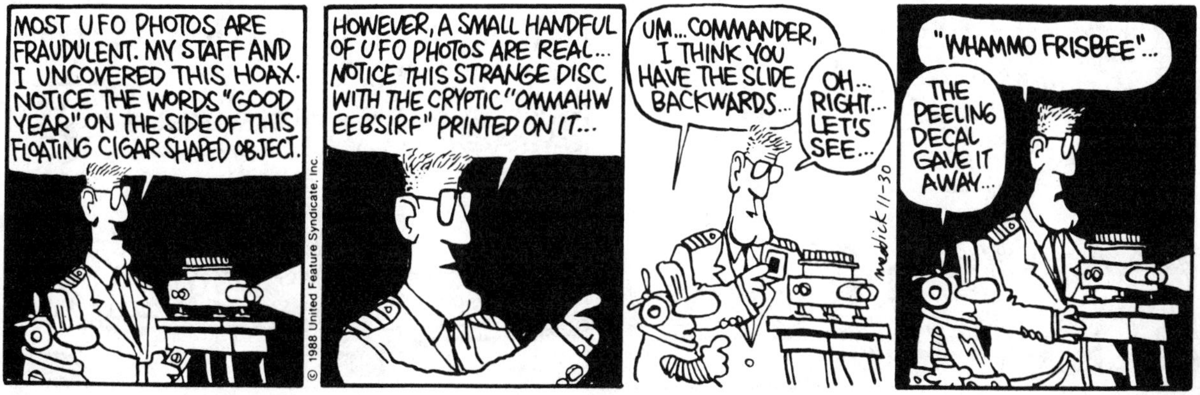
MOST UFO PHOTOS ARE FRAUDULENT. MY STAFF AND I UNCOVERED THIS HOAX. NOTICE THE WORDS "GOOD YEAR" ON THE SIDE OF THIS FLOATING CIGAR SHAPED OBJECT.
© 1988 United Feature Syndicate, Inc.
HOWEVER, A SMALL HANDFUL OF UFO PHOTOS ARE REAL... NOTICE THIS STRANGE DISC WITH THE CRYPTIC "OMMAHW EEBSIRF" PRINTED ON IT...
UM... COMMANDER, I THINK YOU HAVE THE SLIDE BACKWARDS...
OH... RIGHT... LET'S SEE...
meddick 11-30
"WHAMMO FRISBEE"...
THE PEELING DECAL GAVE IT AWAY...

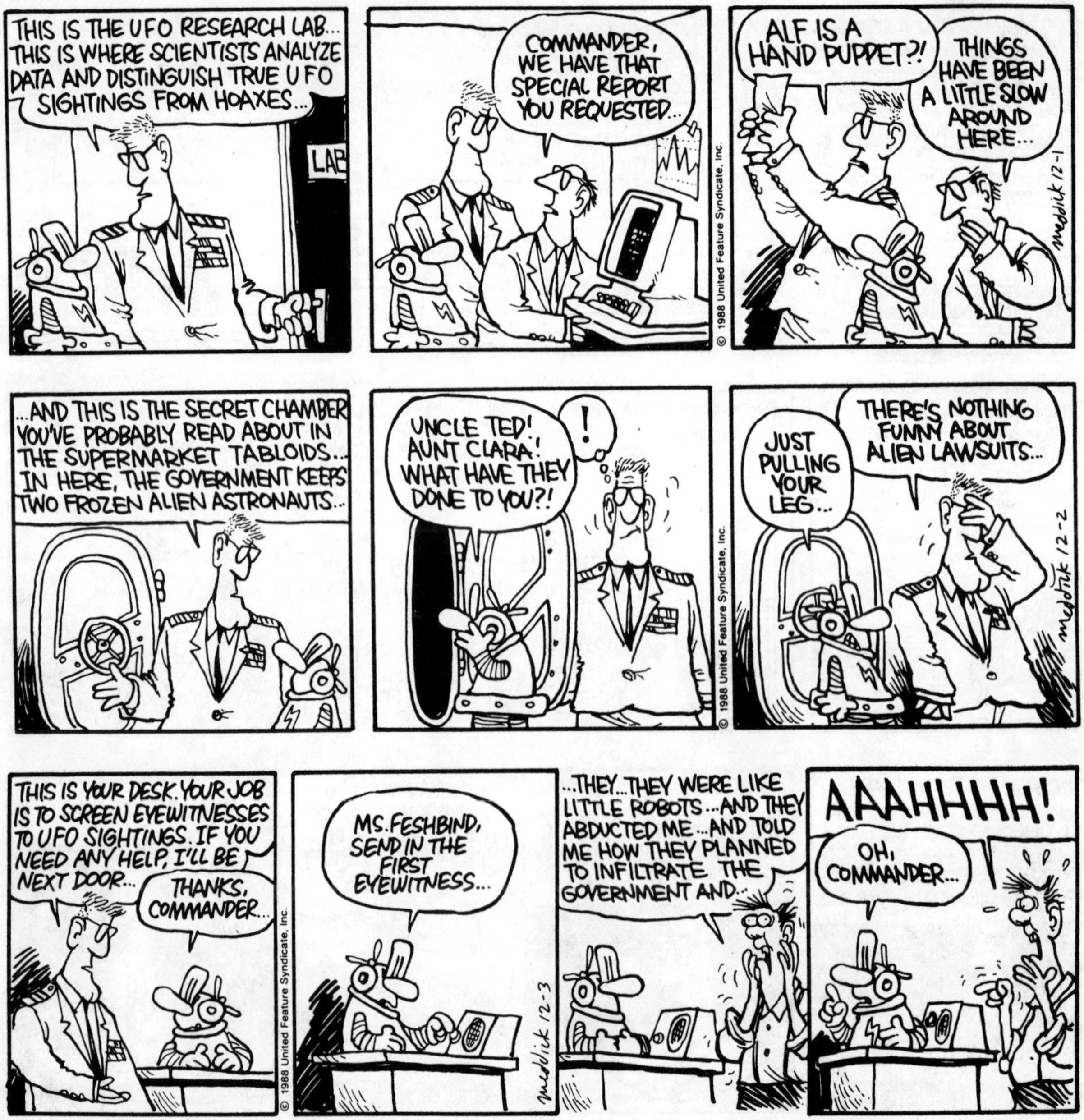
THIS IS THE UFO RESEARCH LAB... THIS IS WHERE SCIENTISTS ANALYZE DATA AND DISTINGUISH TRUE UFO SIGHTINGS FROM HOAXES...
LAB
COMMANDER, WE HAVE THAT SPECIAL REPORT YOU REQUESTED...
© 1988 United Feature Syndicate, Inc.
ALF IS A HAND PUPPET?!
THINGS HAVE BEEN A LITTLE SLOW AROUND HERE...
meddick 12-1
...AND THIS IS THE SECRET CHAMBER YOU'VE PROBABLY READ ABOUT IN THE SUPERMARKET TABLOIDS... IN HERE, THE GOVERNMENT KEEPS TWO FROZEN ALIEN ASTRONAUTS...
UNCLE TED! AUNT CLARA! WHAT HAVE THEY DONE TO YOU?!
!
© 1988 United Feature Syndicate, Inc.
JUST PULLING YOUR LEG...
THERE'S NOTHING FUNNY ABOUT ALIEN LAWSUITS...
meddick 12-2
THIS IS YOUR DESK. YOUR JOB IS TO SCREEN EYEWITNESSES TO UFO SIGHTINGS. IF YOU NEED ANY HELP, I'LL BE NEXT DOOR...
THANKS, COMMANDER...
© 1988 United Feature Syndicate, Inc.
MS. FESHBIND, SEND IN THE FIRST EYEWITNESS...
meddick 12-3
...THEY...THEY WERE LIKE LITTLE ROBOTS...AND THEY ABDUCTED ME...AND TOLD ME HOW THEY PLANNED TO INFILTRATE THE GOVERNMENT AND...
AAAHHHH!
OH, COMMANDER...

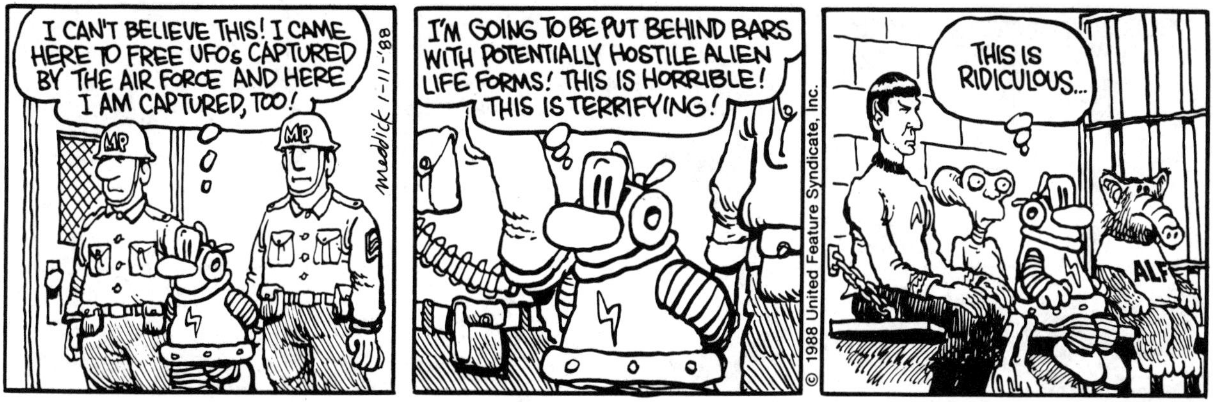
I CAN'T BELIEVE THIS! I CAME HERE TO FREE UFOs CAPTURED BY THE AIR FORCE AND HERE I AM CAPTURED, TOO!
MP
MP
maddick 1-11-'88
I'M GOING TO BE PUT BEHIND BARS WITH POTENTIALLY HOSTILE ALIEN LIFE FORMS! THIS IS HORRIBLE! THIS IS TERRIFYING!
© 1988 United Feature Syndicate, Inc.
THIS IS RIDICULOUS...
ALF

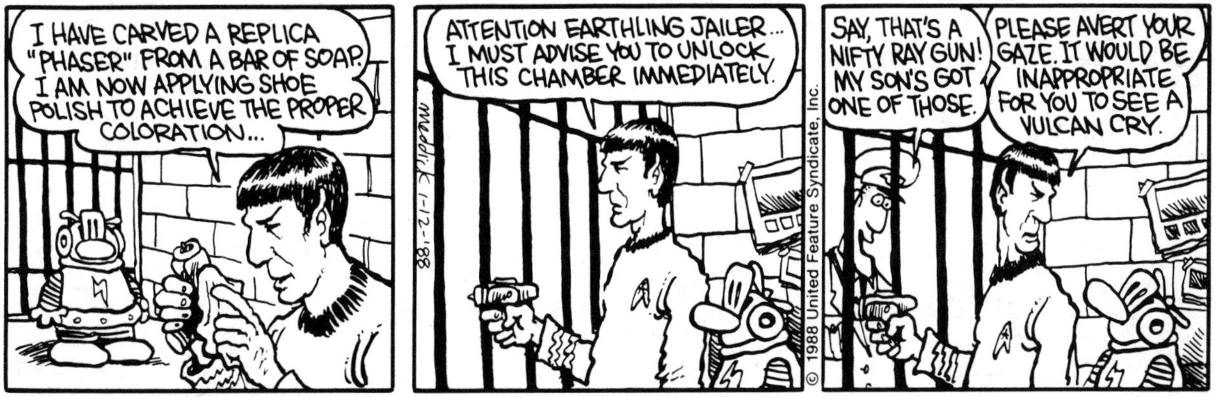
I HAVE CARVED A REPLICA "PHASER" FROM A BAR OF SOAP. I AM NOW APPLYING SHOE POLISH TO ACHIEVE THE PROPER COLORATION...
maddick 1-12-'88
ATTENTION EARTHLING JAILER... I MUST ADVISE YOU TO UNLOCK THIS CHAMBER IMMEDIATELY.
© 1988 United Feature Syndicate, Inc.
SAY, THAT'S A NIFTY RAY GUN! MY SON'S GOT ONE OF THOSE.
PLEASE AVERT YOUR GAZE. IT WOULD BE INAPPROPRIATE FOR YOU TO SEE A VULCAN CRY.

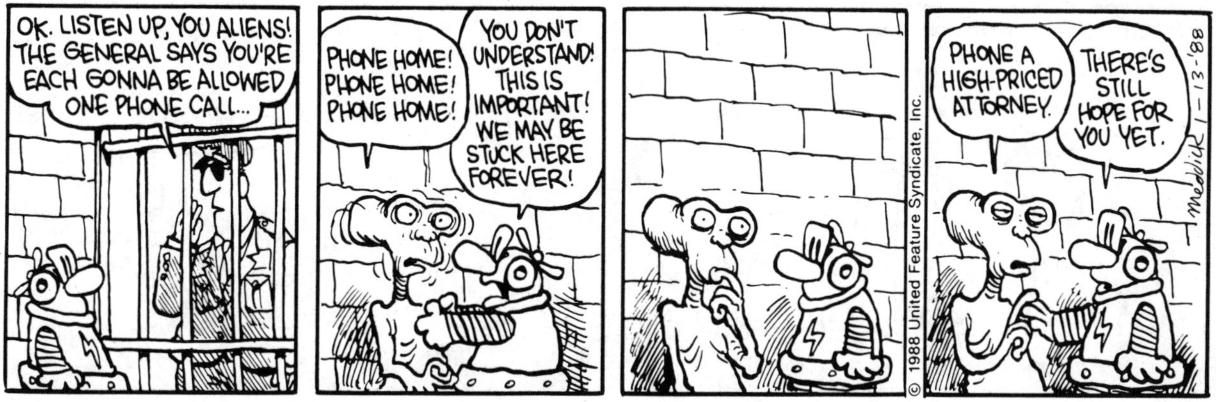
OK. LISTEN UP, YOU ALIENS! THE GENERAL SAYS YOU'RE EACH GONNA BE ALLOWED ONE PHONE CALL...
PHONE HOME! PHONE HOME! PHONE HOME!
YOU DON'T UNDERSTAND! THIS IS IMPORTANT! WE MAY BE STUCK HERE FOREVER!
© 1988 United Feature Syndicate, Inc.
PHONE A HIGH-PRICED ATTORNEY.
THERE'S STILL HOPE FOR YOU YET.
maddick 1-13-'88

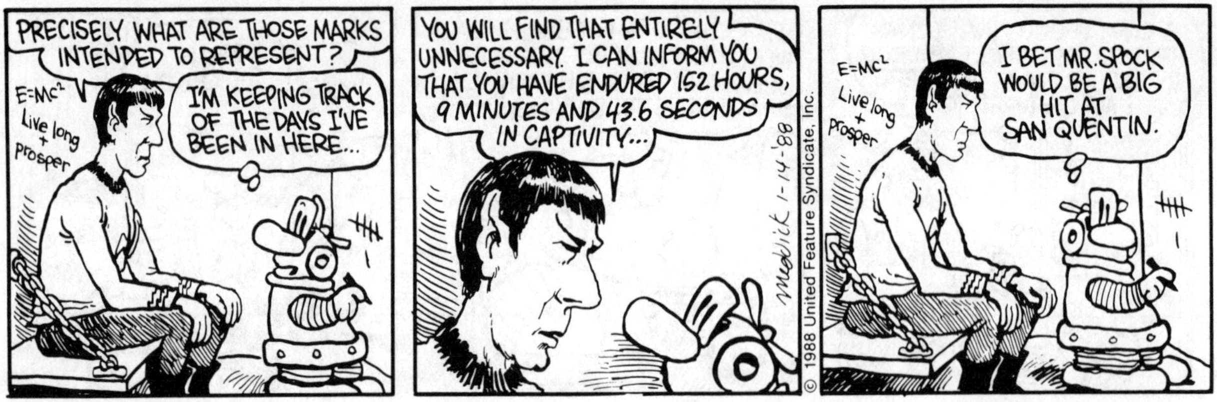
PRECISELY WHAT ARE THOSE MARKS INTENDED TO REPRESENT?
E=MC²
Live long + prosper
I'M KEEPING TRACK OF THE DAYS I'VE BEEN IN HERE...
YOU WILL FIND THAT ENTIRELY UNNECESSARY. I CAN INFORM YOU THAT YOU HAVE ENDURED 152 HOURS, 9 MINUTES AND 43.6 SECONDS IN CAPTIVITY...
meddick 1-14-'88
© 1988 United Feature Syndicate, Inc.
E=MC²
Live long + prosper
I BET MR.SPOCK WOULD BE A BIG HIT AT SAN QUENTIN.

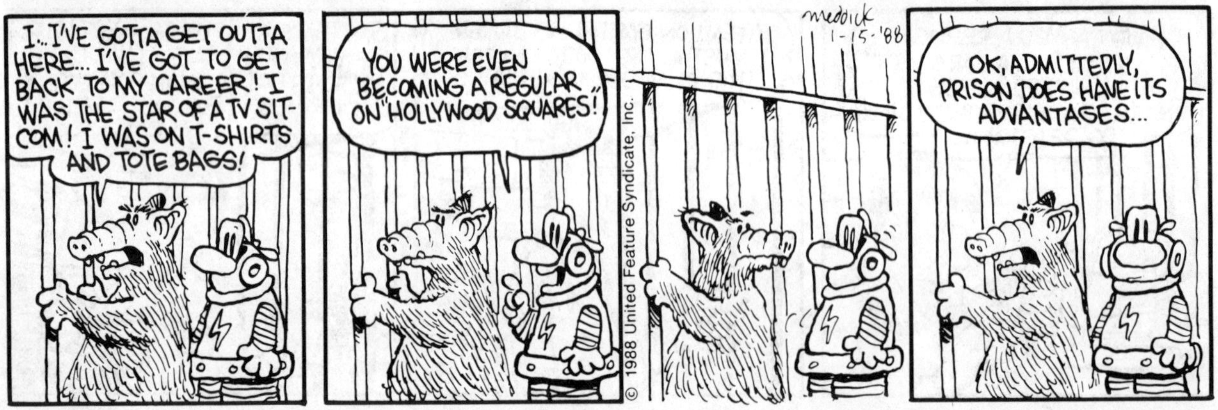
I...I'VE GOTTA GET OUTTA HERE... I'VE GOT TO GET BACK TO MY CAREER! I WAS THE STAR OF A TV SIT-COM! I WAS ON T-SHIRTS AND TOTE BAGS!
YOU WERE EVEN BECOMING A REGULAR ON "HOLLYWOOD SQUARES!"
© 1988 United Feature Syndicate, Inc.
meddick 1-15-'88
OK, ADMITTEDLY, PRISON DOES HAVE ITS ADVANTAGES...

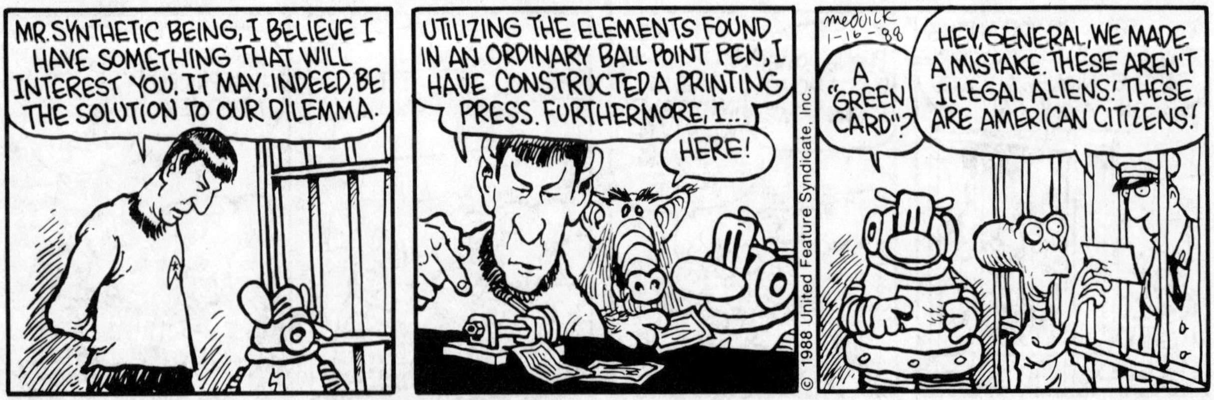
MR.SYNTHETIC BEING, I BELIEVE I HAVE SOMETHING THAT WILL INTEREST YOU. IT MAY, INDEED, BE THE SOLUTION TO OUR DILEMMA.
UTILIZING THE ELEMENTS FOUND IN AN ORDINARY BALL POINT PEN, I HAVE CONSTRUCTED A PRINTING PRESS. FURTHERMORE, I...
HERE!
© 1988 United Feature Syndicate, Inc.
meddick 1-16-88
A "GREEN CARD"?
HEY, GENERAL, WE MADE A MISTAKE. THESE AREN'T ILLEGAL ALIENS! THESE ARE AMERICAN CITIZENS!

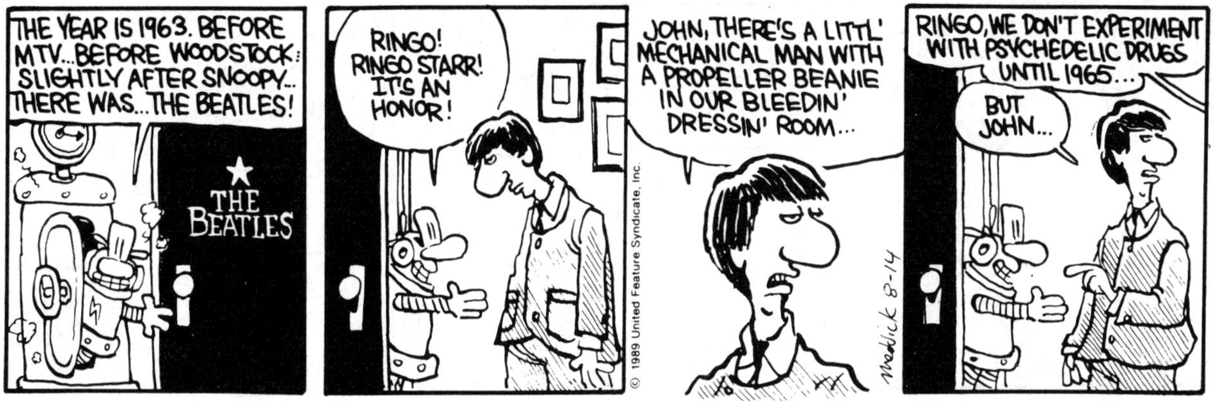
THE YEAR IS 1963. BEFORE MTV...BEFORE WOODSTOCK... SLIGHTLY AFTER SNOOPY... THERE WAS...THE BEATLES!
THE BEATLES
RINGO! RINGO STARR! IT'S AN HONOR!
© 1989 United Feature Syndicate, Inc.
JOHN, THERE'S A LITTL' MECHANICAL MAN WITH A PROPELLER BEANIE IN OUR BLEEDIN' DRESSIN' ROOM...
RINGO, WE DON'T EXPERIMENT WITH PSYCHEDELIC DRUGS UNTIL 1965...
BUT JOHN...

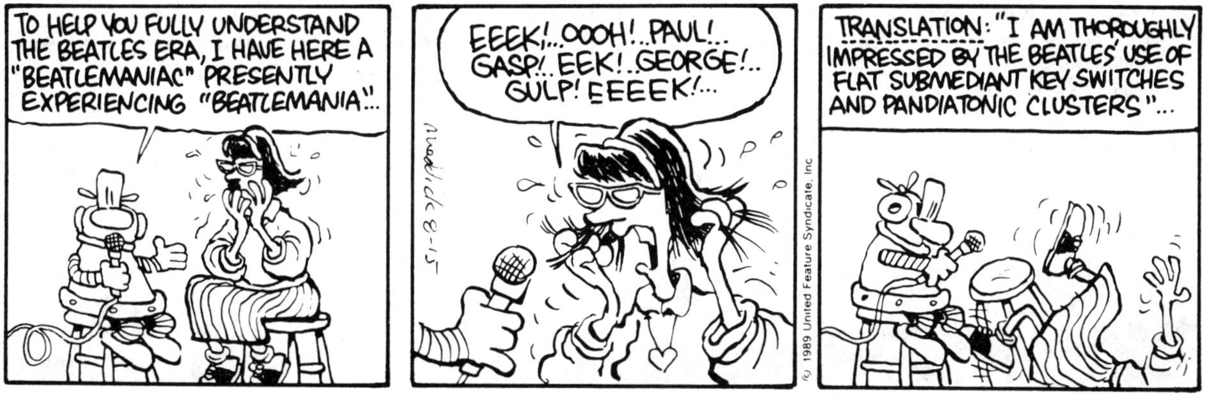
TO HELP YOU FULLY UNDERSTAND THE BEATLES ERA, I HAVE HERE A "BEATLEMANIAC" PRESENTLY EXPERIENCING "BEATLEMANIA"...
EEEK!...OOOH!...PAUL!... GASP!...EEK!...GEORGE!... GULP! EEEEK!...
© 1989 United Feature Syndicate, Inc
TRANSLATION: "I AM THOROUGHLY IMPRESSED BY THE BEATLES' USE OF FLAT SUBMEDIANT KEY SWITCHES AND PANDIATONIC CLUSTERS"...

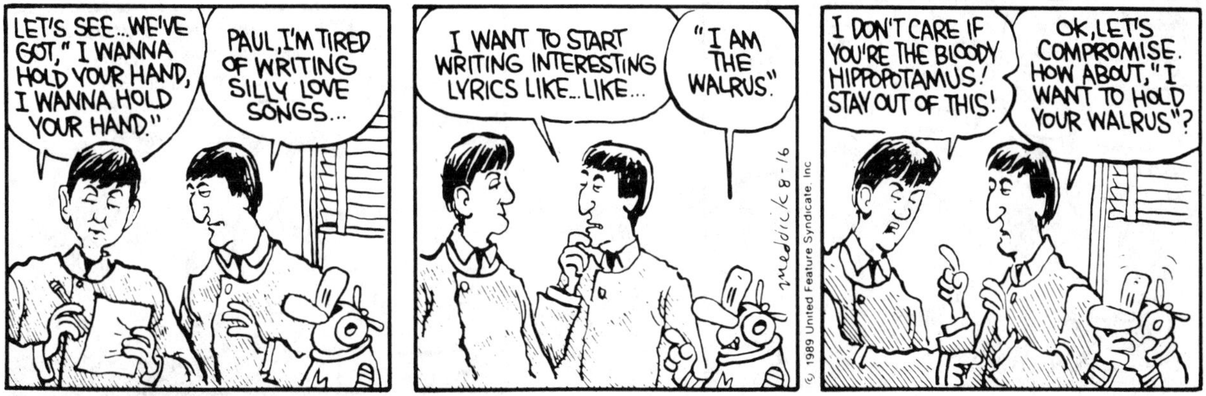
LET'S SEE...WE'VE GOT, "I WANNA HOLD YOUR HAND, I WANNA HOLD YOUR HAND."
PAUL, I'M TIRED OF WRITING SILLY LOVE SONGS...
I WANT TO START WRITING INTERESTING LYRICS LIKE...LIKE...
"I AM THE WALRUS."
© 1989 United Feature Syndicate, Inc.
I DON'T CARE IF YOU'RE THE BLOODY HIPPOPOTAMUS! STAY OUT OF THIS!
OK, LET'S COMPROMISE. HOW ABOUT, "I WANT TO HOLD YOUR WALRUS"?

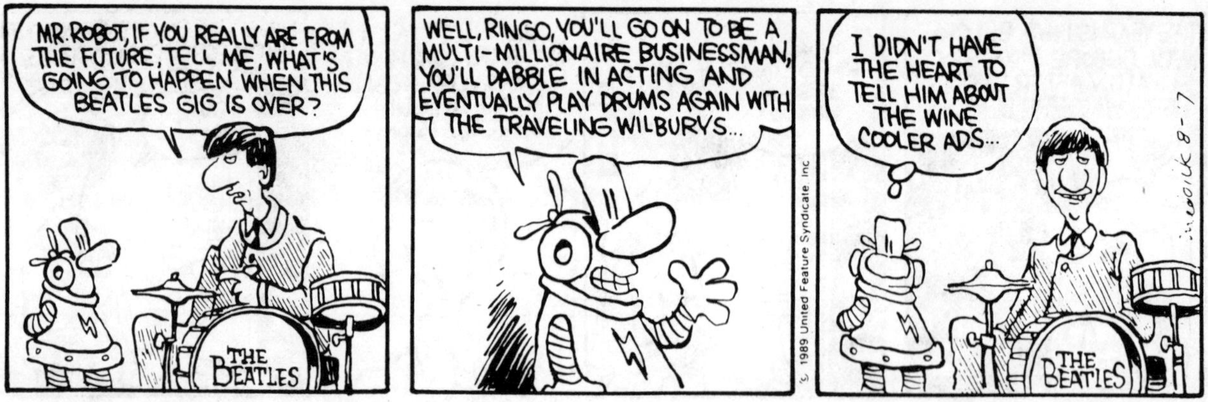
MR. ROBOT, IF YOU REALLY ARE FROM THE FUTURE, TELL ME, WHAT'S GOING TO HAPPEN WHEN THIS BEATLES GIG IS OVER?
THE BEATLES
WELL, RINGO, YOU'LL GO ON TO BE A MULTI-MILLIONAIRE BUSINESSMAN, YOU'LL DABBLE IN ACTING AND EVENTUALLY PLAY DRUMS AGAIN WITH THE TRAVELING WILBURYS...
© 1989 United Feature Syndicate, Inc
I DIDN'T HAVE THE HEART TO TELL HIM ABOUT THE WINE COOLER ADS...
THE BEATLES

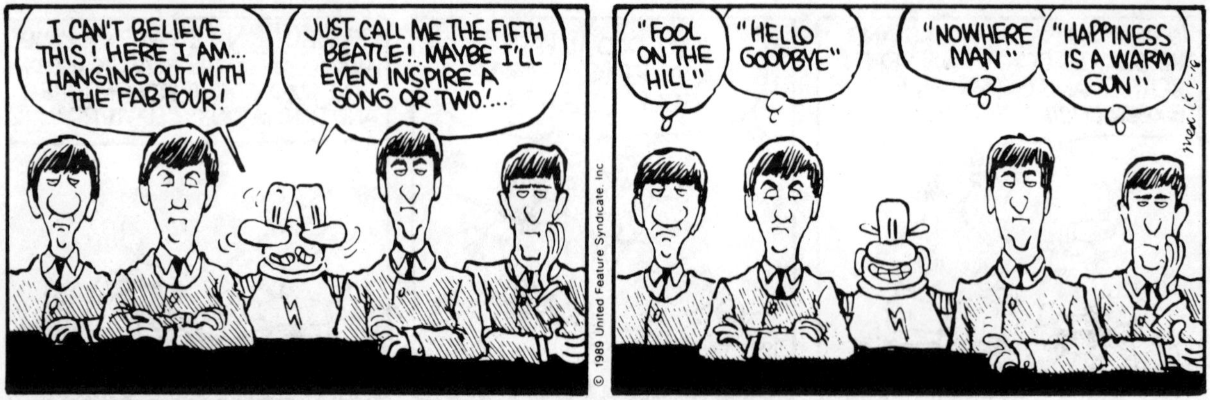
I CAN'T BELIEVE THIS! HERE I AM... HANGING OUT WITH THE FAB FOUR!
JUST CALL ME THE FIFTH BEATLE!.. MAYBE I'LL EVEN INSPIRE A SONG OR TWO!...
© 1989 United Feature Syndicate, Inc
"FOOL ON THE HILL"
"HELLO GOODBYE"
"NOWHERE MAN"
"HAPPINESS IS A WARM GUN"

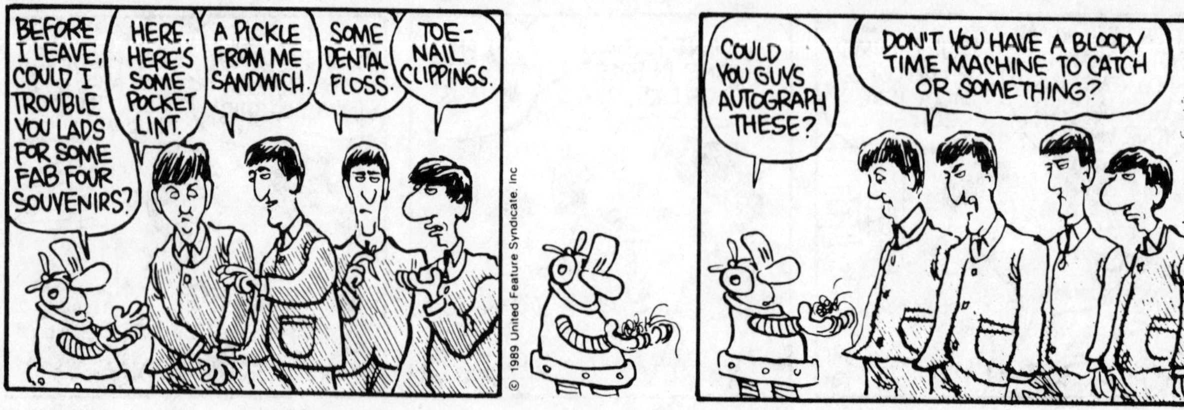
BEFORE I LEAVE, COULD I TROUBLE YOU LADS FOR SOME FAB FOUR SOUVENIRS?
HERE. HERE'S SOME POCKET LINT.
A PICKLE FROM ME SANDWICH.
SOME DENTAL FLOSS.
TOE-NAIL CLIPPINGS.
© 1989 United Feature Syndicate, Inc
COULD YOU GUYS AUTOGRAPH THESE?
DON'T YOU HAVE A BLOODY TIME MACHINE TO CATCH OR SOMETHING?

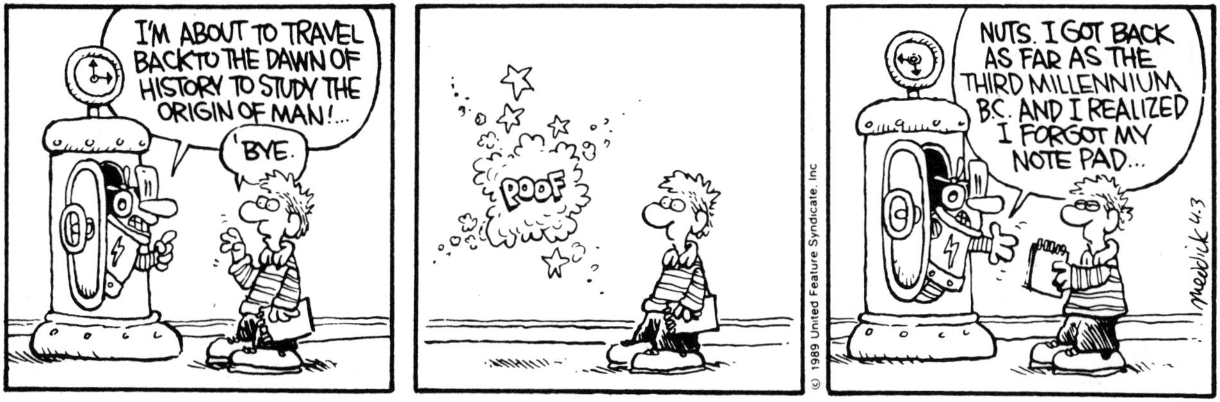
I'M ABOUT TO TRAVEL BACK TO THE DAWN OF HISTORY TO STUDY THE ORIGIN OF MAN!...
BYE.
POOF
© 1989 United Feature Syndicate, Inc
NUTS. I GOT BACK AS FAR AS THE THIRD MILLENNIUM B.C. AND I REALIZED I FORGOT MY NOTE PAD...

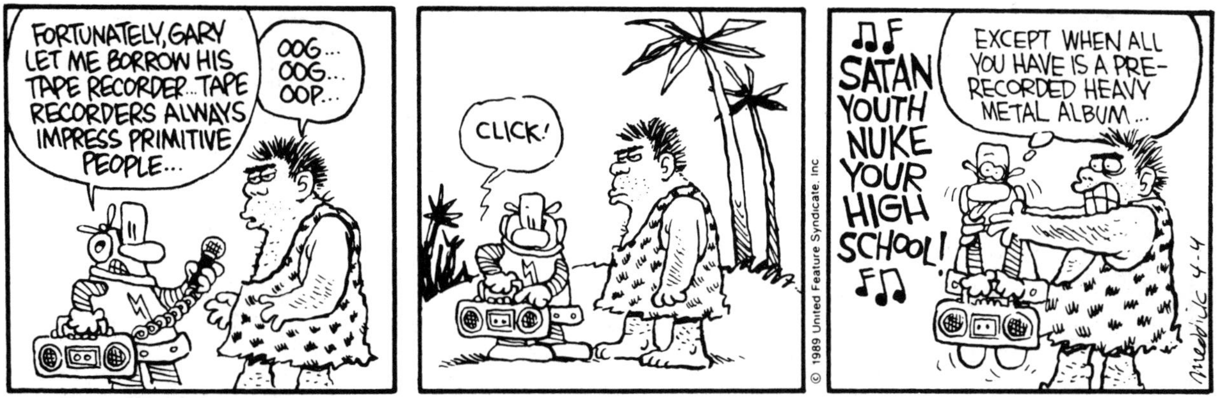
FORTUNATELY, GARY LET ME BORROW HIS TAPE RECORDER... TAPE RECORDERS ALWAYS IMPRESS PRIMITIVE PEOPLE...
OOG... OOG... OOP...
CLICK!
© 1989 United Feature Syndicate, Inc
SATAN YOUTH NUKE YOUR HIGH SCHOOL!
EXCEPT WHEN ALL YOU HAVE IS A PRE-RECORDED HEAVY METAL ALBUM...

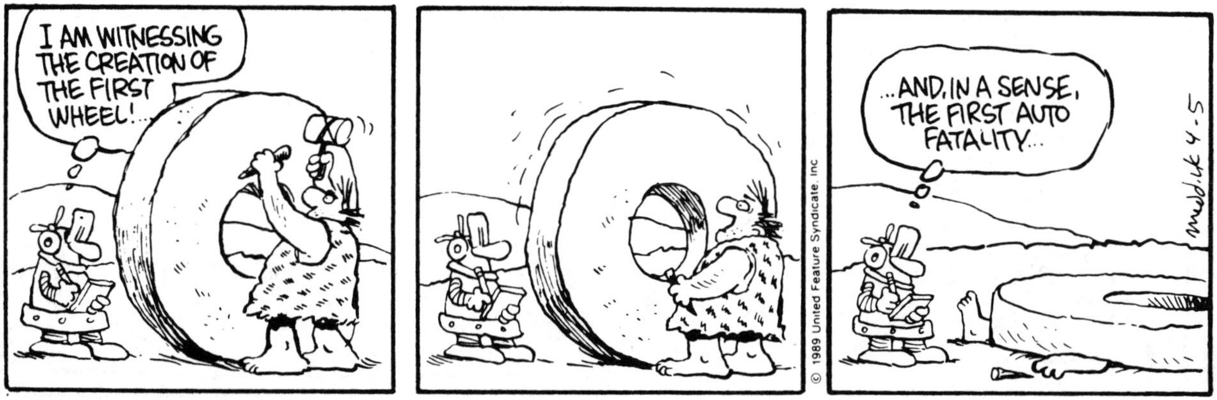
I AM WITNESSING THE CREATION OF THE FIRST WHEEL!...
© 1989 United Feature Syndicate, Inc
...AND, IN A SENSE, THE FIRST AUTO FATALITY...

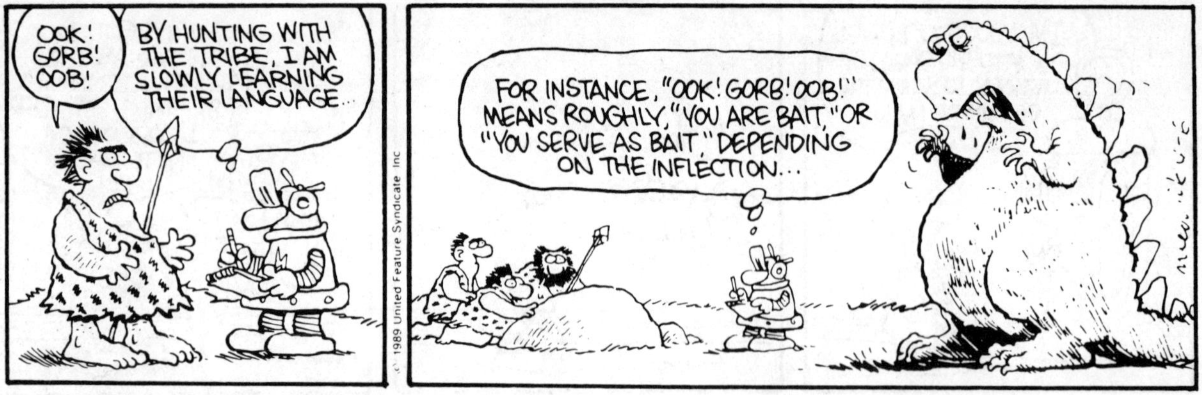
OOK! GORB! OOB!
BY HUNTING WITH THE TRIBE, I AM SLOWLY LEARNING THEIR LANGUAGE...
© 1989 United Feature Syndicate, Inc
FOR INSTANCE, "OOK! GORB! OOB!" MEANS ROUGHLY, "YOU ARE BAIT," OR "YOU SERVE AS BAIT," DEPENDING ON THE INFLECTION...

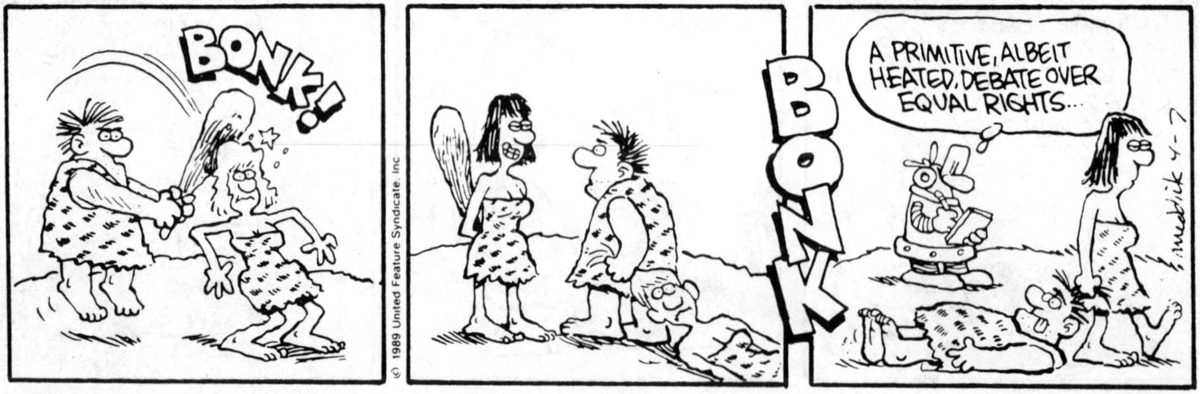
BONK!
© 1989 United Feature Syndicate, Inc
BONK
A PRIMITIVE, ALBEIT HEATED, DEBATE OVER EQUAL RIGHTS...

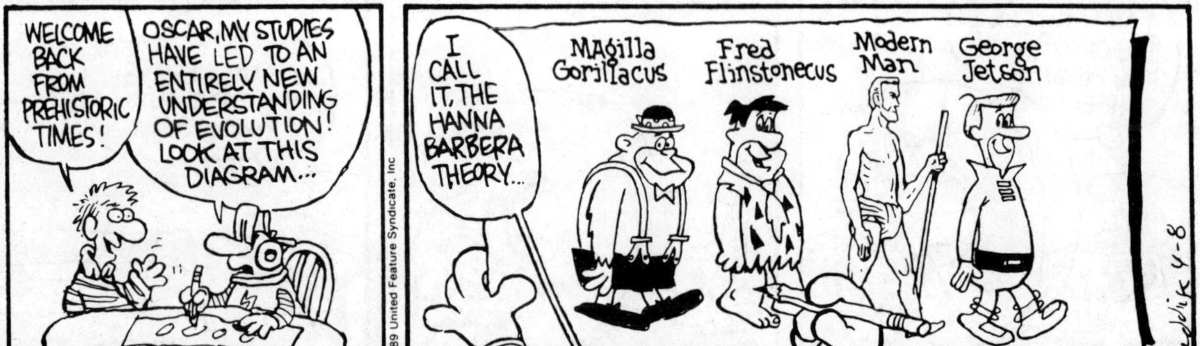
WELCOME BACK FROM PREHISTORIC TIMES!
OSCAR, MY STUDIES HAVE LED TO AN ENTIRELY NEW UNDERSTANDING OF EVOLUTION! LOOK AT THIS DIAGRAM...
© 1989 United Feature Syndicate, Inc
I CALL IT, THE HANNA BARBERA THEORY...
MAgilla Gorillacus
Fred Flinstonecus
Modern Man
George Jetson

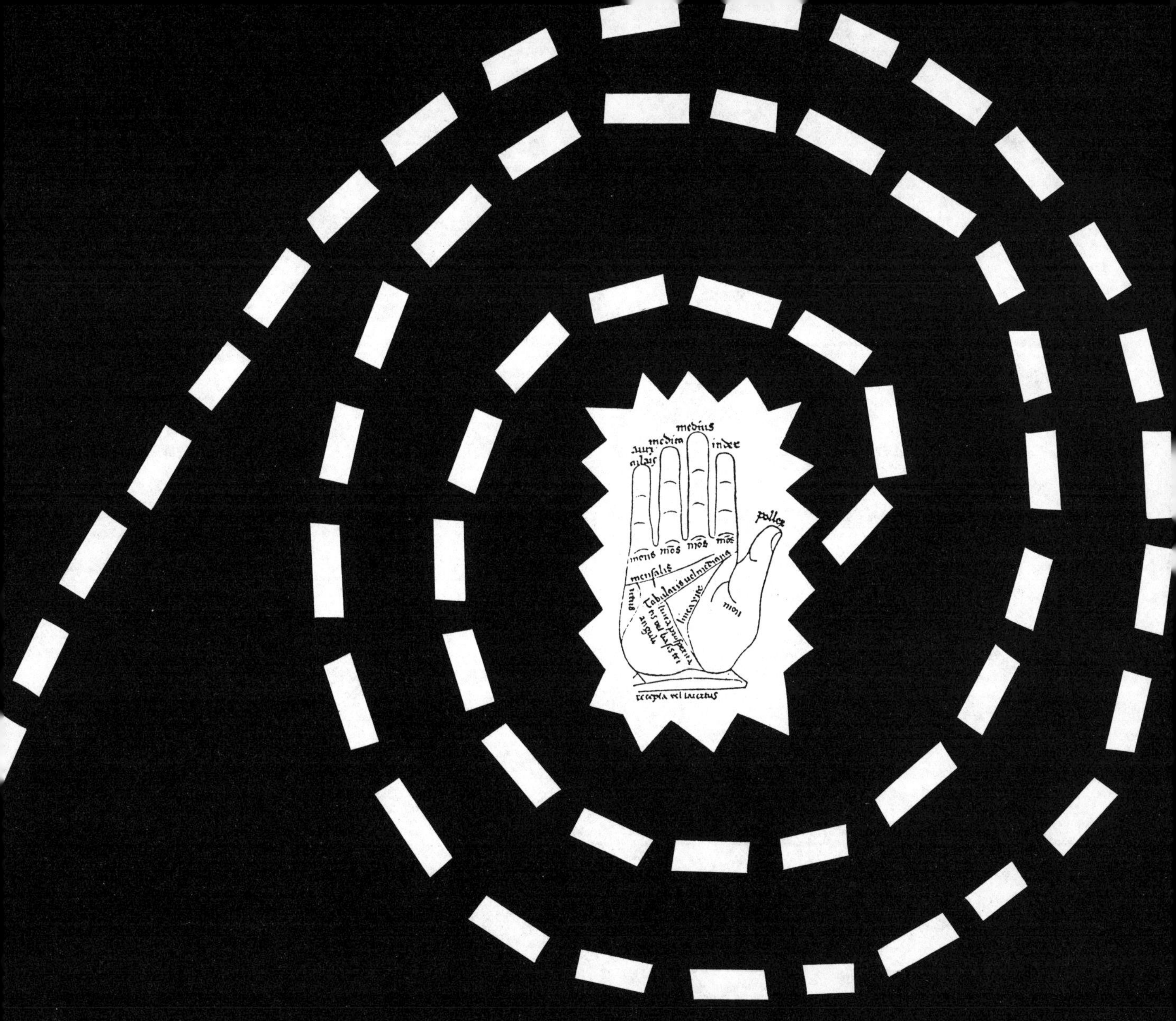
medius
media
index
pollex
mensalis
Tabularis uel mediana
linea vite
recepta vel lacertus

PSUEDO - SCIENCE

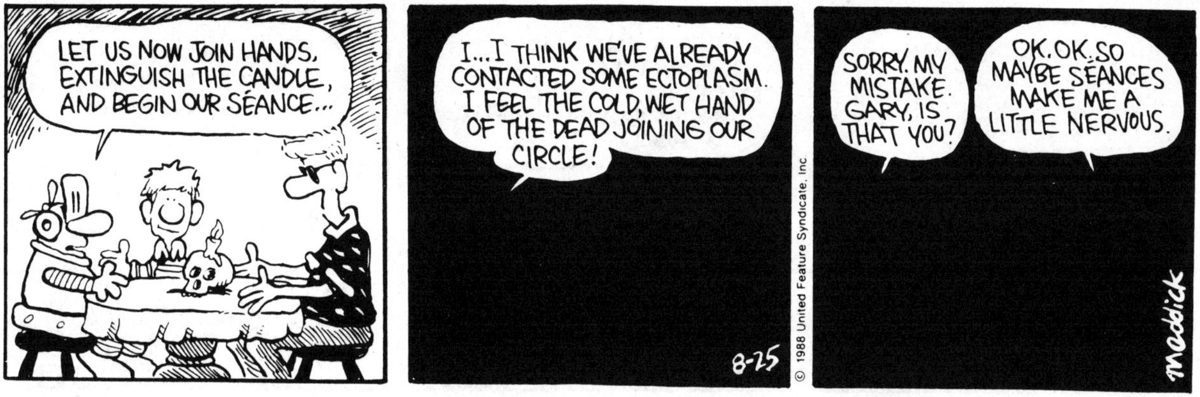
LET US NOW JOIN HANDS, EXTINGUISH THE CANDLE, AND BEGIN OUR SÉANCE...
I... I THINK WE'VE ALREADY CONTACTED SOME ECTOPLASM. I FEEL THE COLD, WET HAND OF THE DEAD JOINING OUR CIRCLE!
8-25
© 1988 United Feature Syndicate, Inc
SORRY. MY MISTAKE. GARY, IS THAT YOU?
OK. OK. SO MAYBE SÉANCES MAKE ME A LITTLE NERVOUS.
meddick

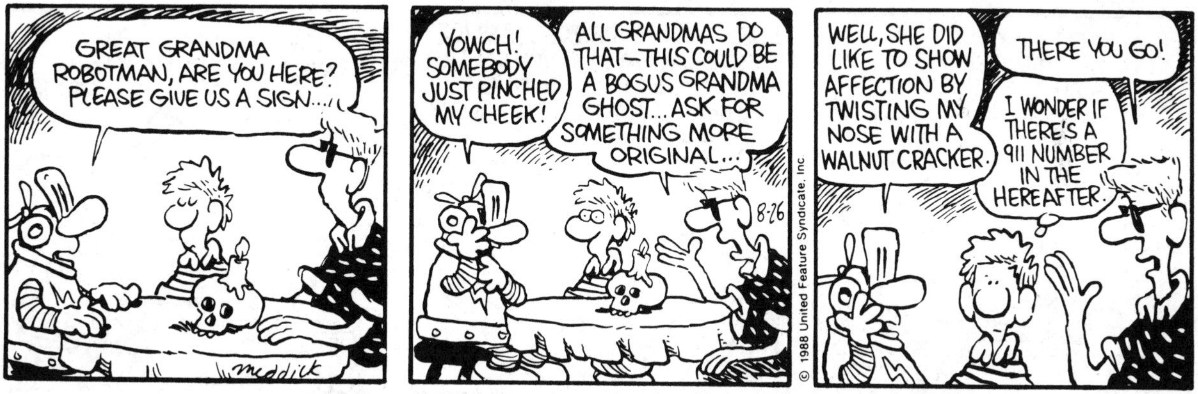
GREAT GRANDMA ROBOTMAN, ARE YOU HERE? PLEASE GIVE US A SIGN...
meddick
YOWCH! SOMEBODY JUST PINCHED MY CHEEK!
ALL GRANDMAS DO THAT—THIS COULD BE A BOGUS GRANDMA GHOST... ASK FOR SOMETHING MORE ORIGINAL...
8-26
© 1988 United Feature Syndicate, Inc
WELL, SHE DID LIKE TO SHOW AFFECTION BY TWISTING MY NOSE WITH A WALNUT CRACKER.
THERE YOU GO!
I WONDER IF THERE'S A 911 NUMBER IN THE HEREAFTER.

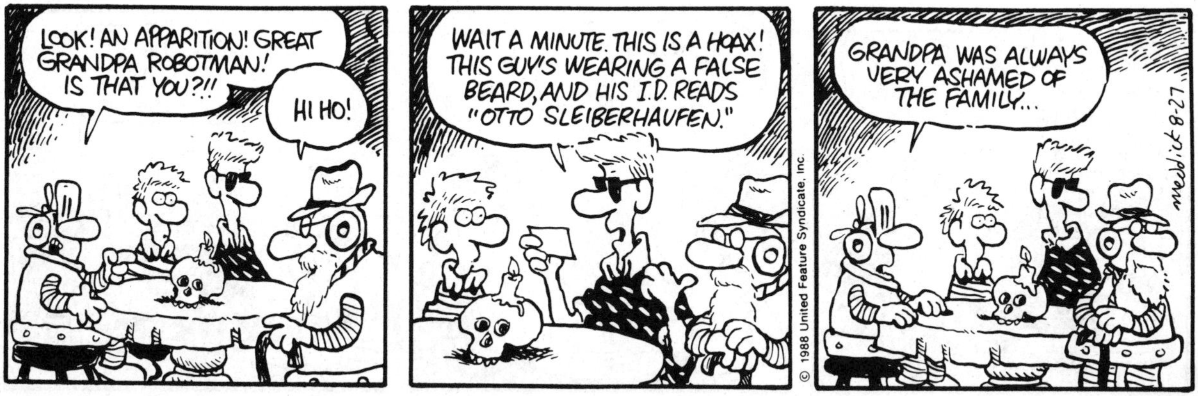
LOOK! AN APPARITION! GREAT GRANDPA ROBOTMAN! IS THAT YOU?!!
HI HO!
WAIT A MINUTE. THIS IS A HOAX! THIS GUY'S WEARING A FALSE BEARD, AND HIS I.D. READS "OTTO SLEIBERHAUFEN."
© 1988 United Feature Syndicate, Inc.
GRANDPA WAS ALWAYS VERY ASHAMED OF THE FAMILY...
meddick 8-27

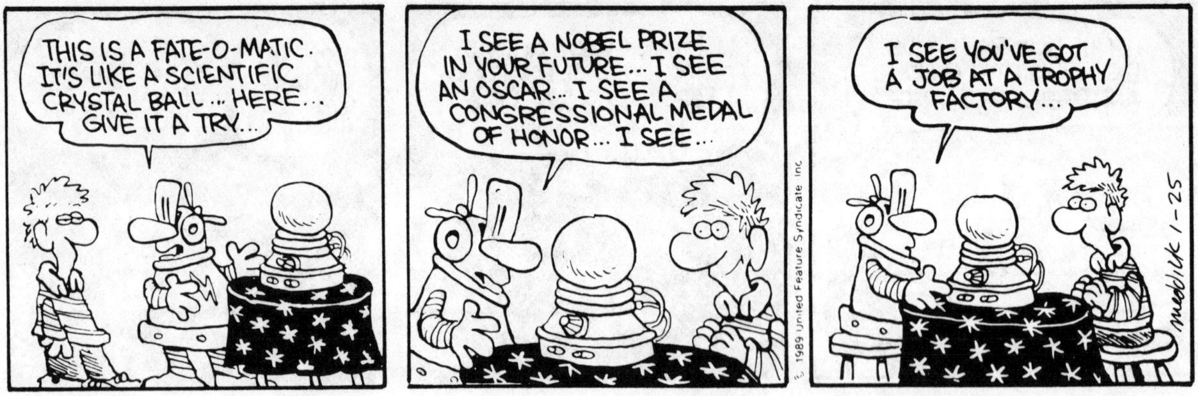
THIS IS A FATE-O-MATIC. IT'S LIKE A SCIENTIFIC CRYSTAL BALL ... HERE... GIVE IT A TRY...
I SEE A NOBEL PRIZE IN YOUR FUTURE... I SEE AN OSCAR... I SEE A CONGRESSIONAL MEDAL OF HONOR... I SEE...
I SEE YOU'VE GOT A JOB AT A TROPHY FACTORY...
© 1989 United Feature Syndicate, Inc.
meddick 1-25

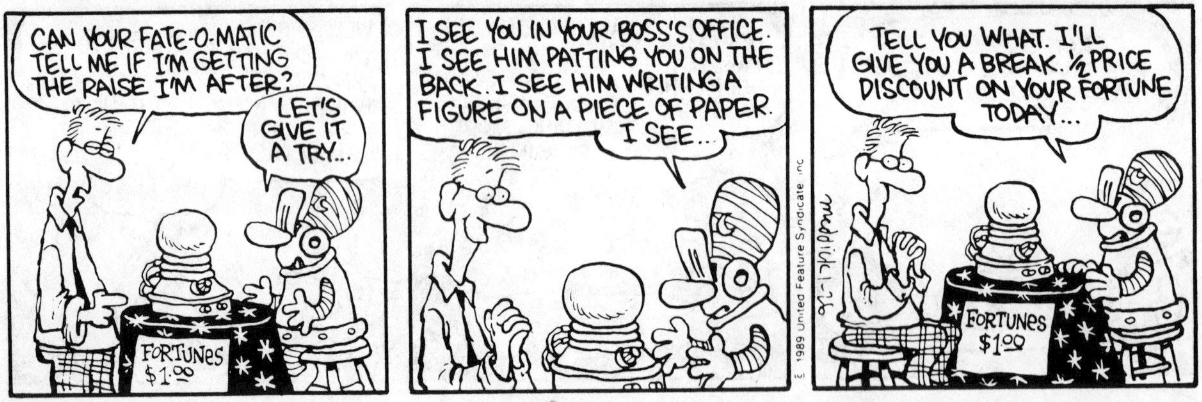
CAN YOUR FATE-O-MATIC TELL ME IF I'M GETTING THE RAISE I'M AFTER?
LET'S GIVE IT A TRY...
FORTUNES $1.00
I SEE YOU IN YOUR BOSS'S OFFICE. I SEE HIM PATTING YOU ON THE BACK. I SEE HIM WRITING A FIGURE ON A PIECE OF PAPER. I SEE...
© 1989 United Feature Syndicate, Inc.
meddick 1-26
TELL YOU WHAT. I'LL GIVE YOU A BREAK. ½ PRICE DISCOUNT ON YOUR FORTUNE TODAY...
FORTUNES $1.00

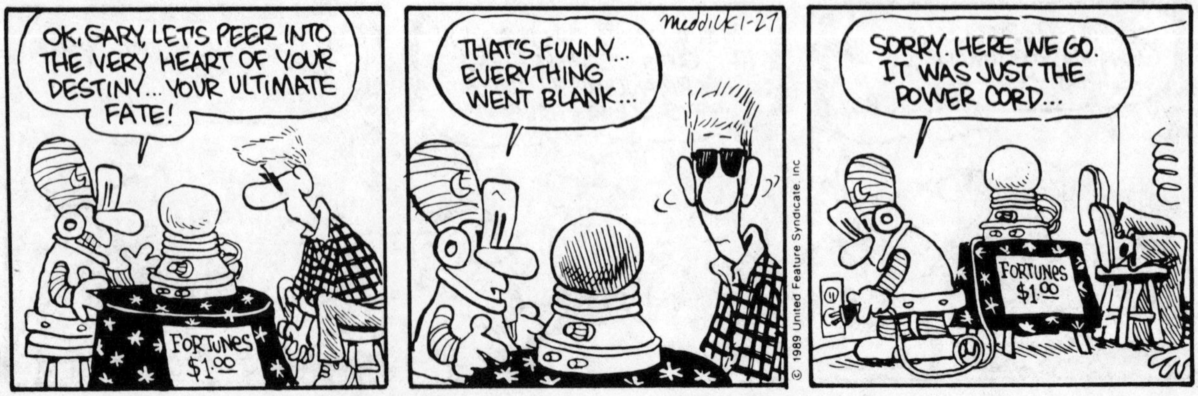
OK, GARY, LET'S PEER INTO THE VERY HEART OF YOUR DESTINY... YOUR ULTIMATE FATE!
FORTUNES $1.00
meddick 1-27
THAT'S FUNNY... EVERYTHING WENT BLANK...
© 1989 United Feature Syndicate, Inc.
SORRY. HERE WE GO. IT WAS JUST THE POWER CORD...
FORTUNES $1.00

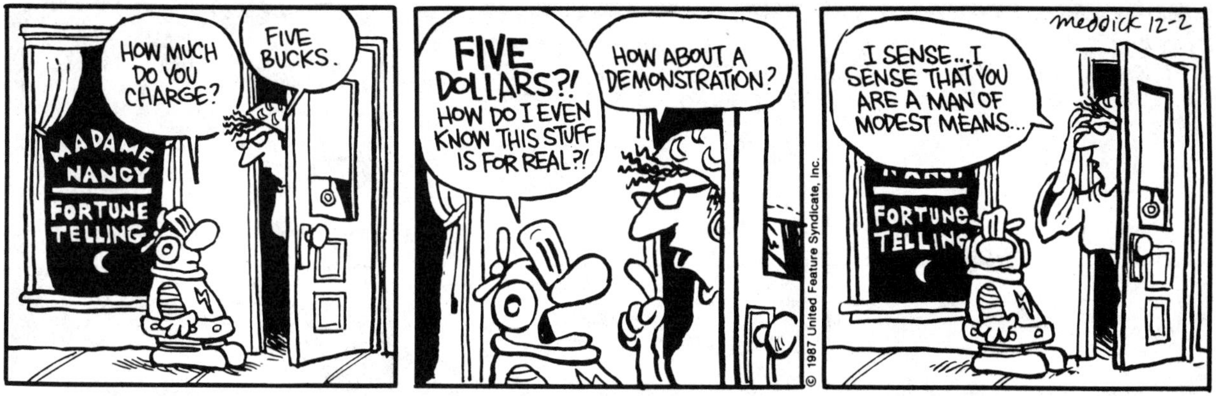
HOW MUCH DO YOU CHARGE?
FIVE BUCKS.
MADAME NANCY
FORTUNE TELLING
FIVE DOLLARS?! HOW DO I EVEN KNOW THIS STUFF IS FOR REAL?!
HOW ABOUT A DEMONSTRATION?
meddick 12-2
I SENSE...I SENSE THAT YOU ARE A MAN OF MODEST MEANS...
FORTUNE TELLING

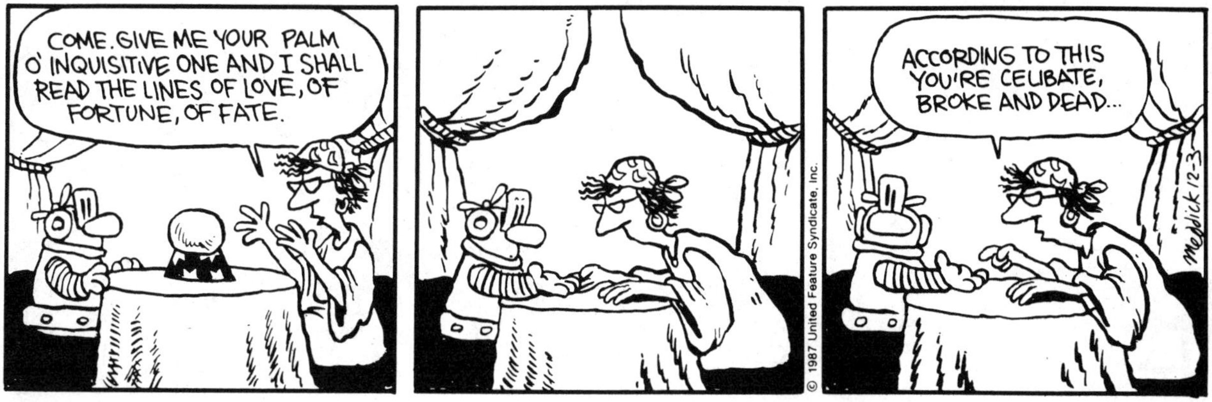
COME. GIVE ME YOUR PALM O' INQUISITIVE ONE AND I SHALL READ THE LINES OF LOVE, OF FORTUNE, OF FATE.
ACCORDING TO THIS YOU'RE CELIBATE, BROKE AND DEAD...
meddick 12-3

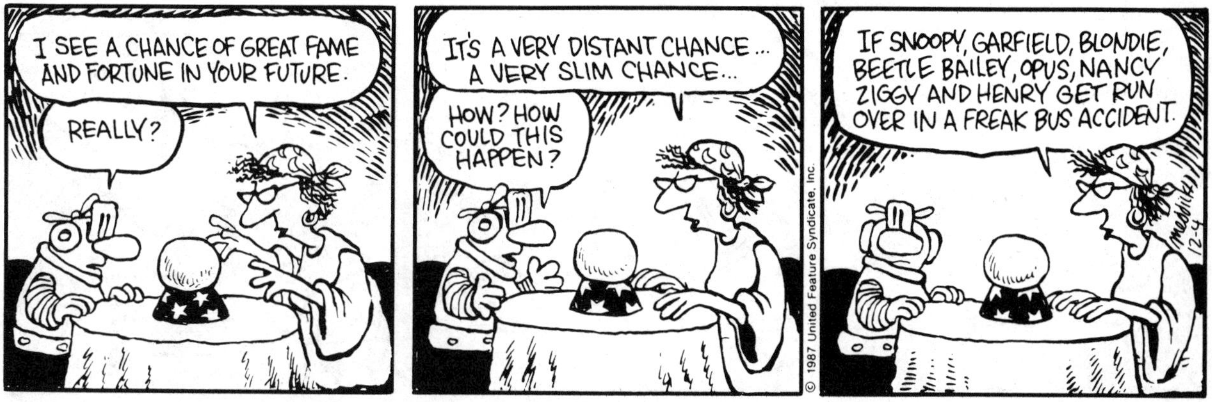
I SEE A CHANCE OF GREAT FAME AND FORTUNE IN YOUR FUTURE.
REALLY?
IT'S A VERY DISTANT CHANCE... A VERY SLIM CHANCE...
HOW? HOW COULD THIS HAPPEN?
IF SNOOPY, GARFIELD, BLONDIE, BEETLE BAILEY, OPUS, NANCY ZIGGY AND HENRY GET RUN OVER IN A FREAK BUS ACCIDENT.
meddick 12-4

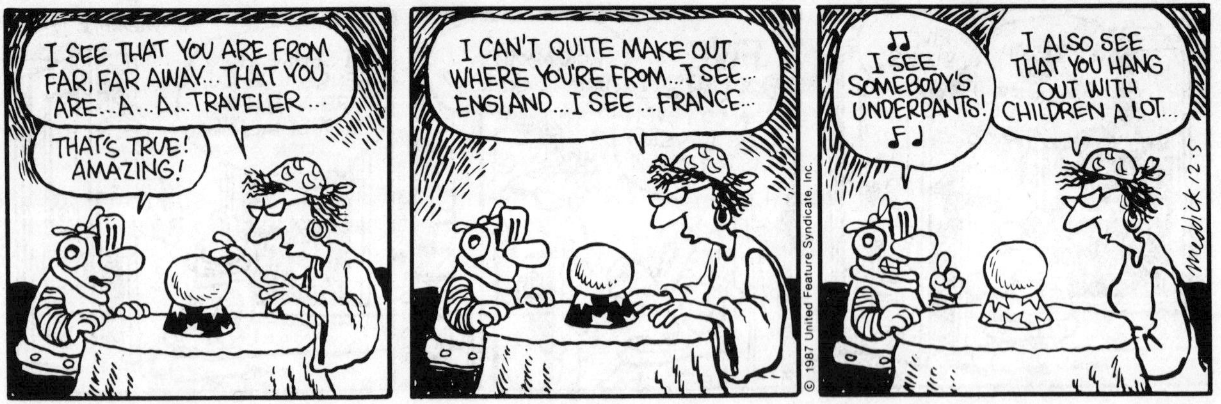
I SEE THAT YOU ARE FROM FAR, FAR AWAY... THAT YOU ARE... A... A... TRAVELER...
THAT'S TRUE! AMAZING!
I CAN'T QUITE MAKE OUT WHERE YOU'RE FROM... I SEE... ENGLAND... I SEE ... FRANCE...
I SEE SOMEBODY'S UNDERPANTS!
I ALSO SEE THAT YOU HANG OUT WITH CHILDREN A LOT...
© 1987 United Feature Syndicate, Inc.

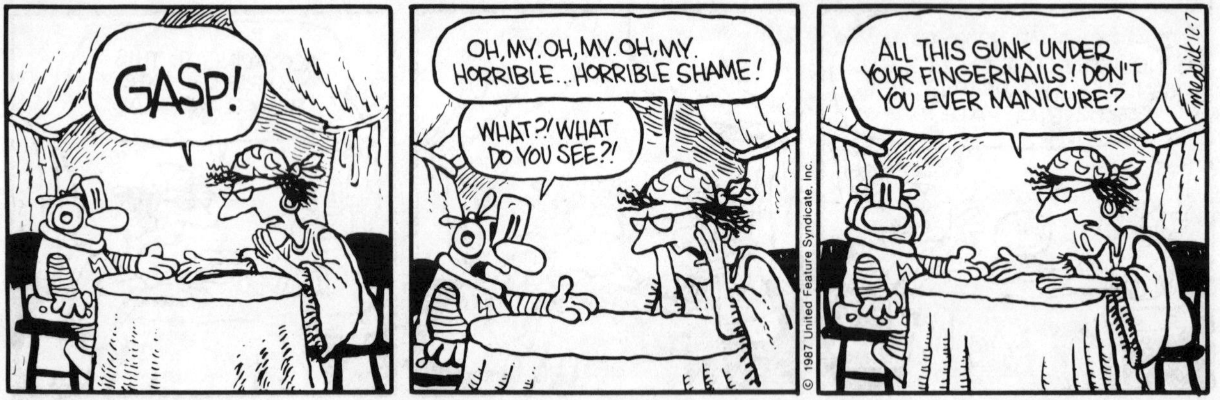
GASP!
OH, MY. OH, MY. OH, MY. HORRIBLE... HORRIBLE SHAME!
WHAT?! WHAT DO YOU SEE?!
ALL THIS GUNK UNDER YOUR FINGERNAILS! DON'T YOU EVER MANICURE?
© 1987 United Feature Syndicate, Inc.

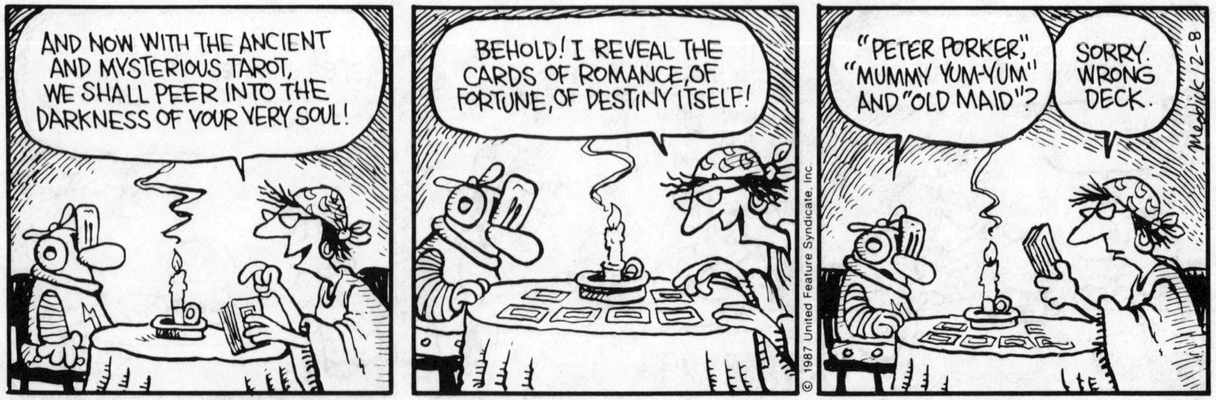
AND NOW WITH THE ANCIENT AND MYSTERIOUS TAROT, WE SHALL PEER INTO THE DARKNESS OF YOUR VERY SOUL!
BEHOLD! I REVEAL THE CARDS OF ROMANCE, OF FORTUNE, OF DESTINY ITSELF!
"PETER PORKER," "MUMMY YUM-YUM" AND "OLD MAID"?
SORRY. WRONG DECK.
© 1987 United Feature Syndicate, Inc.

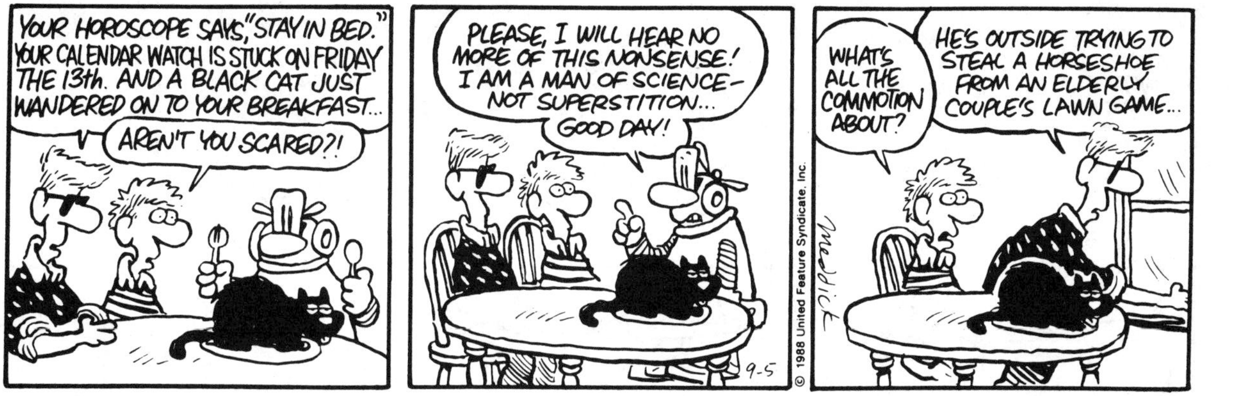
YOUR HOROSCOPE SAYS, "STAY IN BED." YOUR CALENDAR WATCH IS STUCK ON FRIDAY THE 13th. AND A BLACK CAT JUST WANDERED ON TO YOUR BREAKFAST...
AREN'T YOU SCARED?!
PLEASE, I WILL HEAR NO MORE OF THIS NONSENSE! I AM A MAN OF SCIENCE- NOT SUPERSTITION...
GOOD DAY!
9-5
© 1988 United Feature Syndicate, Inc.
WHAT'S ALL THE COMMOTION ABOUT?
HE'S OUTSIDE TRYING TO STEAL A HORSESHOE FROM AN ELDERLY COUPLE'S LAWN GAME...

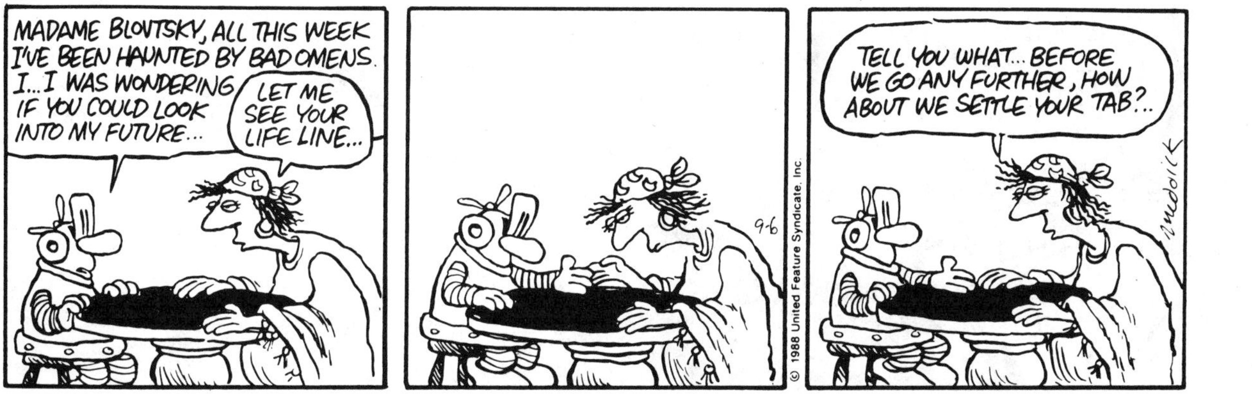
MADAME BLOVTSKY, ALL THIS WEEK I'VE BEEN HAUNTED BY BAD OMENS. I...I WAS WONDERING IF YOU COULD LOOK INTO MY FUTURE...
LET ME SEE YOUR LIFE LINE...
9-6
© 1988 United Feature Syndicate, Inc.
TELL YOU WHAT... BEFORE WE GO ANY FURTHER, HOW ABOUT WE SETTLE YOUR TAB?..

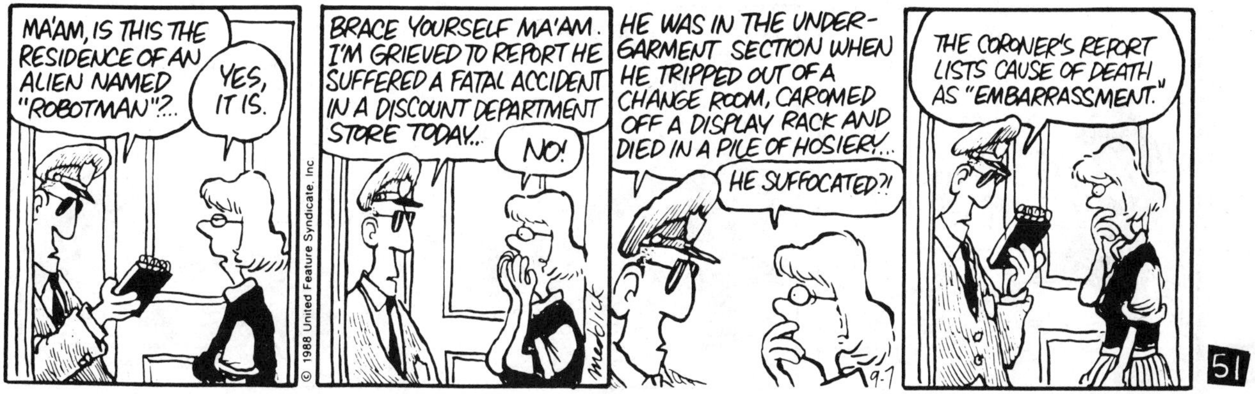
MA'AM, IS THIS THE RESIDENCE OF AN ALIEN NAMED "ROBOTMAN"?..
YES, IT IS.
© 1988 United Feature Syndicate, Inc.
BRACE YOURSELF MA'AM. I'M GRIEVED TO REPORT HE SUFFERED A FATAL ACCIDENT IN A DISCOUNT DEPARTMENT STORE TODAY...
NO!
HE WAS IN THE UNDER-GARMENT SECTION WHEN HE TRIPPED OUT OF A CHANGE ROOM, CAROMED OFF A DISPLAY RACK AND DIED IN A PILE OF HOSIERY...
HE SUFFOCATED?!
9-7
THE CORONER'S REPORT LISTS CAUSE OF DEATH AS "EMBARRASSMENT."

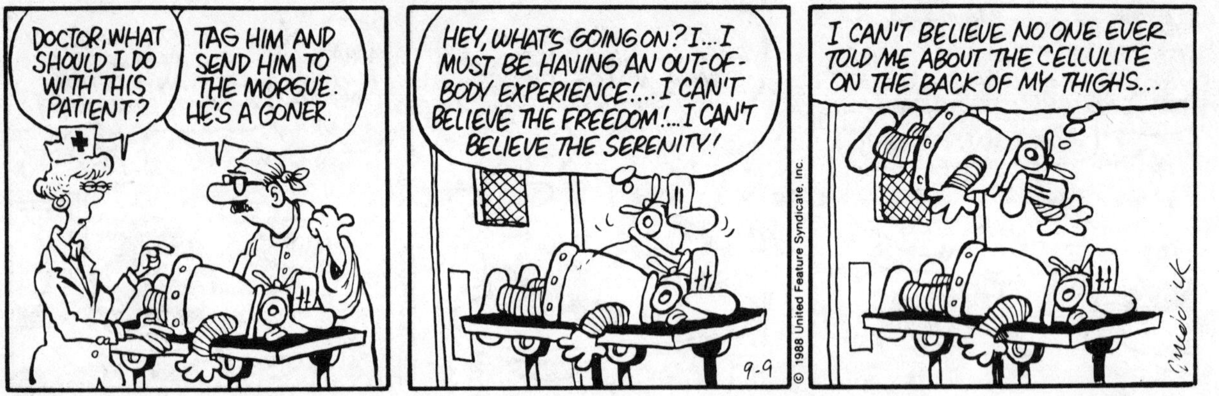
DOCTOR, WHAT SHOULD I DO WITH THIS PATIENT?
TAG HIM AND SEND HIM TO THE MORGUE. HE'S A GONER.
HEY, WHAT'S GOING ON? I... I MUST BE HAVING AN OUT-OF-BODY EXPERIENCE!... I CAN'T BELIEVE THE FREEDOM!... I CAN'T BELIEVE THE SERENITY!
9-9
© 1988 United Feature Syndicate, Inc.
I CAN'T BELIEVE NO ONE EVER TOLD ME ABOUT THE CELLULITE ON THE BACK OF MY THIGHS...

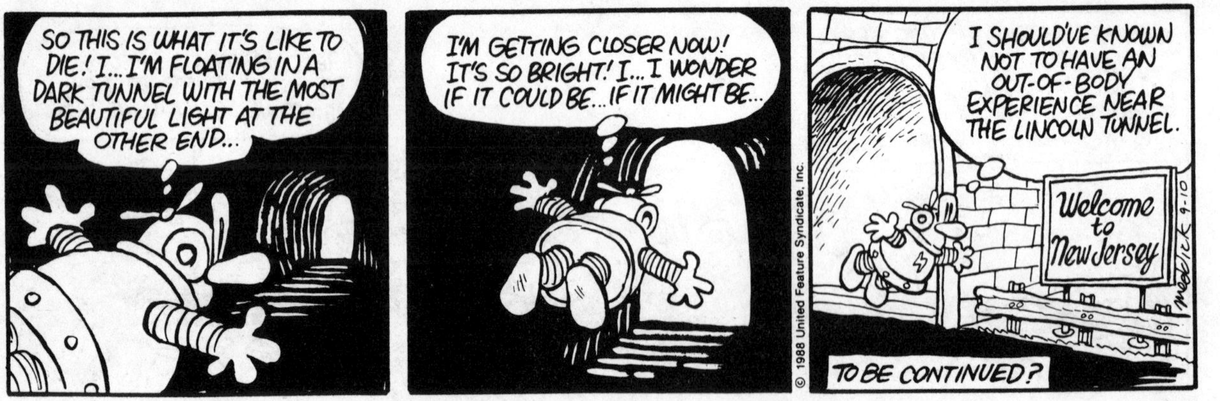
SO THIS IS WHAT IT'S LIKE TO DIE! I... I'M FLOATING IN A DARK TUNNEL WITH THE MOST BEAUTIFUL LIGHT AT THE OTHER END...
I'M GETTING CLOSER NOW! IT'S SO BRIGHT! I... I WONDER IF IT COULD BE... IF IT MIGHT BE...
© 1988 United Feature Syndicate, Inc.
I SHOULD'VE KNOWN NOT TO HAVE AN OUT-OF-BODY EXPERIENCE NEAR THE LINCOLN TUNNEL.
Welcome to New Jersey
9-10
TO BE CONTINUED?

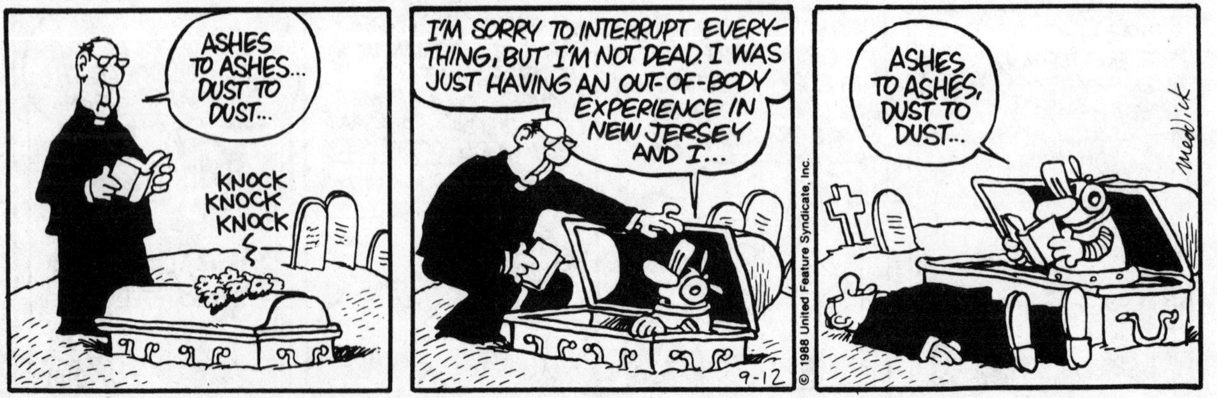
ASHES TO ASHES... DUST TO DUST...
KNOCK KNOCK KNOCK
I'M SORRY TO INTERRUPT EVERYTHING, BUT I'M NOT DEAD. I WAS JUST HAVING AN OUT-OF-BODY EXPERIENCE IN NEW JERSEY AND I...
9-12
© 1988 United Feature Syndicate, Inc.
ASHES TO ASHES, DUST TO DUST...

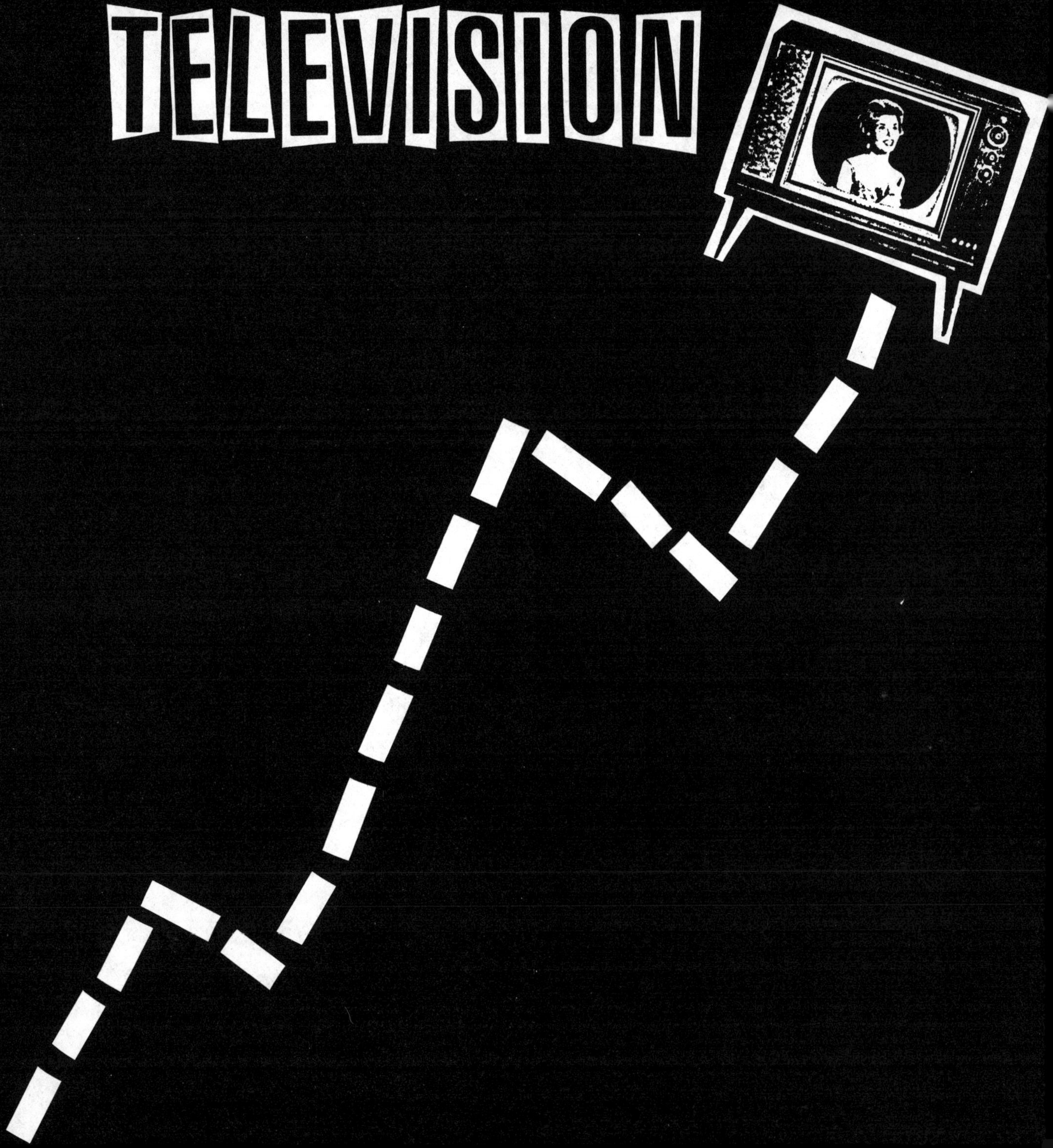
TELEVISION

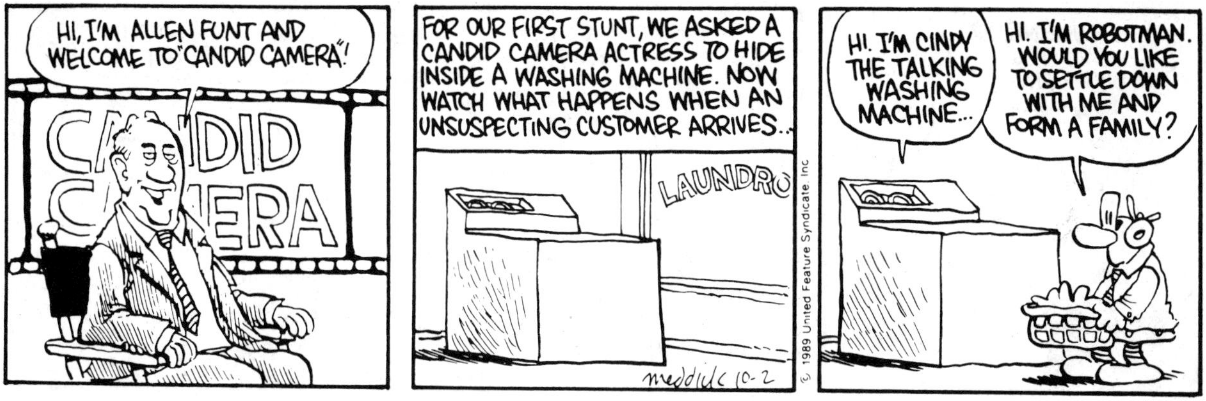
HI, I'M ALLEN FUNT AND WELCOME TO "CANDID CAMERA"!
CANDID CAMERA
FOR OUR FIRST STUNT, WE ASKED A CANDID CAMERA ACTRESS TO HIDE INSIDE A WASHING MACHINE. NOW WATCH WHAT HAPPENS WHEN AN UNSUSPECTING CUSTOMER ARRIVES...
LAUNDRO
© 1989 United Feature Syndicate Inc
HI. I'M CINDY THE TALKING WASHING MACHINE...
HI. I'M ROBOTMAN. WOULD YOU LIKE TO SETTLE DOWN WITH ME AND FORM A FAMILY?

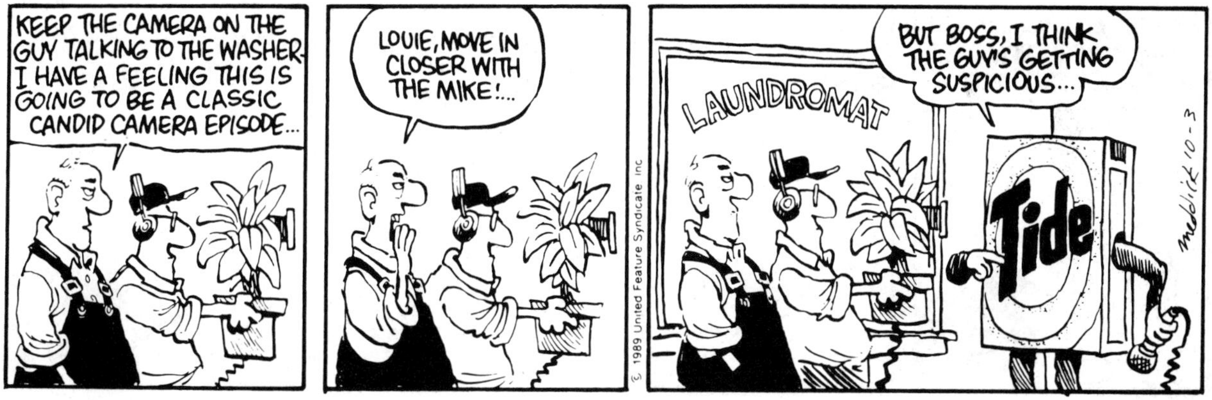
KEEP THE CAMERA ON THE GUY TALKING TO THE WASHER. I HAVE A FEELING THIS IS GOING TO BE A CLASSIC CANDID CAMERA EPISODE...
LOUIE, MOVE IN CLOSER WITH THE MIKE!...
© 1989 United Feature Syndicate Inc
LAUNDROMAT
BUT BOSS, I THINK THE GUY'S GETTING SUSPICIOUS...
Tide

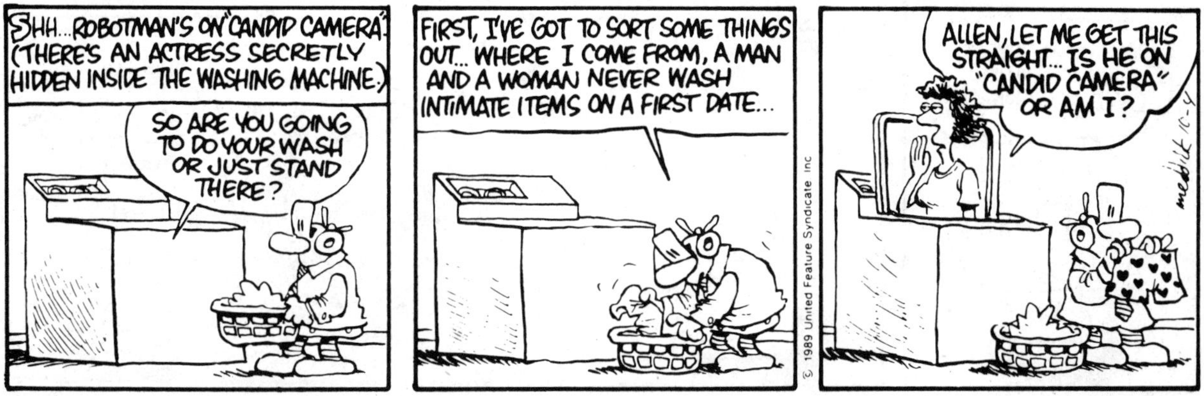
SHH...ROBOTMAN'S ON "CANDID CAMERA". (THERE'S AN ACTRESS SECRETLY HIDDEN INSIDE THE WASHING MACHINE.)
SO ARE YOU GOING TO DO YOUR WASH OR JUST STAND THERE?
FIRST, I'VE GOT TO SORT SOME THINGS OUT... WHERE I COME FROM, A MAN AND A WOMAN NEVER WASH INTIMATE ITEMS ON A FIRST DATE...
© 1989 United Feature Syndicate Inc
ALLEN, LET ME GET THIS STRAIGHT... IS HE ON "CANDID CAMERA" OR AM I?

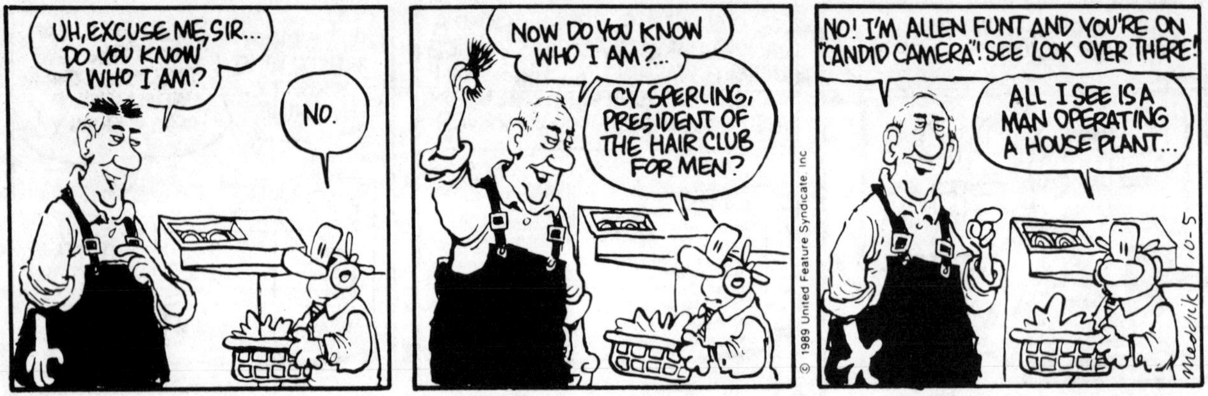
UH, EXCUSE ME, SIR... DO YOU KNOW WHO I AM?
NO.
NOW DO YOU KNOW WHO I AM?...
CY SPERLING, PRESIDENT OF THE HAIR CLUB FOR MEN?
© 1989 United Feature Syndicate, Inc.
NO! I'M ALLEN FUNT AND YOU'RE ON "CANDID CAMERA"! SEE LOOK OVER THERE!
ALL I SEE IS A MAN OPERATING A HOUSE PLANT...
meddick 10-5

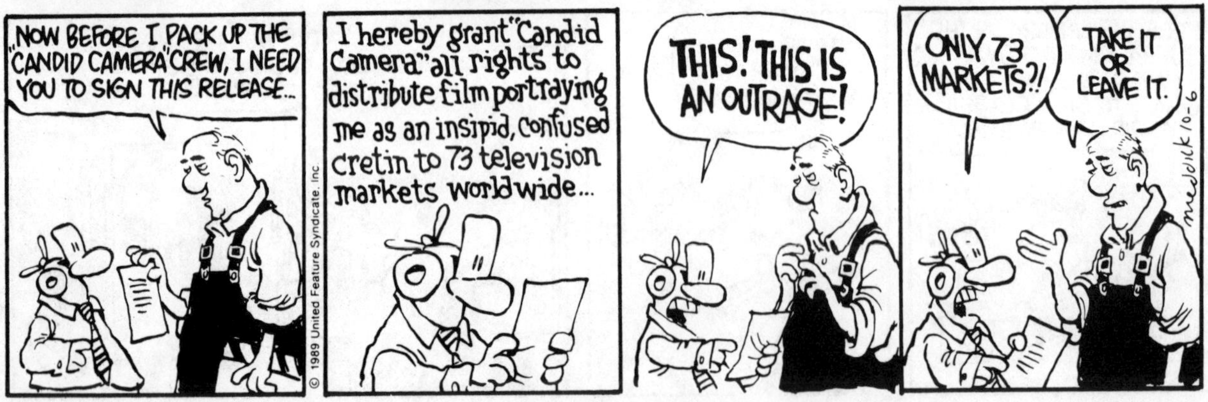
NOW BEFORE I PACK UP THE "CANDID CAMERA" CREW, I NEED YOU TO SIGN THIS RELEASE...
© 1989 United Feature Syndicate, Inc.
I hereby grant "Candid Camera" all rights to distribute film portraying me as an insipid, confused cretin to 73 television markets worldwide...
THIS! THIS IS AN OUTRAGE!
ONLY 73 MARKETS?!
TAKE IT OR LEAVE IT.
meddick 10-6

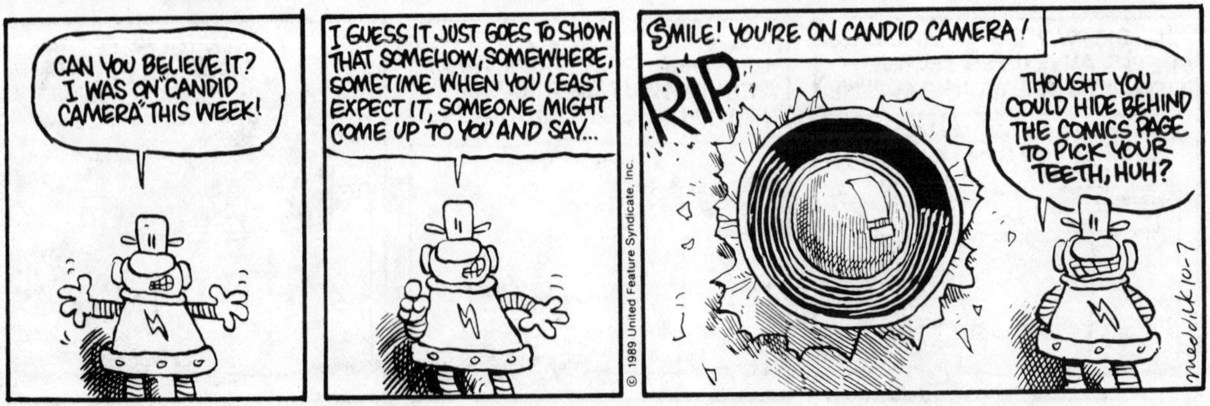
CAN YOU BELIEVE IT? I WAS ON "CANDID CAMERA" THIS WEEK!
I GUESS IT JUST GOES TO SHOW THAT SOMEHOW, SOMEWHERE, SOMETIME WHEN YOU LEAST EXPECT IT, SOMEONE MIGHT COME UP TO YOU AND SAY...
© 1989 United Feature Syndicate, Inc.
SMILE! YOU'RE ON CANDID CAMERA!
RIP
THOUGHT YOU COULD HIDE BEHIND THE COMICS PAGE TO PICK YOUR TEETH, HUH?
meddick 10-7

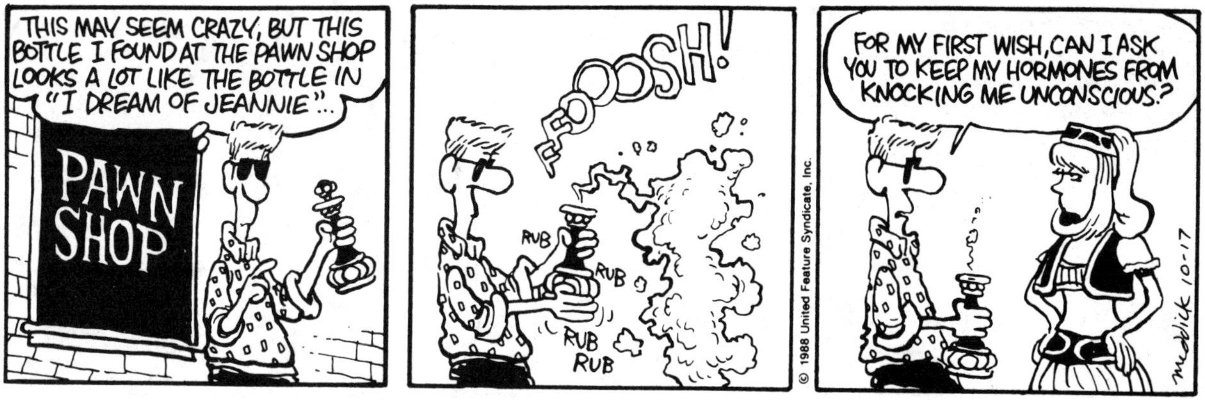
THIS MAY SEEM CRAZY, BUT THIS BOTTLE I FOUND AT THE PAWN SHOP LOOKS A LOT LIKE THE BOTTLE IN "I DREAM OF JEANNIE"...
PAWN SHOP
RUB
RUB
RUB
RUB
FROOOSH!
© 1988 United Feature Syndicate, Inc.
FOR MY FIRST WISH, CAN I ASK YOU TO KEEP MY HORMONES FROM KNOCKING ME UNCONSCIOUS?

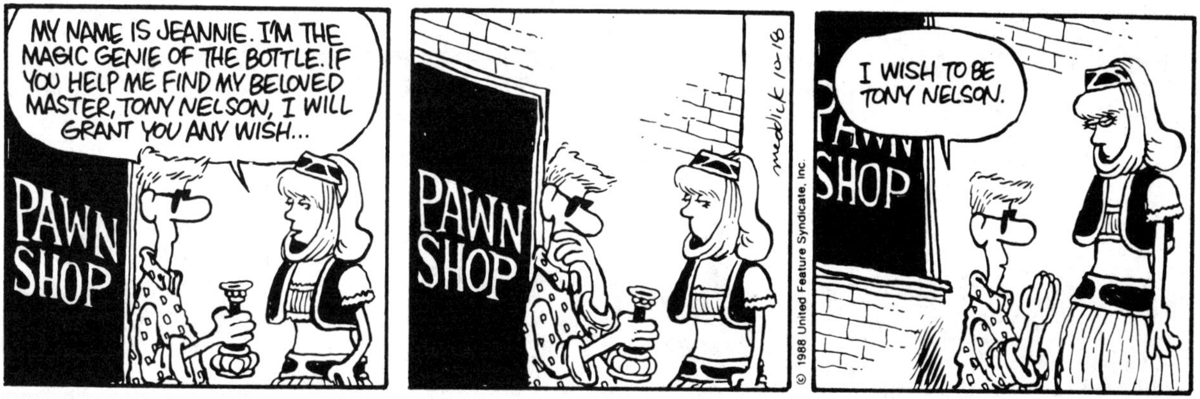
MY NAME IS JEANNIE. I'M THE MAGIC GENIE OF THE BOTTLE. IF YOU HELP ME FIND MY BELOVED MASTER, TONY NELSON, I WILL GRANT YOU ANY WISH...
PAWN SHOP
PAWN SHOP
© 1988 United Feature Syndicate, Inc.
I WISH TO BE TONY NELSON.
SHOP

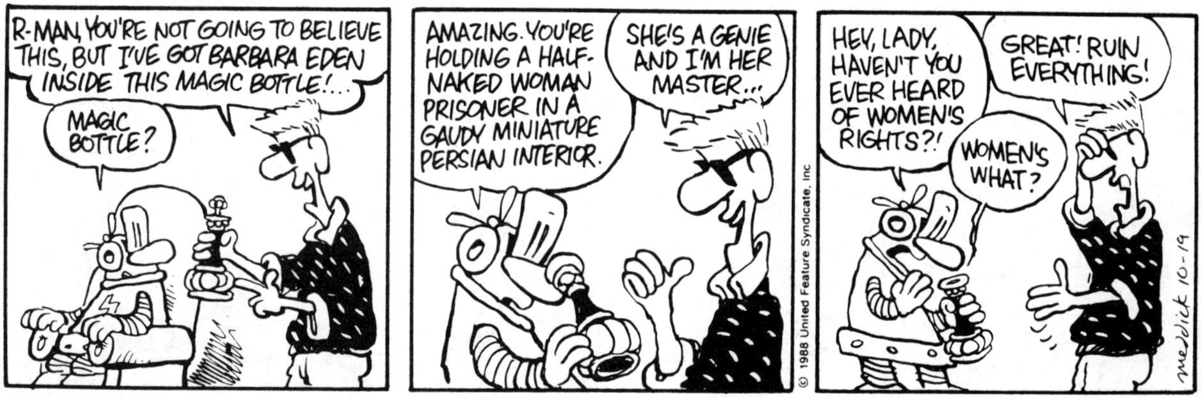
R-MAN, YOU'RE NOT GOING TO BELIEVE THIS, BUT I'VE GOT BARBARA EDEN INSIDE THIS MAGIC BOTTLE!...
MAGIC BOTTLE?
AMAZING. YOU'RE HOLDING A HALF-NAKED WOMAN PRISONER IN A GAUDY MINIATURE PERSIAN INTERIOR.
SHE'S A GENIE AND I'M HER MASTER...
© 1988 United Feature Syndicate, Inc.
HEY, LADY, HAVEN'T YOU EVER HEARD OF WOMEN'S RIGHTS?!
GREAT! RUIN EVERYTHING!
WOMEN'S WHAT?

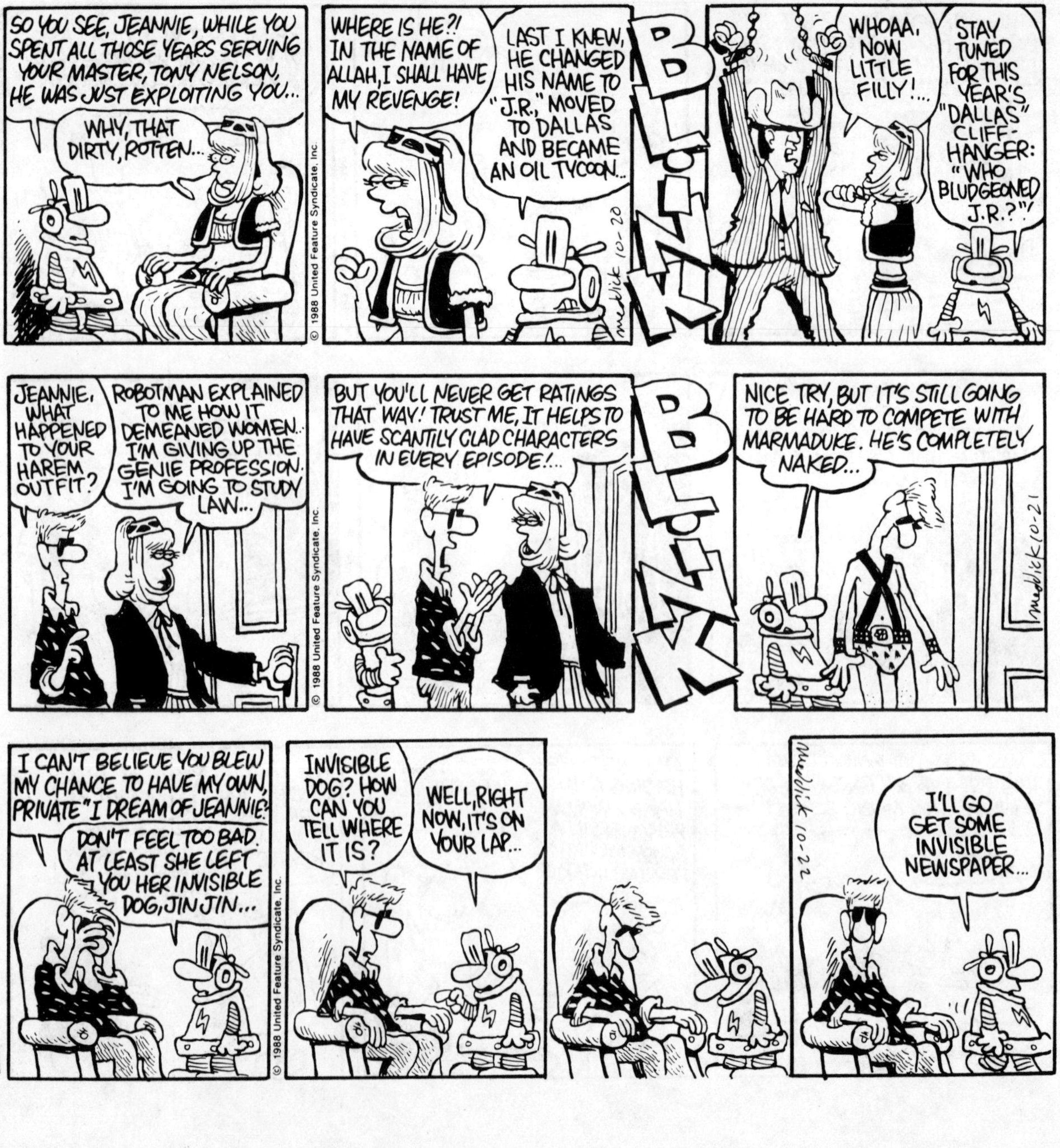
SO YOU SEE, JEANNIE, WHILE YOU SPENT ALL THOSE YEARS SERVING YOUR MASTER, TONY NELSON, HE WAS JUST EXPLOITING YOU...
WHY, THAT DIRTY, ROTTEN...
WHERE IS HE?! IN THE NAME OF ALLAH, I SHALL HAVE MY REVENGE!
LAST I KNEW, HE CHANGED HIS NAME TO "J.R.," MOVED TO DALLAS AND BECAME AN OIL TYCOON...
BLINK
WHOAA, NOW LITTLE FILLY!...
STAY TUNED FOR THIS YEAR'S "DALLAS" CLIFF-HANGER: "WHO BLUDGEONED J.R.?"!
JEANNIE, WHAT HAPPENED TO YOUR HAREM OUTFIT?
ROBOTMAN EXPLAINED TO ME HOW IT DEMEANED WOMEN... I'M GIVING UP THE GENIE PROFESSION. I'M GOING TO STUDY LAW...
BUT YOU'LL NEVER GET RATINGS THAT WAY! TRUST ME, IT HELPS TO HAVE SCANTILY CLAD CHARACTERS IN EVERY EPISODE!...
BLINK
NICE TRY, BUT IT'S STILL GOING TO BE HARD TO COMPETE WITH MARMADUKE. HE'S COMPLETELY NAKED...
I CAN'T BELIEVE YOU BLEW MY CHANCE TO HAVE MY OWN, PRIVATE "I DREAM OF JEANNIE"
DON'T FEEL TOO BAD. AT LEAST SHE LEFT YOU HER INVISIBLE DOG, JIN JIN...
INVISIBLE DOG? HOW CAN YOU TELL WHERE IT IS?
WELL, RIGHT NOW, IT'S ON YOUR LAP...
I'LL GO GET SOME INVISIBLE NEWSPAPER...

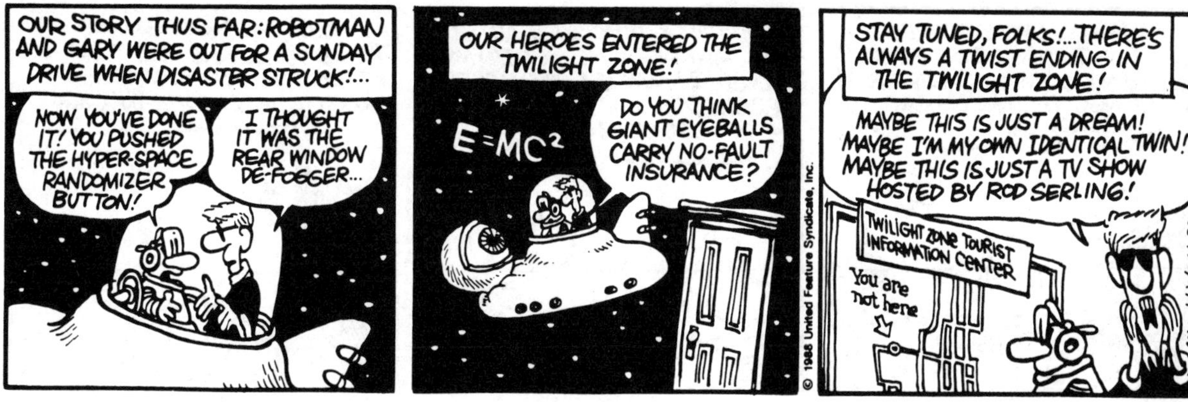
OUR STORY THUS FAR: ROBOTMAN AND GARY WERE OUT FOR A SUNDAY DRIVE WHEN DISASTER STRUCK!...
NOW YOU'VE DONE IT! YOU PUSHED THE HYPER-SPACE RANDOMIZER BUTTON!
I THOUGHT IT WAS THE REAR WINDOW DE-FOGGER...
OUR HEROES ENTERED THE TWILIGHT ZONE!
E=MC²
DO YOU THINK GIANT EYEBALLS CARRY NO-FAULT INSURANCE?
© 1988 United Feature Syndicate, Inc.
STAY TUNED, FOLKS!...THERE'S ALWAYS A TWIST ENDING IN THE TWILIGHT ZONE!
MAYBE THIS IS JUST A DREAM! MAYBE I'M MY OWN IDENTICAL TWIN! MAYBE THIS IS JUST A TV SHOW HOSTED BY ROD SERLING!
TWILIGHT ZONE TOURIST INFORMATION CENTER
You are not here
meddick 4-25

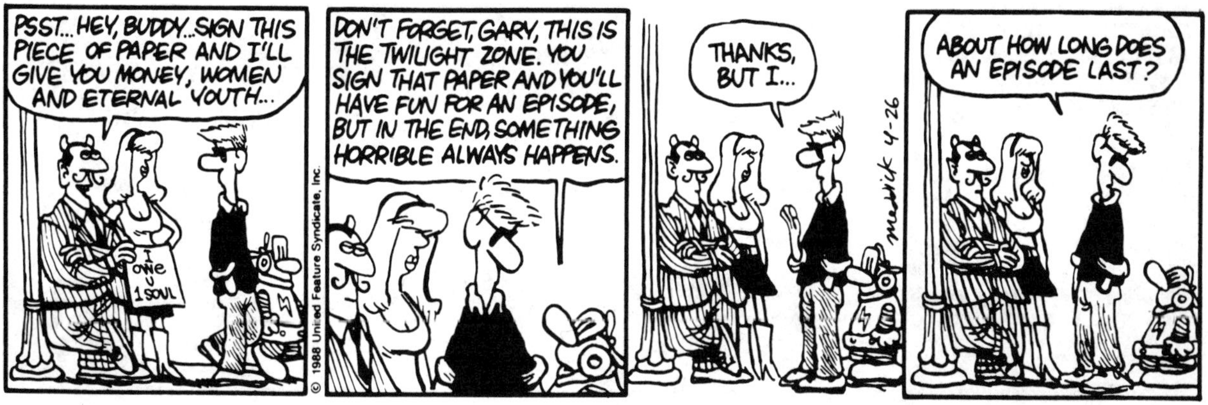
PSST... HEY, BUDDY...SIGN THIS PIECE OF PAPER AND I'LL GIVE YOU MONEY, WOMEN AND ETERNAL YOUTH...
I OWE U 1 SOUL
© 1988 United Feature Syndicate, Inc.
DON'T FORGET, GARY, THIS IS THE TWILIGHT ZONE. YOU SIGN THAT PAPER AND YOU'LL HAVE FUN FOR AN EPISODE, BUT IN THE END, SOMETHING HORRIBLE ALWAYS HAPPENS.
THANKS, BUT I...
meddick 4-26
ABOUT HOW LONG DOES AN EPISODE LAST?

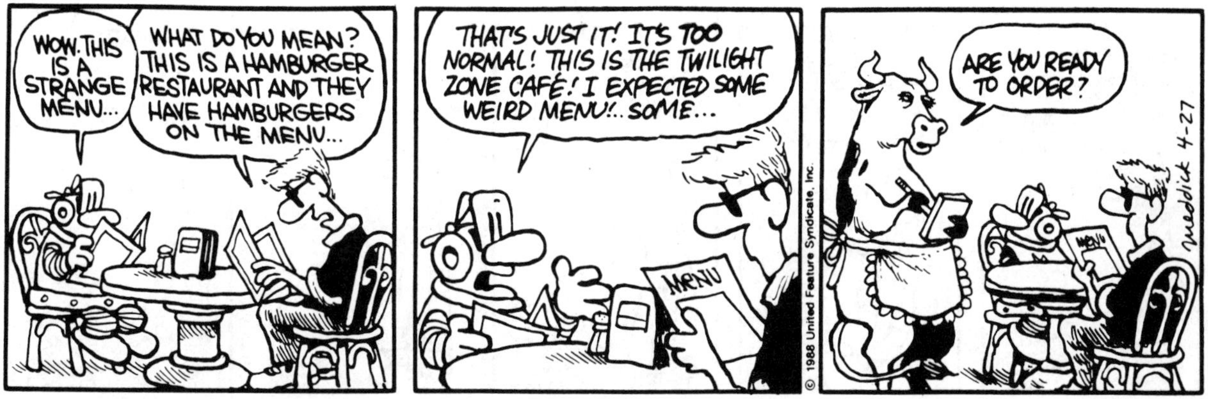
WOW. THIS IS A STRANGE MENU...
WHAT DO YOU MEAN? THIS IS A HAMBURGER RESTAURANT AND THEY HAVE HAMBURGERS ON THE MENU...
THAT'S JUST IT! IT'S TOO NORMAL! THIS IS THE TWILIGHT ZONE CAFÉ! I EXPECTED SOME WEIRD MENU!.. SOME...
MENU
© 1988 United Feature Syndicate, Inc.
ARE YOU READY TO ORDER?
MENU
meddick 4-27

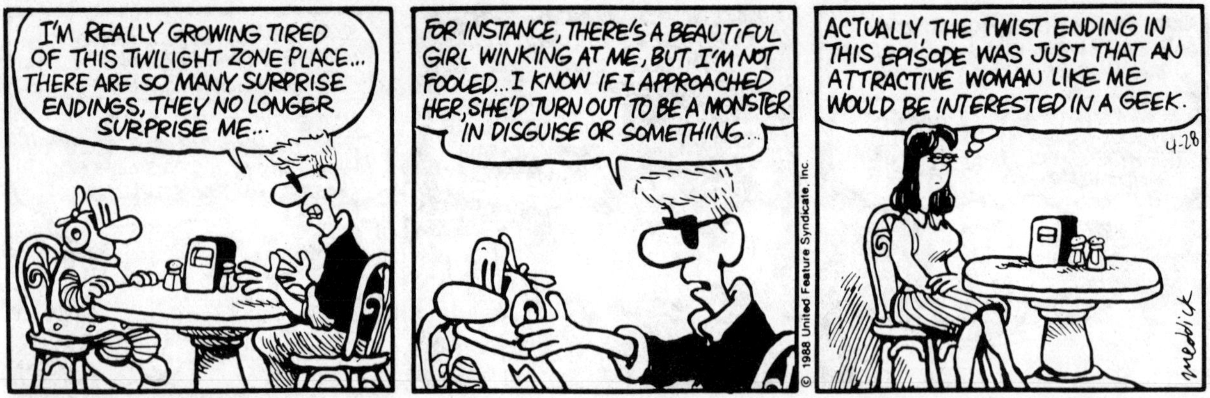
I'M REALLY GROWING TIRED OF THIS TWILIGHT ZONE PLACE... THERE ARE SO MANY SURPRISE ENDINGS, THEY NO LONGER SURPRISE ME...
FOR INSTANCE, THERE'S A BEAUTIFUL GIRL WINKING AT ME, BUT I'M NOT FOOLED... I KNOW IF I APPROACHED HER, SHE'D TURN OUT TO BE A MONSTER IN DISGUISE OR SOMETHING...
© 1988 United Feature Syndicate, Inc.
ACTUALLY, THE TWIST ENDING IN THIS EPISODE WAS JUST THAT AN ATTRACTIVE WOMAN LIKE ME WOULD BE INTERESTED IN A GEEK.
4-28
meddick

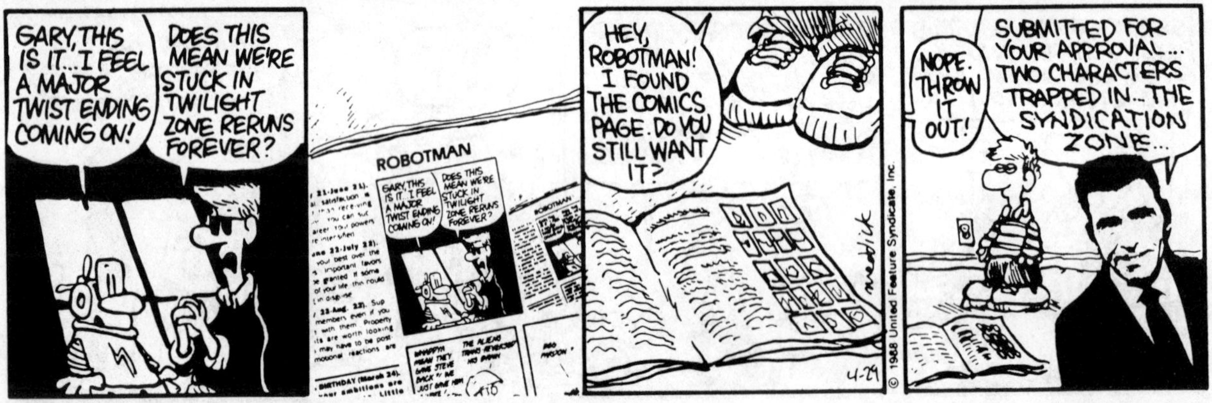
GARY, THIS IS IT... I FEEL A MAJOR TWIST ENDING COMING ON!
DOES THIS MEAN WE'RE STUCK IN TWILIGHT ZONE RERUNS FOREVER?
ROBOTMAN
HEY, ROBOTMAN! I FOUND THE COMICS PAGE. DO YOU STILL WANT IT?
meddick
4-29
© 1988 United Feature Syndicate, Inc.
NOPE. THROW IT OUT!
SUBMITTED FOR YOUR APPROVAL... TWO CHARACTERS TRAPPED IN... THE SYNDICATION ZONE...

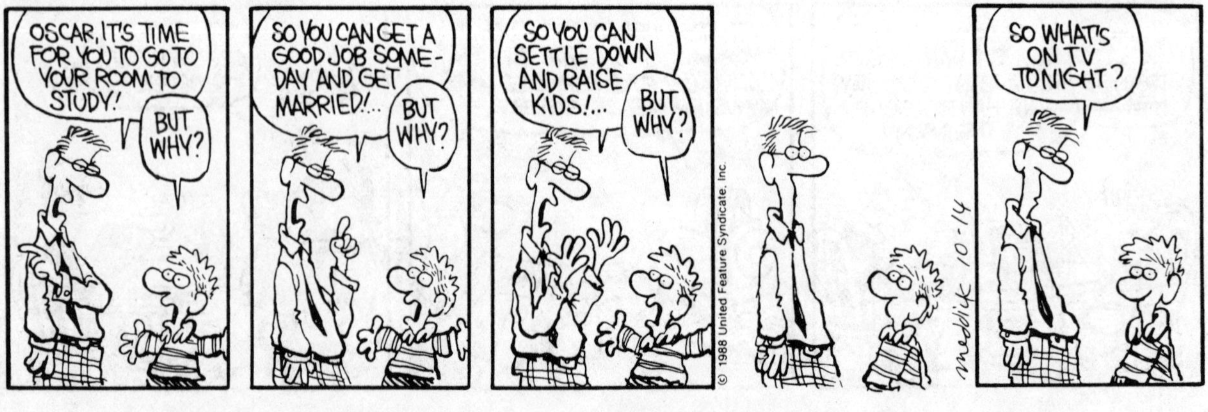
OSCAR, IT'S TIME FOR YOU TO GO TO YOUR ROOM TO STUDY!
BUT WHY?
SO YOU CAN GET A GOOD JOB SOME-DAY AND GET MARRIED!...
BUT WHY?
SO YOU CAN SETTLE DOWN AND RAISE KIDS!...
BUT WHY?
© 1988 United Feature Syndicate, Inc.
meddick 10-14
SO WHAT'S ON TV TONIGHT?

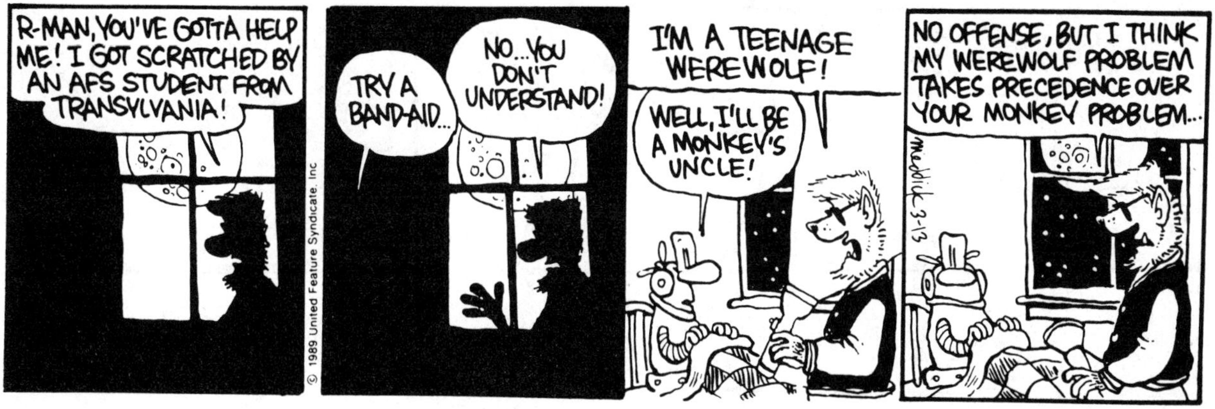
R-MAN, YOU'VE GOTTA HELP ME! I GOT SCRATCHED BY AN AFS STUDENT FROM TRANSYLVANIA!
© 1989 United Feature Syndicate, Inc
TRY A BAND-AID...
NO...YOU DON'T UNDERSTAND!
I'M A TEENAGE WEREWOLF!
WELL, I'LL BE A MONKEY'S UNCLE!
NO OFFENSE, BUT I THINK MY WEREWOLF PROBLEM TAKES PRECEDENCE OVER YOUR MONKEY PROBLEM...

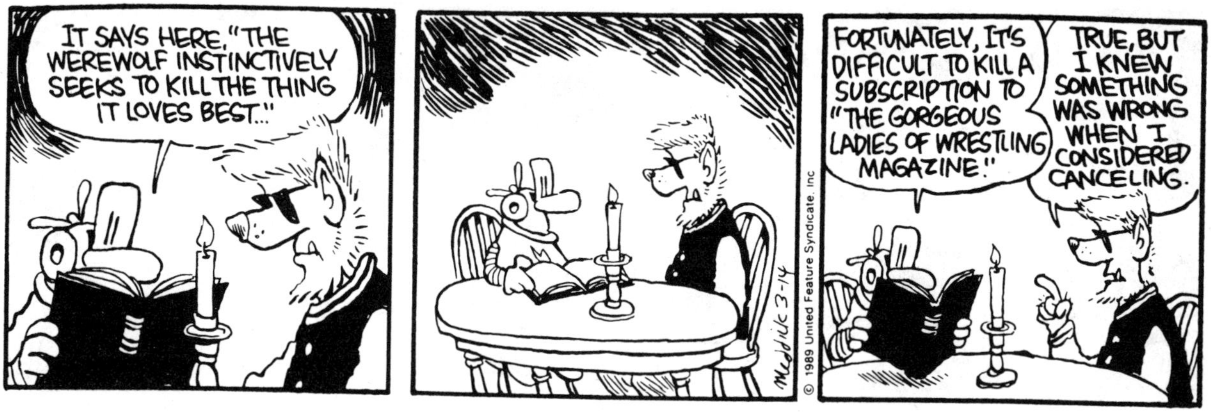
IT SAYS HERE, "THE WEREWOLF INSTINCTIVELY SEEKS TO KILL THE THING IT LOVES BEST..."
© 1989 United Feature Syndicate, Inc
FORTUNATELY, IT'S DIFFICULT TO KILL A SUBSCRIPTION TO "THE GORGEOUS LADIES OF WRESTLING MAGAZINE."
TRUE, BUT I KNEW SOMETHING WAS WRONG WHEN I CONSIDERED CANCELING.

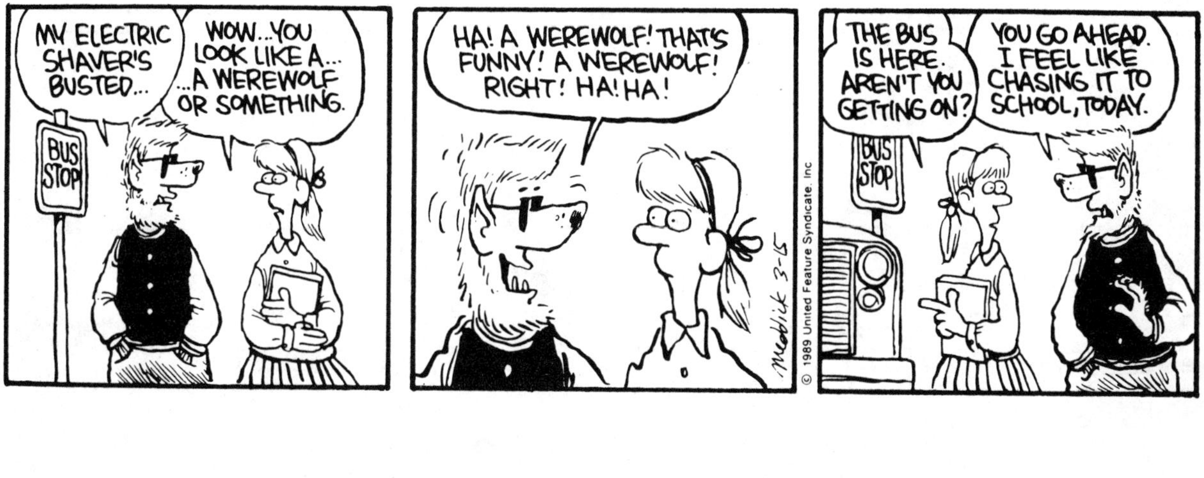
MY ELECTRIC SHAVER'S BUSTED...
WOW...YOU LOOK LIKE A... ...A WEREWOLF OR SOMETHING.
BUS STOP
HA! A WEREWOLF! THAT'S FUNNY! A WEREWOLF! RIGHT! HA! HA!
© 1989 United Feature Syndicate, Inc
THE BUS IS HERE. AREN'T YOU GETTING ON?
YOU GO AHEAD. I FEEL LIKE CHASING IT TO SCHOOL, TODAY.
BUS STOP

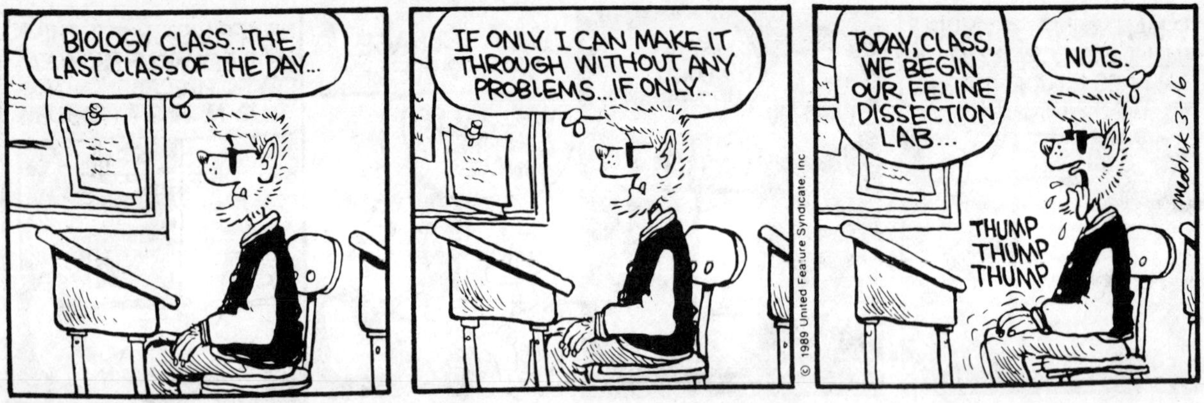
BIOLOGY CLASS...THE LAST CLASS OF THE DAY...
IF ONLY I CAN MAKE IT THROUGH WITHOUT ANY PROBLEMS...IF ONLY...
© 1989 United Feature Syndicate, Inc.
TODAY, CLASS, WE BEGIN OUR FELINE DISSECTION LAB...
NUTS.
THUMP THUMP THUMP
meddick 3-16

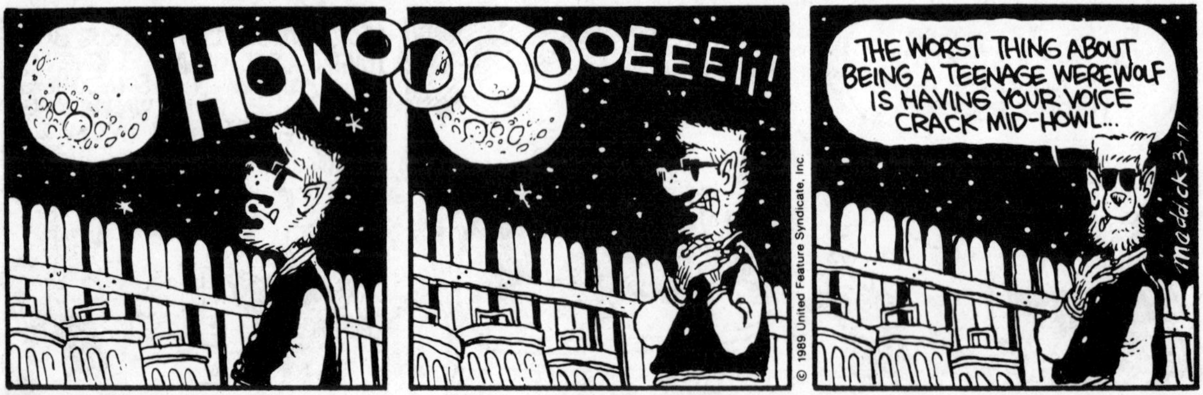
HOWOOOOOOEEEii!
© 1989 United Feature Syndicate, Inc.
THE WORST THING ABOUT BEING A TEENAGE WEREWOLF IS HAVING YOUR VOICE CRACK MID-HOWL...
meddick 3-17

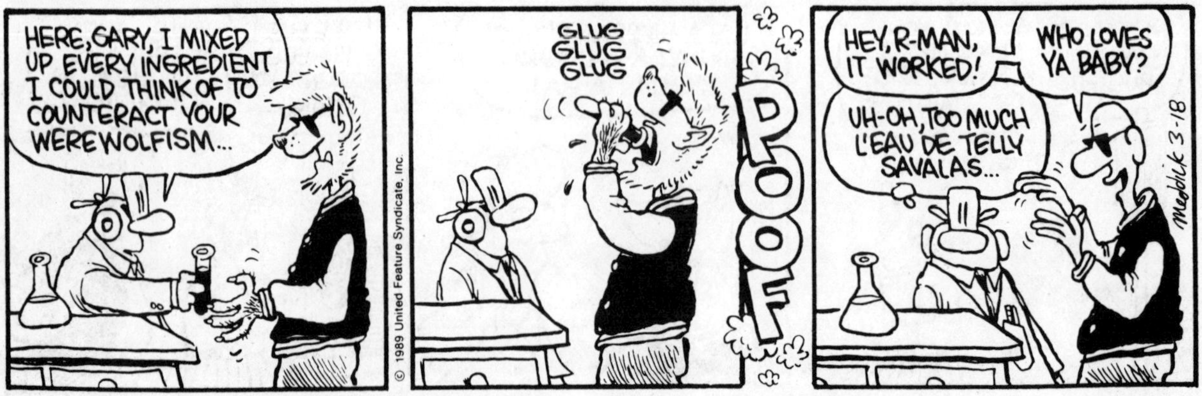
HERE, GARY, I MIXED UP EVERY INGREDIENT I COULD THINK OF TO COUNTERACT YOUR WEREWOLFISM...
© 1989 United Feature Syndicate, Inc.
GLUG GLUG GLUG
POOOF
HEY, R-MAN, IT WORKED!
WHO LOVES YA BABY?
UH-OH, TOO MUCH L'EAU DE TELLY SAVALAS...
meddick 3-18

MOVIES

Film magazine

Lens

Tripod head

MITCHELL
BNC REFLEX

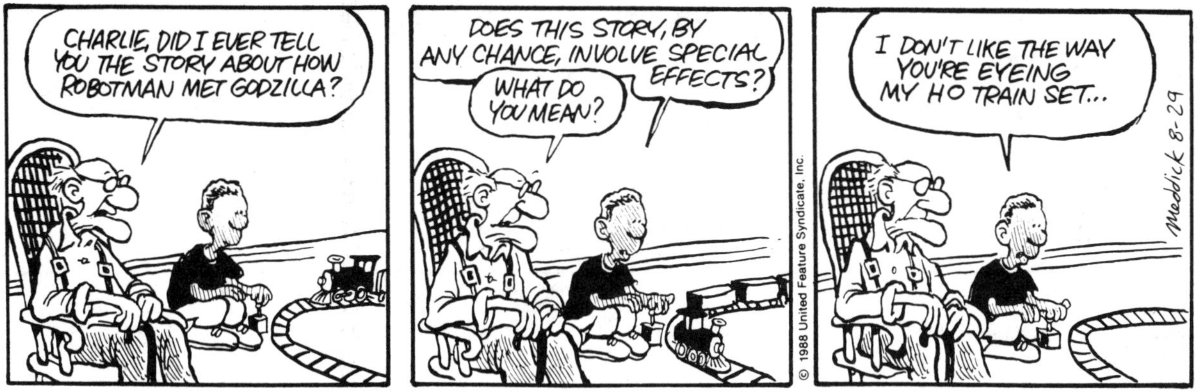
CHARLIE, DID I EVER TELL YOU THE STORY ABOUT HOW ROBOTMAN MET GODZILLA?
DOES THIS STORY, BY ANY CHANCE, INVOLVE SPECIAL EFFECTS?
WHAT DO YOU MEAN?
I DON'T LIKE THE WAY YOU'RE EYEING MY HO TRAIN SET...
meddick 8-29
© 1988 United Feature Syndicate, Inc.

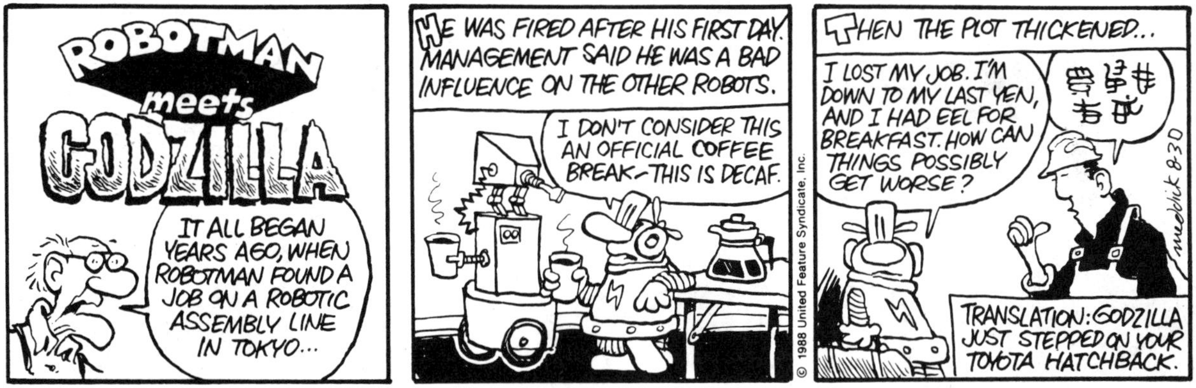
ROBOTMAN meets GODZILLA
IT ALL BEGAN YEARS AGO, WHEN ROBOTMAN FOUND A JOB ON A ROBOTIC ASSEMBLY LINE IN TOKYO...
HE WAS FIRED AFTER HIS FIRST DAY. MANAGEMENT SAID HE WAS A BAD INFLUENCE ON THE OTHER ROBOTS.
I DON'T CONSIDER THIS AN OFFICIAL COFFEE BREAK— THIS IS DECAF.
THEN THE PLOT THICKENED...
I LOST MY JOB. I'M DOWN TO MY LAST YEN, AND I HAD EEL FOR BREAKFAST. HOW CAN THINGS POSSIBLY GET WORSE?
TRANSLATION: GODZILLA JUST STEPPED ON YOUR TOYOTA HATCHBACK.
meddick 8-30
© 1988 United Feature Syndicate, Inc.

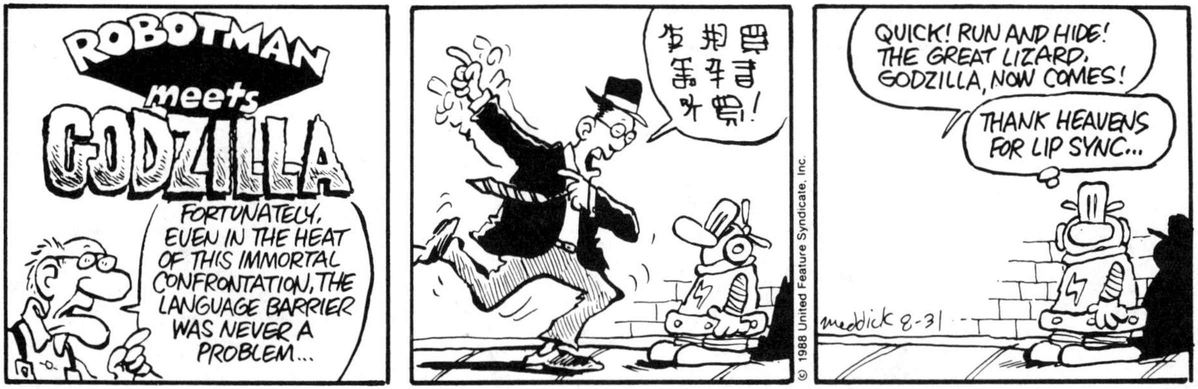
ROBOTMAN meets GODZILLA
FORTUNATELY, EVEN IN THE HEAT OF THIS IMMORTAL CONFRONTATION, THE LANGUAGE BARRIER WAS NEVER A PROBLEM...
QUICK! RUN AND HIDE! THE GREAT LIZARD, GODZILLA, NOW COMES!
THANK HEAVENS FOR LIP SYNC...
meddick 8-31
© 1988 United Feature Syndicate, Inc.

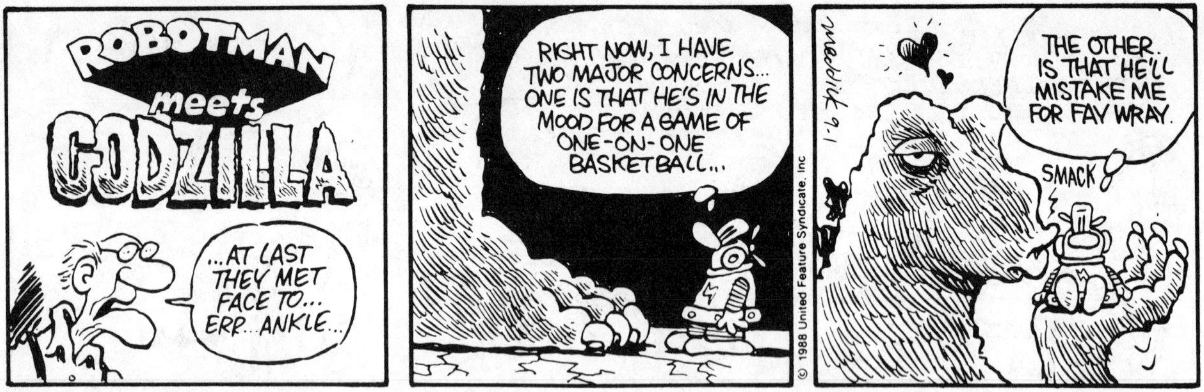
ROBOTMAN meets GODZILLA
...AT LAST THEY MET FACE TO... ERP...ANKLE...
RIGHT NOW, I HAVE TWO MAJOR CONCERNS... ONE IS THAT HE'S IN THE MOOD FOR A GAME OF ONE-ON-ONE BASKETBALL...
© 1988 United Feature Syndicate, Inc.
meddick 9-1
THE OTHER. IS THAT HE'LL MISTAKE ME FOR FAY WRAY.
SMACK

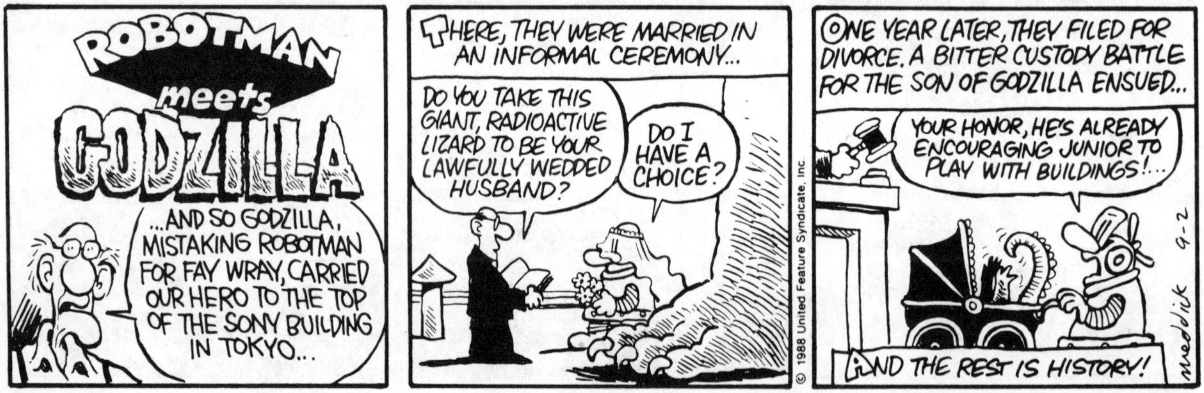
ROBOTMAN meets GODZILLA
...AND SO GODZILLA, MISTAKING ROBOTMAN FOR FAY WRAY, CARRIED OUR HERO TO THE TOP OF THE SONY BUILDING IN TOKYO...
THERE, THEY WERE MARRIED IN AN INFORMAL CEREMONY...
DO YOU TAKE THIS GIANT, RADIOACTIVE LIZARD TO BE YOUR LAWFULLY WEDDED HUSBAND?
DO I HAVE A CHOICE?
© 1988 United Feature Syndicate, Inc.
ONE YEAR LATER, THEY FILED FOR DIVORCE. A BITTER CUSTODY BATTLE FOR THE SON OF GODZILLA ENSUED...
YOUR HONOR, HE'S ALREADY ENCOURAGING JUNIOR TO PLAY WITH BUILDINGS!...
AND THE REST IS HISTORY!
meddick 9-2

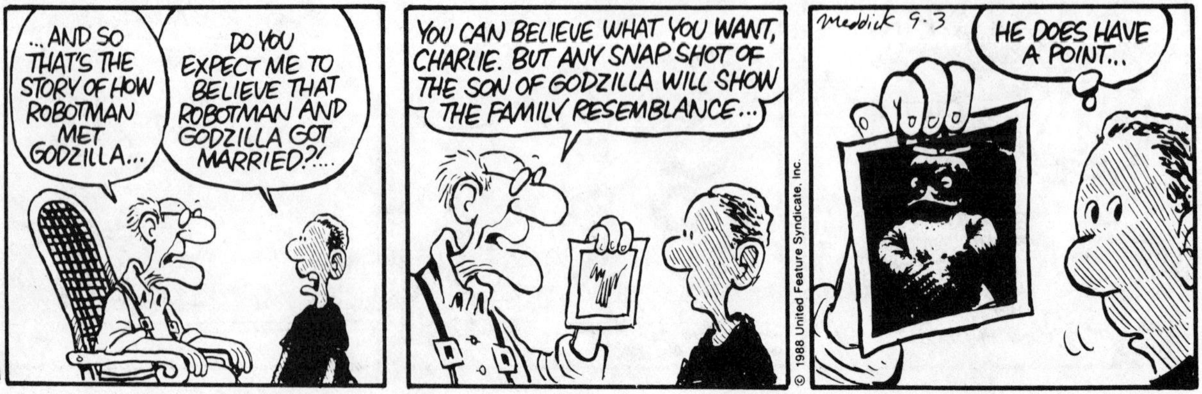
...AND SO THAT'S THE STORY OF HOW ROBOTMAN MET GODZILLA...
DO YOU EXPECT ME TO BELIEVE THAT ROBOTMAN AND GODZILLA GOT MARRIED?!...
YOU CAN BELIEVE WHAT YOU WANT, CHARLIE. BUT ANY SNAP SHOT OF THE SON OF GODZILLA WILL SHOW THE FAMILY RESEMBLANCE...
© 1988 United Feature Syndicate, Inc.
meddick 9-3
HE DOES HAVE A POINT...

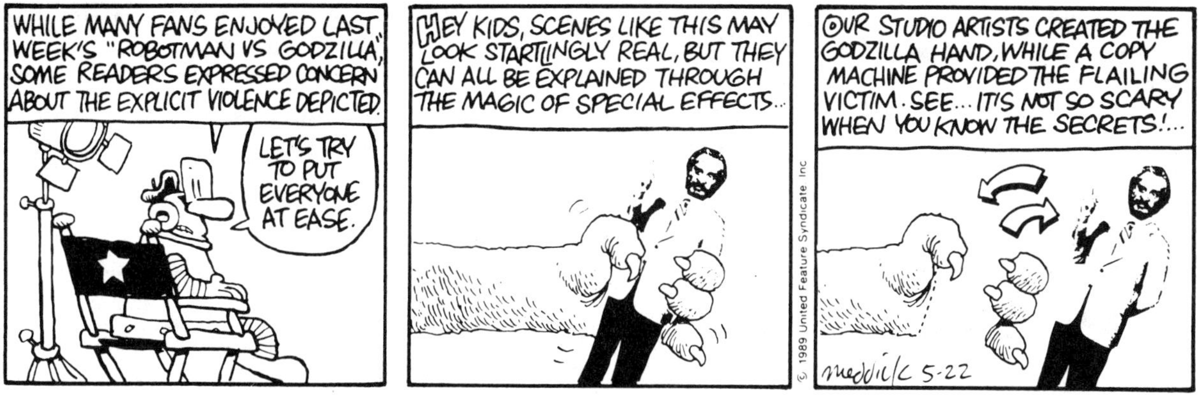
WHILE MANY FANS ENJOYED LAST WEEK'S "ROBOTMAN VS GODZILLA", SOME READERS EXPRESSED CONCERN ABOUT THE EXPLICIT VIOLENCE DEPICTED.
LET'S TRY TO PUT EVERYONE AT EASE.
HEY KIDS, SCENES LIKE THIS MAY LOOK STARTLINGLY REAL, BUT THEY CAN ALL BE EXPLAINED THROUGH THE MAGIC OF SPECIAL EFFECTS...
OUR STUDIO ARTISTS CREATED THE GODZILLA HAND, WHILE A COPY MACHINE PROVIDED THE FLAILING VICTIM. SEE... IT'S NOT SO SCARY WHEN YOU KNOW THE SECRETS!...
© 1989 United Feature Syndicate, Inc
meddick 5-22

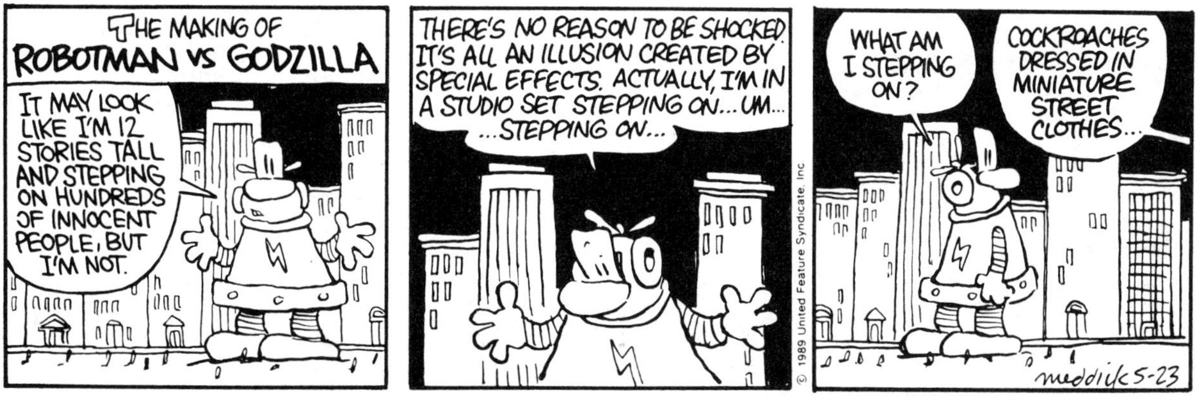
THE MAKING OF
ROBOTMAN VS GODZILLA
IT MAY LOOK LIKE I'M 12 STORIES TALL AND STEPPING ON HUNDREDS OF INNOCENT PEOPLE, BUT I'M NOT.
THERE'S NO REASON TO BE SHOCKED. IT'S ALL AN ILLUSION CREATED BY SPECIAL EFFECTS. ACTUALLY, I'M IN A STUDIO SET STEPPING ON... UM...
...STEPPING ON...
WHAT AM I STEPPING ON?
COCKROACHES DRESSED IN MINIATURE STREET CLOTHES...
© 1989 United Feature Syndicate, Inc
meddick 5-23

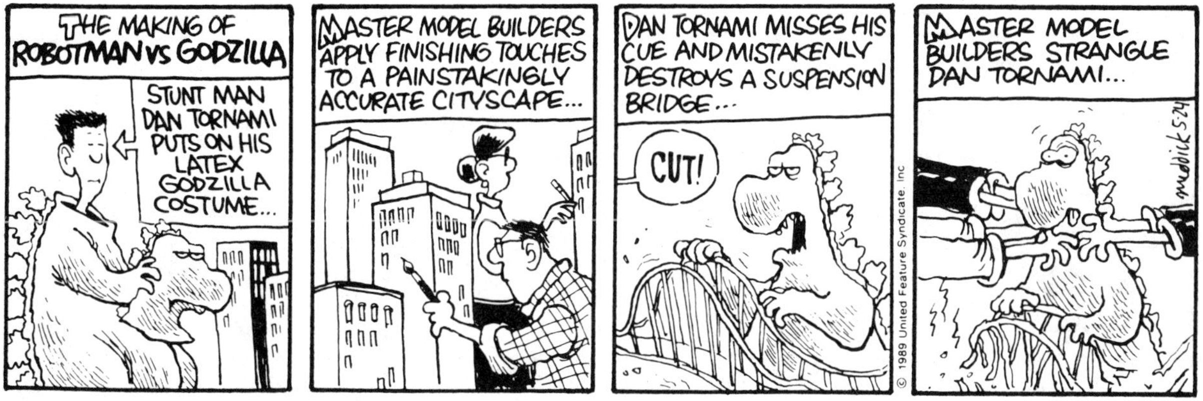
THE MAKING OF
ROBOTMAN VS GODZILLA
STUNT MAN DAN TORNAMI PUTS ON HIS LATEX GODZILLA COSTUME...
MASTER MODEL BUILDERS APPLY FINISHING TOUCHES TO A PAINSTAKINGLY ACCURATE CITYSCAPE...
DAN TORNAMI MISSES HIS CUE AND MISTAKENLY DESTROYS A SUSPENSION BRIDGE...
CUT!
MASTER MODEL BUILDERS STRANGLE DAN TORNAMI...
© 1989 United Feature Syndicate, Inc
meddick 5-24

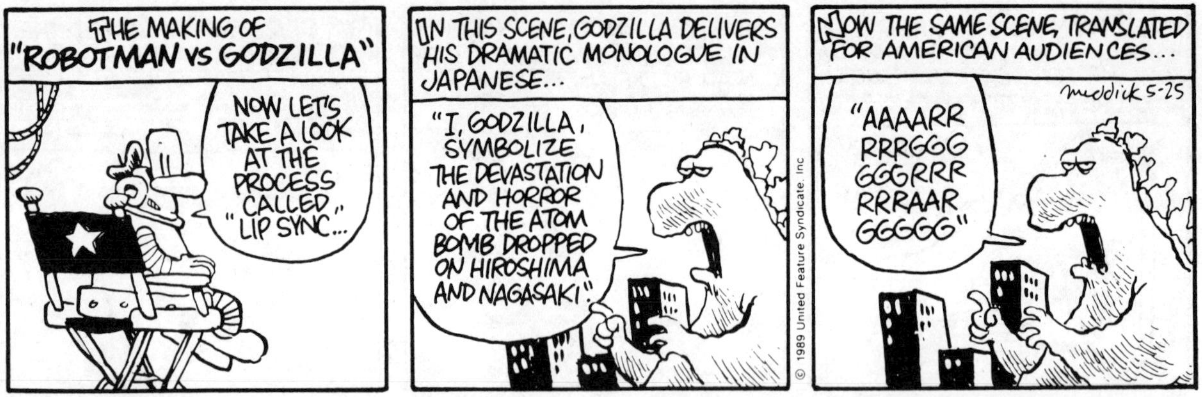
THE MAKING OF "ROBOTMAN VS GODZILLA"
NOW LET'S TAKE A LOOK AT THE PROCESS CALLED "LIP SYNC"...
IN THIS SCENE, GODZILLA DELIVERS HIS DRAMATIC MONOLOGUE IN JAPANESE...
"I, GODZILLA, SYMBOLIZE THE DEVASTATION AND HORROR OF THE ATOM BOMB DROPPED ON HIROSHIMA AND NAGASAKI."
© 1989 United Feature Syndicate, Inc.
NOW THE SAME SCENE, TRANSLATED FOR AMERICAN AUDIENCES...
meddick 5-25
"AAAARR RRRGGG GGGRRR RRRAAR GGGGG"

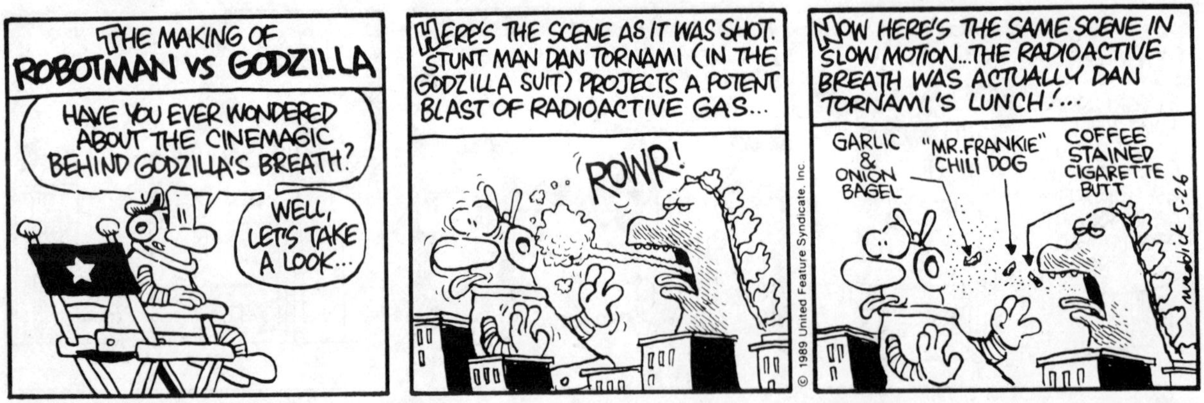
THE MAKING OF ROBOTMAN VS GODZILLA
HAVE YOU EVER WONDERED ABOUT THE CINEMAGIC BEHIND GODZILLA'S BREATH?
WELL, LET'S TAKE A LOOK...
HERE'S THE SCENE AS IT WAS SHOT. STUNT MAN DAN TORNAMI (IN THE GODZILLA SUIT) PROJECTS A POTENT BLAST OF RADIOACTIVE GAS...
ROWR!
© 1989 United Feature Syndicate, Inc.
NOW HERE'S THE SAME SCENE IN SLOW MOTION...THE RADIOACTIVE BREATH WAS ACTUALLY DAN TORNAMI'S LUNCH!...
GARLIC & ONION BAGEL
"MR. FRANKIE" CHILI DOG
COFFEE STAINED CIGARETTE BUTT
meddick 5-26

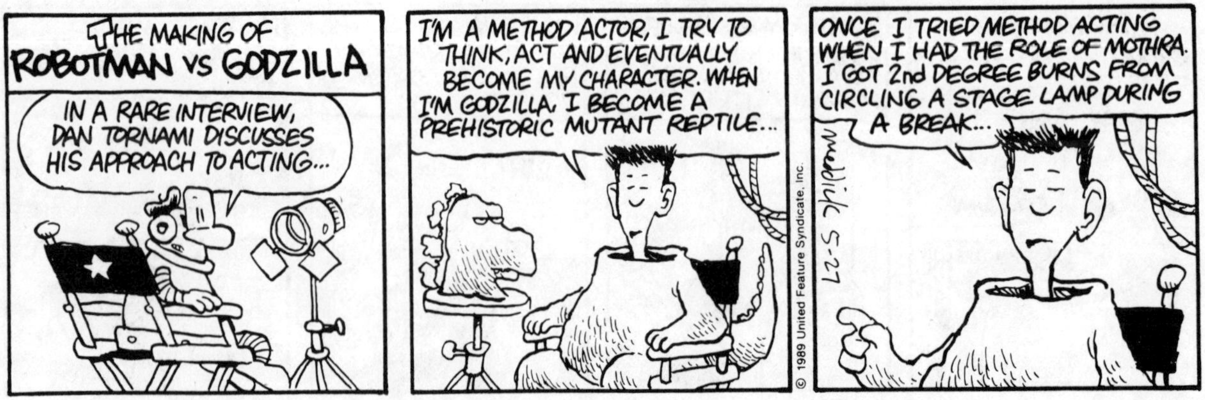
THE MAKING OF ROBOTMAN VS GODZILLA
IN A RARE INTERVIEW, DAN TORNAMI DISCUSSES HIS APPROACH TO ACTING...
I'M A METHOD ACTOR, I TRY TO THINK, ACT AND EVENTUALLY BECOME MY CHARACTER. WHEN I'M GODZILLA, I BECOME A PREHISTORIC MUTANT REPTILE...
© 1989 United Feature Syndicate, Inc.
meddick 5-27
ONCE I TRIED METHOD ACTING WHEN I HAD THE ROLE OF MOTHRA. I GOT 2nd DEGREE BURNS FROM CIRCLING A STAGE LAMP DURING A BREAK...

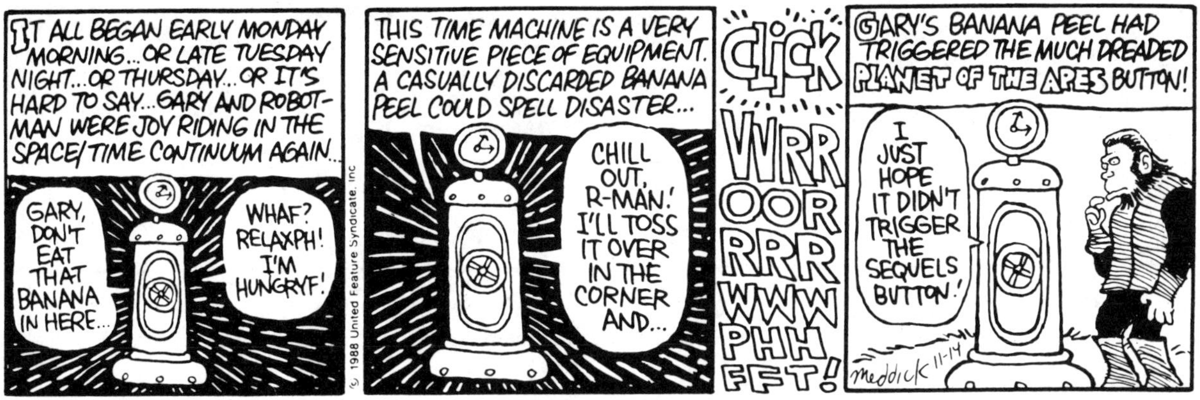
IT ALL BEGAN EARLY MONDAY MORNING...OR LATE TUESDAY NIGHT...OR THURSDAY...OR IT'S HARD TO SAY...GARY AND ROBOT-MAN WERE JOY RIDING IN THE SPACE/TIME CONTINUUM AGAIN...
GARY, DON'T EAT THAT BANANA IN HERE...
WHAF? RELAXPH! I'M HUNGRYF!
© 1988 United Feature Syndicate, Inc
THIS TIME MACHINE IS A VERY SENSITIVE PIECE OF EQUIPMENT. A CASUALLY DISCARDED BANANA PEEL COULD SPELL DISASTER...
CHILL OUT, R-MAN! I'LL TOSS IT OVER IN THE CORNER AND...
CLICK
VVRR OOR RRR WWW PHH FFT!
GARY'S BANANA PEEL HAD TRIGGERED THE MUCH DREADED PLANET OF THE APES BUTTON!
I JUST HOPE IT DIDN'T TRIGGER THE SEQUELS BUTTON!
meddick 11-14

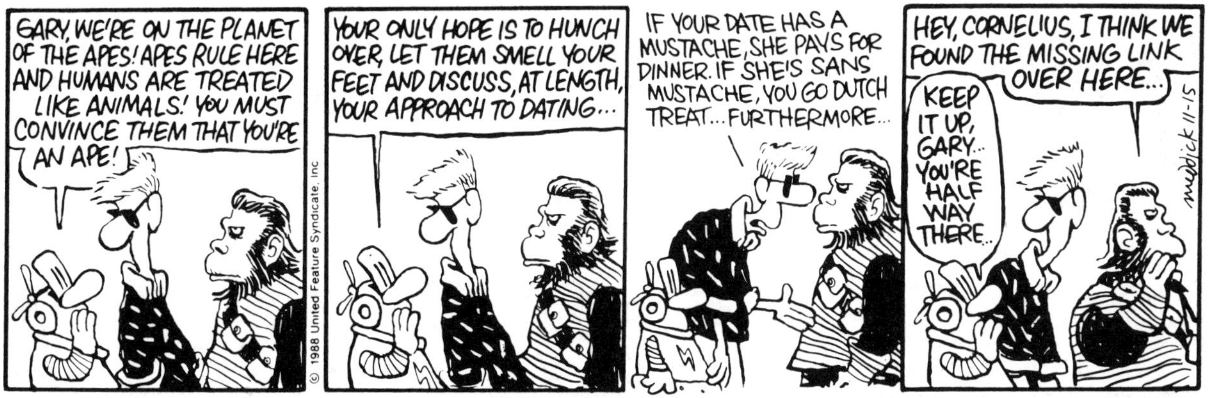
GARY, WE'RE ON THE PLANET OF THE APES! APES RULE HERE AND HUMANS ARE TREATED LIKE ANIMALS! YOU MUST CONVINCE THEM THAT YOU'RE AN APE!
© 1988 United Feature Syndicate, Inc
YOUR ONLY HOPE IS TO HUNCH OVER, LET THEM SMELL YOUR FEET AND DISCUSS, AT LENGTH, YOUR APPROACH TO DATING...
IF YOUR DATE HAS A MUSTACHE, SHE PAYS FOR DINNER. IF SHE'S SANS MUSTACHE, YOU GO DUTCH TREAT... FURTHERMORE...
HEY, CORNELIUS, I THINK WE FOUND THE MISSING LINK OVER HERE...
KEEP IT UP, GARY... YOU'RE HALF WAY THERE...
meddick 11-15

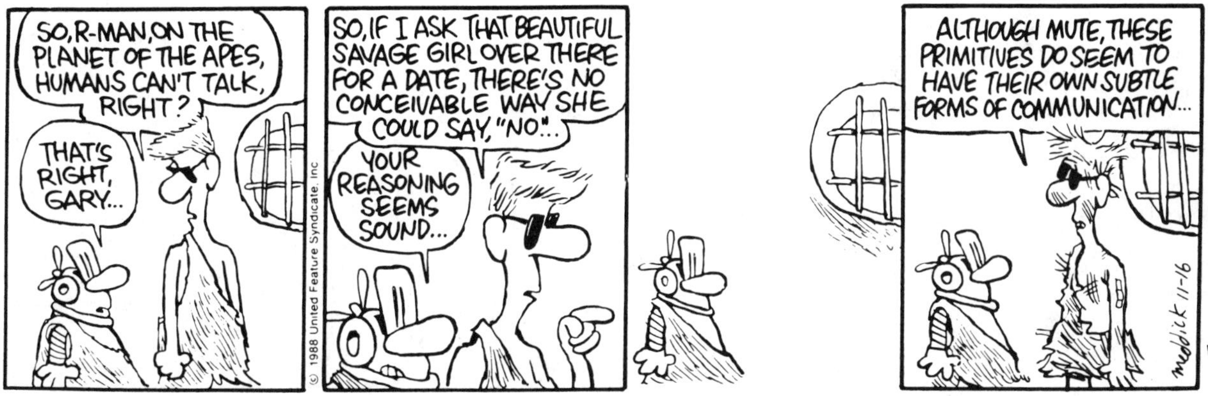
SO, R-MAN, ON THE PLANET OF THE APES, HUMANS CAN'T TALK, RIGHT?
THAT'S RIGHT, GARY...
© 1988 United Feature Syndicate, Inc
SO, IF I ASK THAT BEAUTIFUL SAVAGE GIRL OVER THERE FOR A DATE, THERE'S NO CONCEIVABLE WAY SHE COULD SAY, "NO"...
YOUR REASONING SEEMS SOUND...
ALTHOUGH MUTE, THESE PRIMITIVES DO SEEM TO HAVE THEIR OWN SUBTLE FORMS OF COMMUNICATION...
meddick 11-16

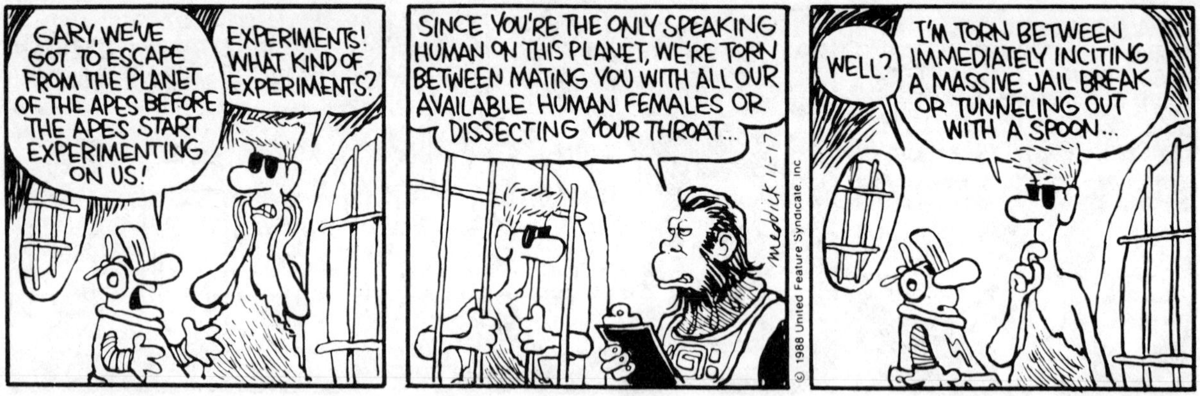
GARY, WE'VE GOT TO ESCAPE FROM THE PLANET OF THE APES BEFORE THE APES START EXPERIMENTING ON US!
EXPERIMENTS! WHAT KIND OF EXPERIMENTS?
SINCE YOU'RE THE ONLY SPEAKING HUMAN ON THIS PLANET, WE'RE TORN BETWEEN MATING YOU WITH ALL OUR AVAILABLE HUMAN FEMALES OR DISSECTING YOUR THROAT...
meddick 11-17
WELL?
I'M TORN BETWEEN IMMEDIATELY INCITING A MASSIVE JAIL BREAK OR TUNNELING OUT WITH A SPOON...

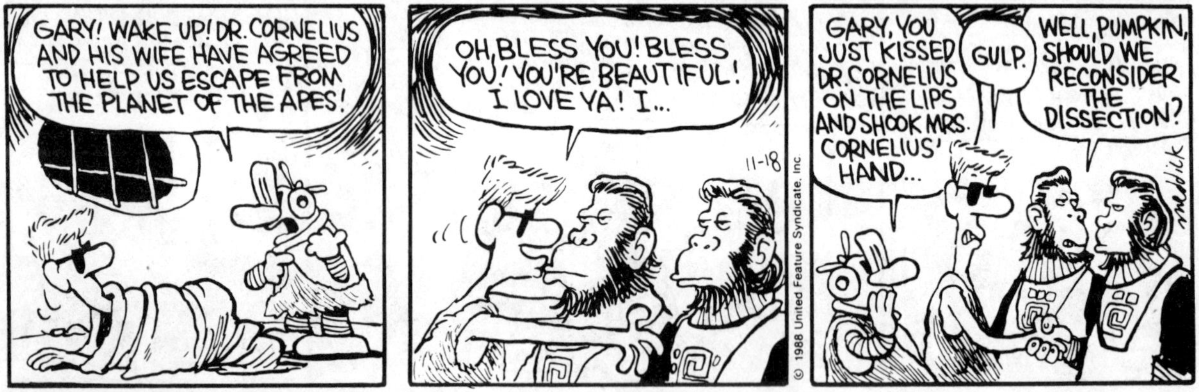
GARY! WAKE UP! DR. CORNELIUS AND HIS WIFE HAVE AGREED TO HELP US ESCAPE FROM THE PLANET OF THE APES!
OH, BLESS YOU! BLESS YOU! YOU'RE BEAUTIFUL! I LOVE YA! I...
11-18
GARY, YOU JUST KISSED DR. CORNELIUS ON THE LIPS AND SHOOK MRS. CORNELIUS' HAND...
GULP.
WELL, PUMPKIN, SHOULD WE RECONSIDER THE DISSECTION?
meddick

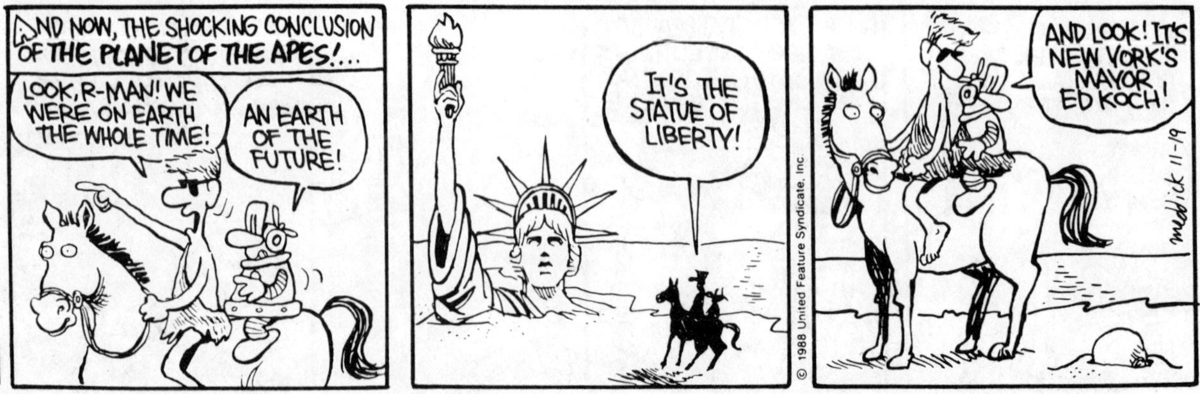
AND NOW, THE SHOCKING CONCLUSION OF THE PLANET OF THE APES!...
LOOK, R-MAN! WE WERE ON EARTH THE WHOLE TIME!
AN EARTH OF THE FUTURE!
IT'S THE STATUE OF LIBERTY!
AND LOOK! IT'S NEW YORK'S MAYOR ED KOCH!
meddick 11-19

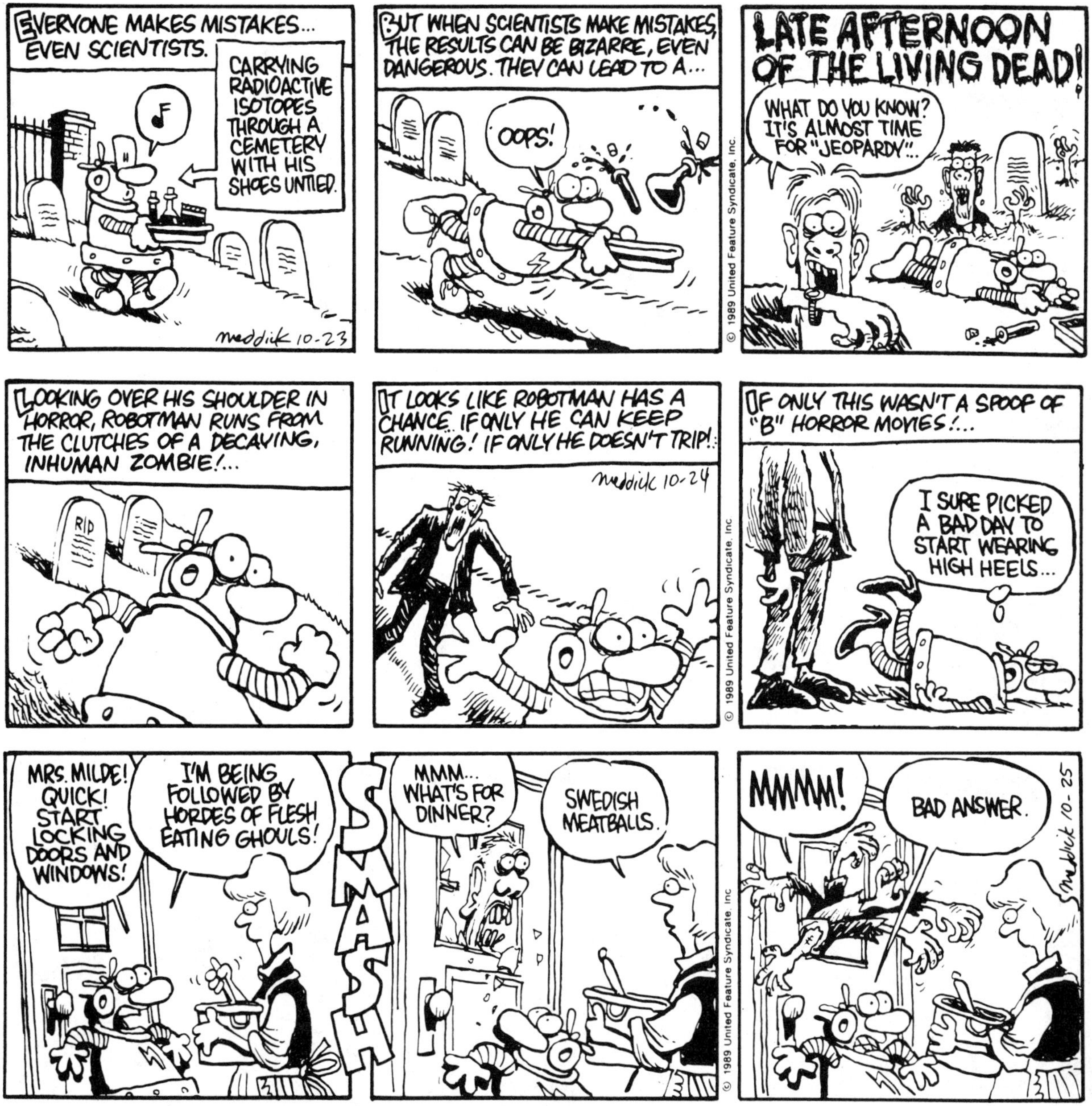
EVERYONE MAKES MISTAKES... EVEN SCIENTISTS.
CARRYING RADIOACTIVE ISOTOPES THROUGH A CEMETERY WITH HIS SHOES UNTIED.
BUT WHEN SCIENTISTS MAKE MISTAKES, THE RESULTS CAN BE BIZARRE, EVEN DANGEROUS. THEY CAN LEAD TO A...
OOPS!
LATE AFTERNOON OF THE LIVING DEAD!
WHAT DO YOU KNOW? IT'S ALMOST TIME FOR "JEOPARDY"...
© 1989 United Feature Syndicate, Inc.
LOOKING OVER HIS SHOULDER IN HORROR, ROBOTMAN RUNS FROM THE CLUTCHES OF A DECAYING, INHUMAN ZOMBIE!...
RIP
IT LOOKS LIKE ROBOTMAN HAS A CHANCE... IF ONLY HE CAN KEEP RUNNING! IF ONLY HE DOESN'T TRIP!...
IF ONLY THIS WASN'T A SPOOF OF "B" HORROR MOVIES!...
I SURE PICKED A BAD DAY TO START WEARING HIGH HEELS...
© 1989 United Feature Syndicate, Inc.
MRS. MILDE! QUICK! START LOCKING DOORS AND WINDOWS!
I'M BEING FOLLOWED BY HORDES OF FLESH EATING GHOULS!
SMASH
MMM... WHAT'S FOR DINNER?
SWEDISH MEATBALLS.
MMMM!
BAD ANSWER.
© 1989 United Feature Syndicate, Inc.

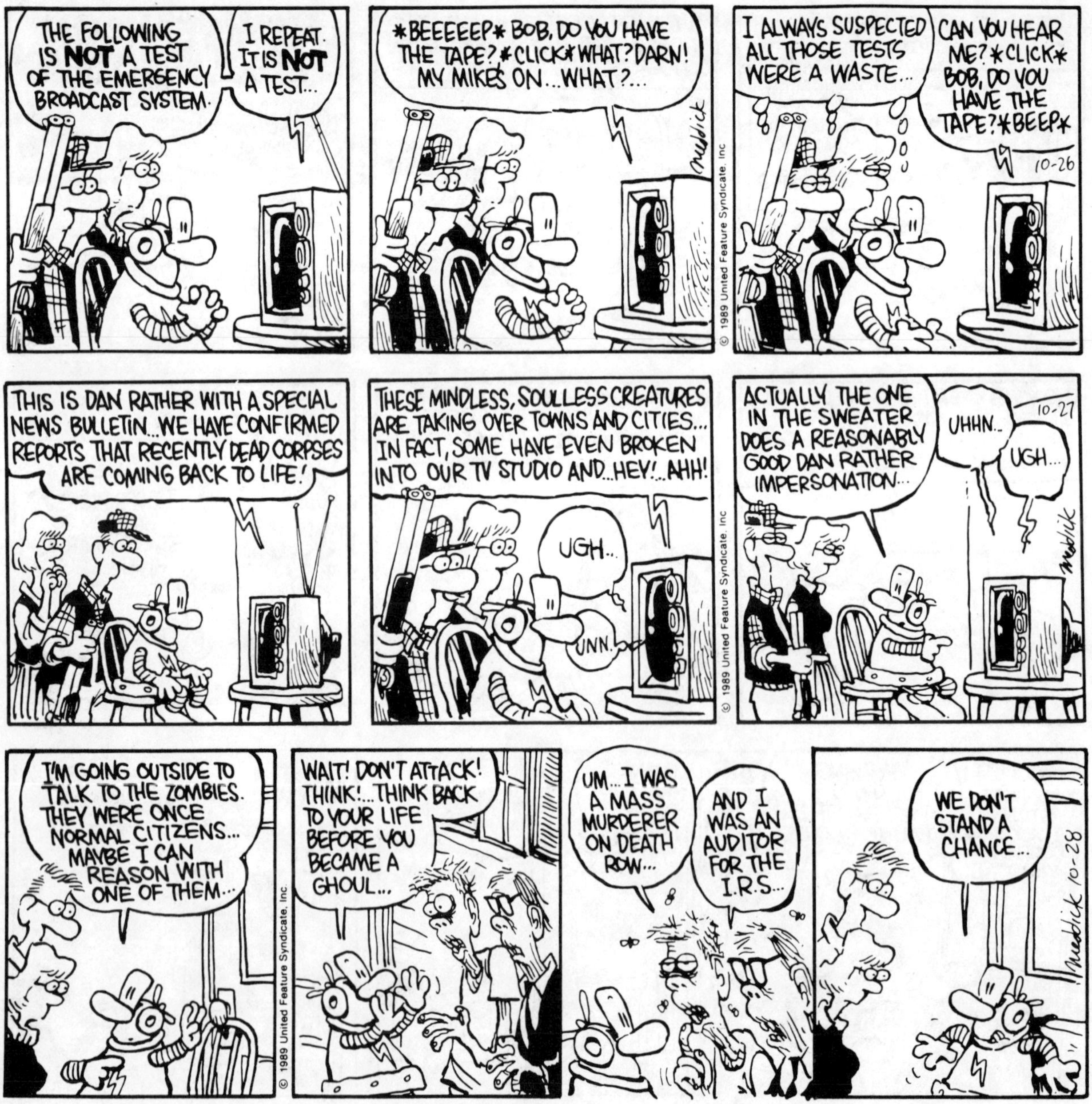
THE FOLLOWING IS NOT A TEST OF THE EMERGENCY BROADCAST SYSTEM.
I REPEAT. IT IS NOT A TEST...
BEEEEEP BOB, DO YOU HAVE THE TAPE? *CLICK* WHAT? DARN! MY MIKE'S ON... WHAT?...
© 1989 United Feature Syndicate, Inc
I ALWAYS SUSPECTED ALL THOSE TESTS WERE A WASTE...
CAN YOU HEAR ME? *CLICK* BOB, DO YOU HAVE THE TAPE? *BEEP*
10-26
THIS IS DAN RATHER WITH A SPECIAL NEWS BULLETIN... WE HAVE CONFIRMED REPORTS THAT RECENTLY DEAD CORPSES ARE COMING BACK TO LIFE!
THESE MINDLESS, SOULLESS CREATURES ARE TAKING OVER TOWNS AND CITIES... IN FACT, SOME HAVE EVEN BROKEN INTO OUR TV STUDIO AND... HEY!.. AHH!
UGH...
UNN...
© 1989 United Feature Syndicate, Inc
ACTUALLY THE ONE IN THE SWEATER DOES A REASONABLY GOOD DAN RATHER IMPERSONATION...
UHHN...
UGH...
10-27
I'M GOING OUTSIDE TO TALK TO THE ZOMBIES. THEY WERE ONCE NORMAL CITIZENS... MAYBE I CAN REASON WITH ONE OF THEM...
© 1989 United Feature Syndicate, Inc
WAIT! DON'T ATTACK! THINK!... THINK BACK TO YOUR LIFE BEFORE YOU BECAME A GHOUL...
UM... I WAS A MASS MURDERER ON DEATH ROW...
AND I WAS AN AUDITOR FOR THE I.R.S...
WE DON'T STAND A CHANCE...
10-28

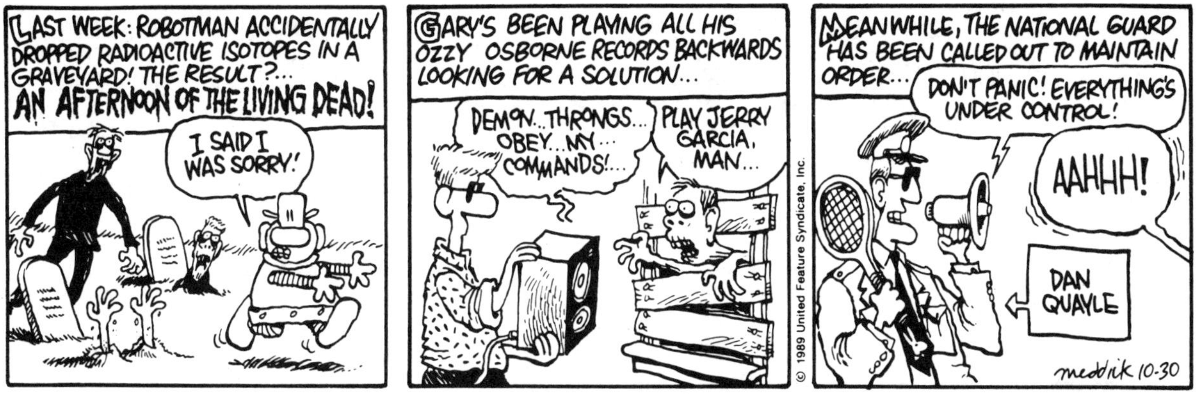
LAST WEEK: ROBOTMAN ACCIDENTALLY DROPPED RADIOACTIVE ISOTOPES IN A GRAVEYARD! THE RESULT?...
AN AFTERNOON OF THE LIVING DEAD!
I SAID I WAS SORRY!
GARY'S BEEN PLAYING ALL HIS OZZY OSBORNE RECORDS BACKWARDS LOOKING FOR A SOLUTION...
DEMON... THRONGS... OBEY... MY... COMMANDS!...
PLAY JERRY GARCIA, MAN...
© 1989 United Feature Syndicate, Inc.
MEANWHILE, THE NATIONAL GUARD HAS BEEN CALLED OUT TO MAINTAIN ORDER...
DON'T PANIC! EVERYTHING'S UNDER CONTROL!
AAHHH!
DAN QUAYLE
meddick 10-30

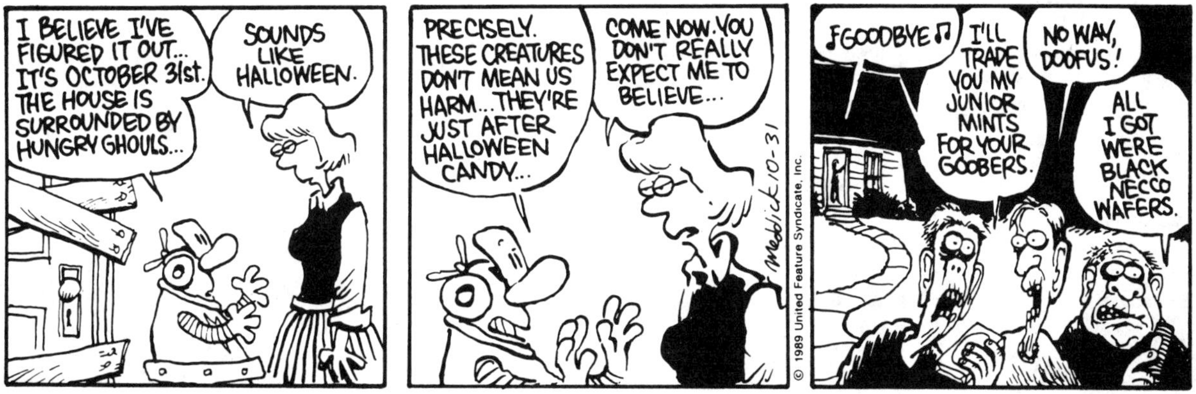
I BELIEVE I'VE FIGURED IT OUT... IT'S OCTOBER 31st. THE HOUSE IS SURROUNDED BY HUNGRY GHOULS...
SOUNDS LIKE HALLOWEEN.
PRECISELY. THESE CREATURES DON'T MEAN US HARM... THEY'RE JUST AFTER HALLOWEEN CANDY...
COME NOW. YOU DON'T REALLY EXPECT ME TO BELIEVE...
meddick 10-31
© 1989 United Feature Syndicate, Inc.
♪GOODBYE♫
I'LL TRADE YOU MY JUNIOR MINTS FOR YOUR GOOBERS.
NO WAY, DOOFUS!
ALL I GOT WERE BLACK NECCO WAFERS.

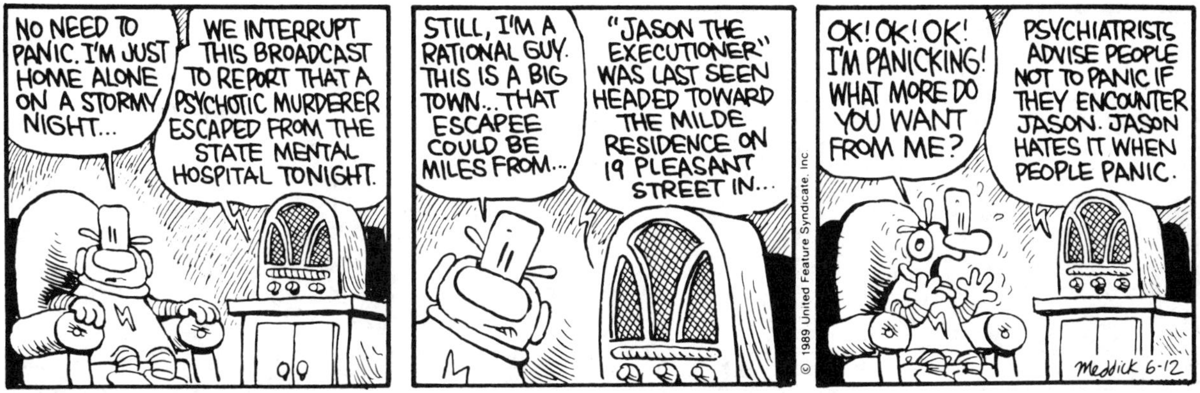
NO NEED TO PANIC. I'M JUST HOME ALONE ON A STORMY NIGHT...
WE INTERRUPT THIS BROADCAST TO REPORT THAT A PSYCHOTIC MURDERER ESCAPED FROM THE STATE MENTAL HOSPITAL TONIGHT.
STILL, I'M A RATIONAL GUY. THIS IS A BIG TOWN... THAT ESCAPEE COULD BE MILES FROM...
"JASON THE EXECUTIONER" WAS LAST SEEN HEADED TOWARD THE MILDE RESIDENCE ON 19 PLEASANT STREET IN...
© 1989 United Feature Syndicate, Inc.
OK! OK! OK! I'M PANICKING! WHAT MORE DO YOU WANT FROM ME?
PSYCHIATRISTS ADVISE PEOPLE NOT TO PANIC IF THEY ENCOUNTER JASON. JASON HATES IT WHEN PEOPLE PANIC.
Meddick 6-12

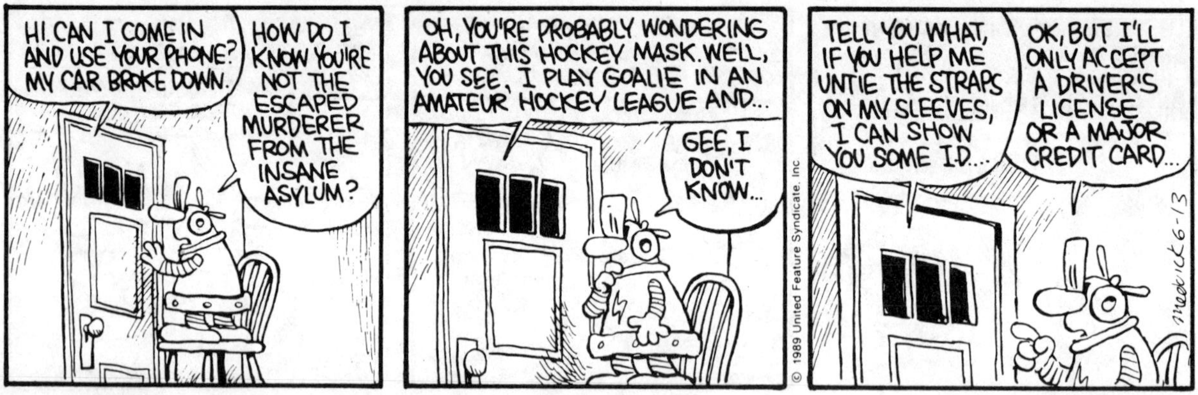
HI. CAN I COME IN AND USE YOUR PHONE? MY CAR BROKE DOWN.
HOW DO I KNOW YOU'RE NOT THE ESCAPED MURDERER FROM THE INSANE ASYLUM?
OH, YOU'RE PROBABLY WONDERING ABOUT THIS HOCKEY MASK. WELL, YOU SEE, I PLAY GOALIE IN AN AMATEUR HOCKEY LEAGUE AND...
GEE, I DON'T KNOW...
© 1989 United Feature Syndicate, Inc
TELL YOU WHAT, IF YOU HELP ME UNTIE THE STRAPS ON MY SLEEVES, I CAN SHOW YOU SOME I.D....
OK, BUT I'LL ONLY ACCEPT A DRIVER'S LICENSE OR A MAJOR CREDIT CARD...

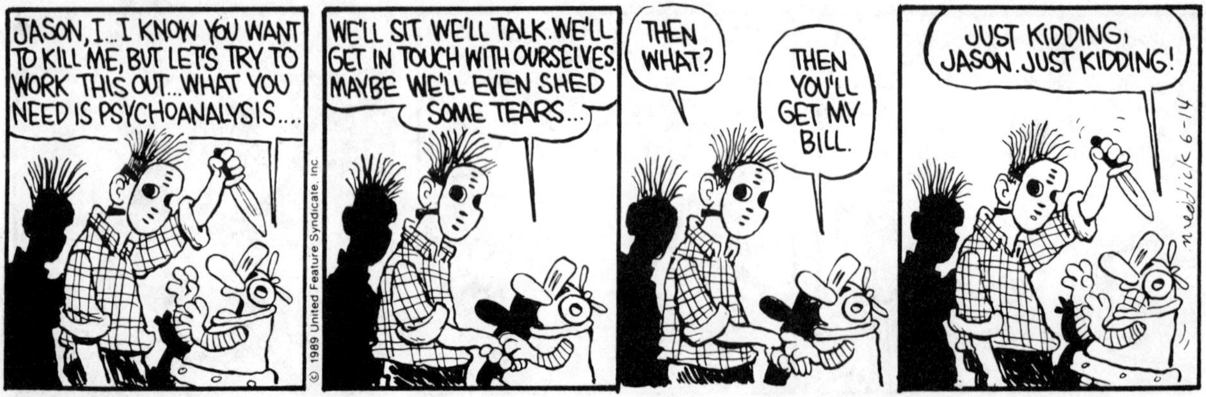
JASON, I...I KNOW YOU WANT TO KILL ME, BUT LET'S TRY TO WORK THIS OUT...WHAT YOU NEED IS PSYCHOANALYSIS....
© 1989 United Feature Syndicate, Inc
WE'LL SIT. WE'LL TALK. WE'LL GET IN TOUCH WITH OURSELVES. MAYBE WE'LL EVEN SHED SOME TEARS...
THEN WHAT?
THEN YOU'LL GET MY BILL.
JUST KIDDING, JASON. JUST KIDDING!

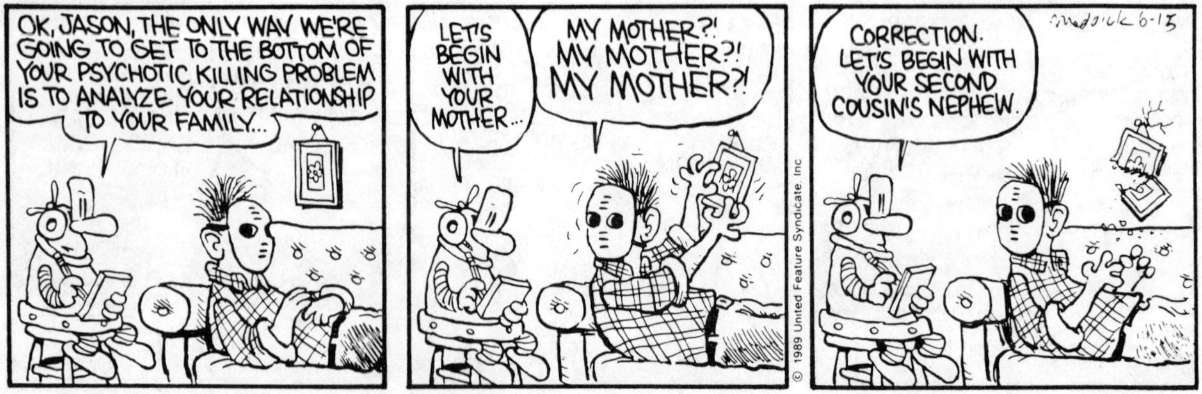
OK, JASON, THE ONLY WAY WE'RE GOING TO GET TO THE BOTTOM OF YOUR PSYCHOTIC KILLING PROBLEM IS TO ANALYZE YOUR RELATIONSHIP TO YOUR FAMILY...
LET'S BEGIN WITH YOUR MOTHER...
MY MOTHER?! MY MOTHER?! MY MOTHER?!
© 1989 United Feature Syndicate, Inc
CORRECTION. LET'S BEGIN WITH YOUR SECOND COUSIN'S NEPHEW.

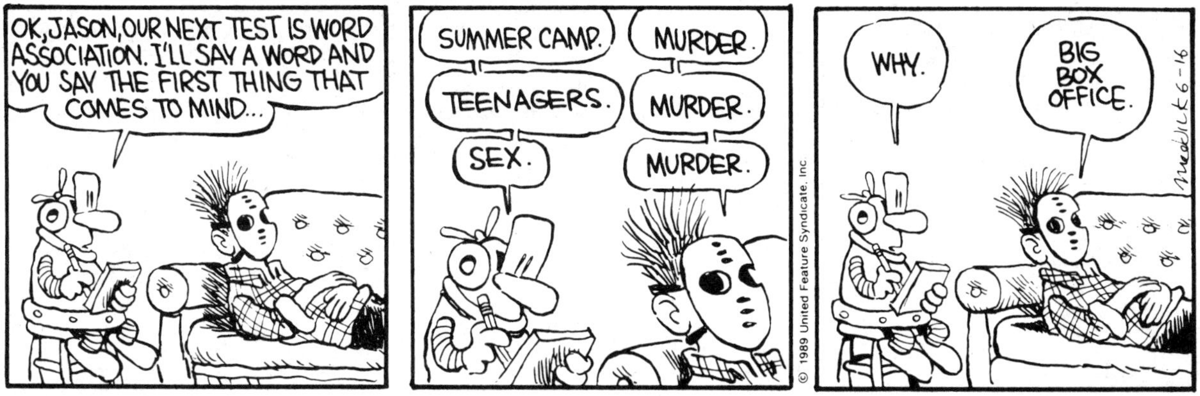
OK, JASON, OUR NEXT TEST IS WORD ASSOCIATION. I'LL SAY A WORD AND YOU SAY THE FIRST THING THAT COMES TO MIND...
SUMMER CAMP.
MURDER.
TEENAGERS.
MURDER.
SEX.
MURDER.
© 1989 United Feature Syndicate, Inc
WHY.
BIG BOX OFFICE.
Meddick 6-16

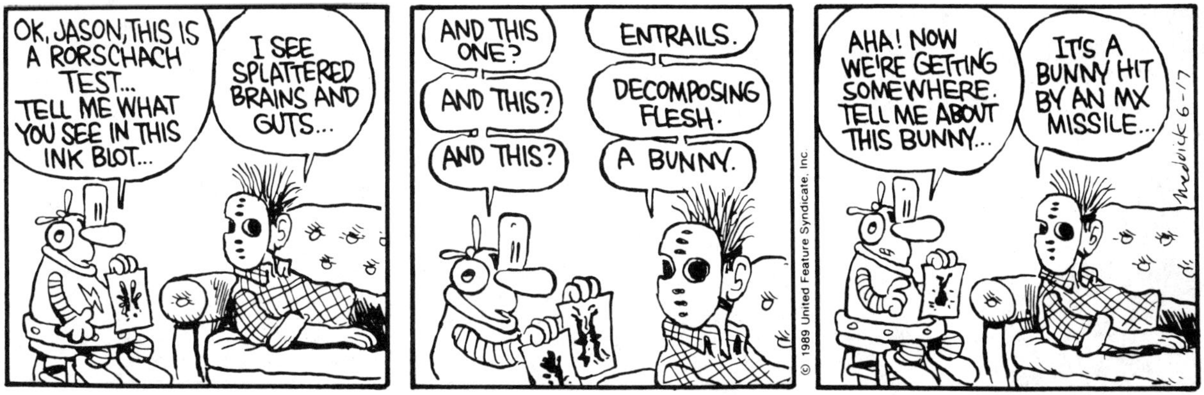
OK, JASON, THIS IS A RORSCHACH TEST... TELL ME WHAT YOU SEE IN THIS INK BLOT...
I SEE SPLATTERED BRAINS AND GUTS...
AND THIS ONE?
ENTRAILS.
AND THIS?
DECOMPOSING FLESH.
AND THIS?
A BUNNY.
© 1989 United Feature Syndicate, Inc.
AHA! NOW WE'RE GETTING SOMEWHERE. TELL ME ABOUT THIS BUNNY...
IT'S A BUNNY HIT BY AN MX MISSILE...
Meddick 6-17

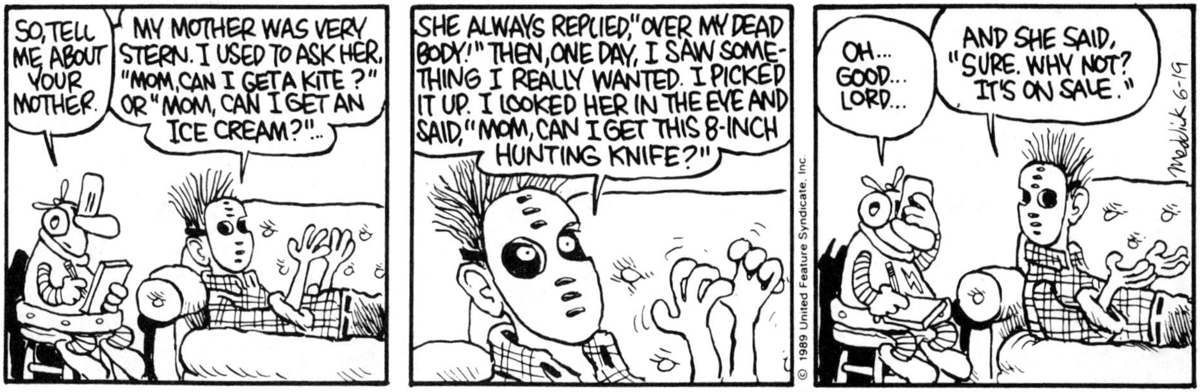
SO, TELL ME ABOUT YOUR MOTHER.
MY MOTHER WAS VERY STERN. I USED TO ASK HER, "MOM, CAN I GET A KITE?" OR "MOM, CAN I GET AN ICE CREAM?"...
SHE ALWAYS REPLIED, "OVER MY DEAD BODY!" THEN, ONE DAY, I SAW SOMETHING I REALLY WANTED. I PICKED IT UP. I LOOKED HER IN THE EYE AND SAID, "MOM, CAN I GET THIS 8-INCH HUNTING KNIFE?"
© 1989 United Feature Syndicate, Inc.
OH... GOOD... LORD...
AND SHE SAID, "SURE. WHY NOT? IT'S ON SALE."
Meddick 6-19

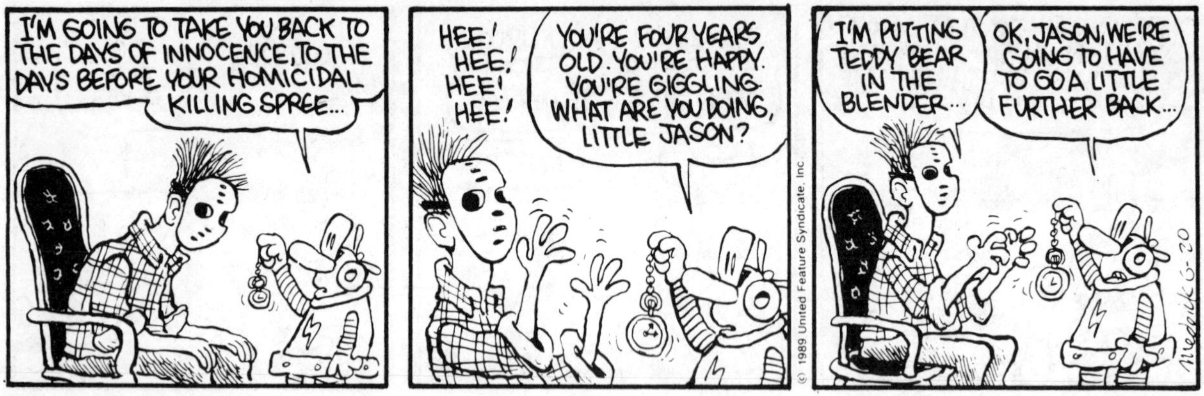
I'M GOING TO TAKE YOU BACK TO THE DAYS OF INNOCENCE, TO THE DAYS BEFORE YOUR HOMICIDAL KILLING SPREE...
HEE! HEE! HEE! HEE!
YOU'RE FOUR YEARS OLD. YOU'RE HAPPY. YOU'RE GIGGLING. WHAT ARE YOU DOING, LITTLE JASON?
© 1989 United Feature Syndicate, Inc
I'M PUTTING TEDDY BEAR IN THE BLENDER...
OK, JASON, WE'RE GOING TO HAVE TO GO A LITTLE FURTHER BACK...
Medrick 6-20

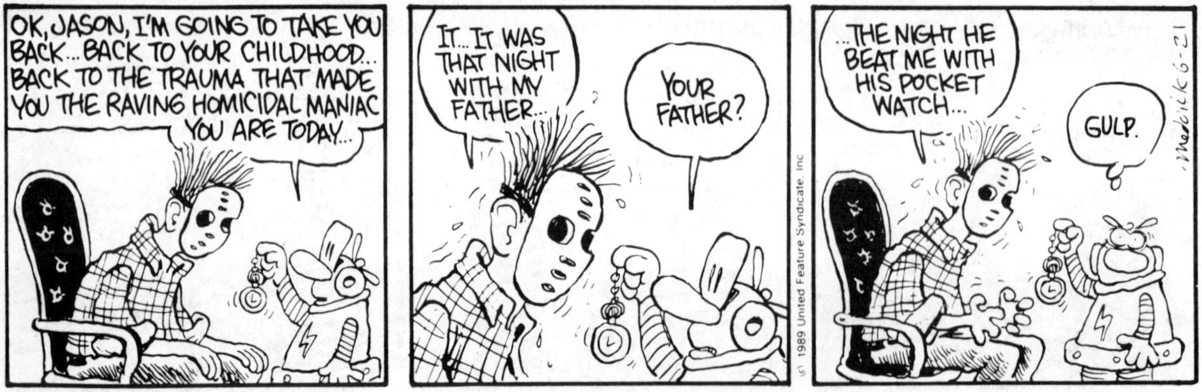
OK, JASON, I'M GOING TO TAKE YOU BACK... BACK TO YOUR CHILDHOOD... BACK TO THE TRAUMA THAT MADE YOU THE RAVING HOMICIDAL MANIAC YOU ARE TODAY...
IT... IT WAS THAT NIGHT WITH MY FATHER...
YOUR FATHER?
© 1989 United Feature Syndicate, Inc
...THE NIGHT HE BEAT ME WITH HIS POCKET WATCH...
GULP.
Medrick 6-21

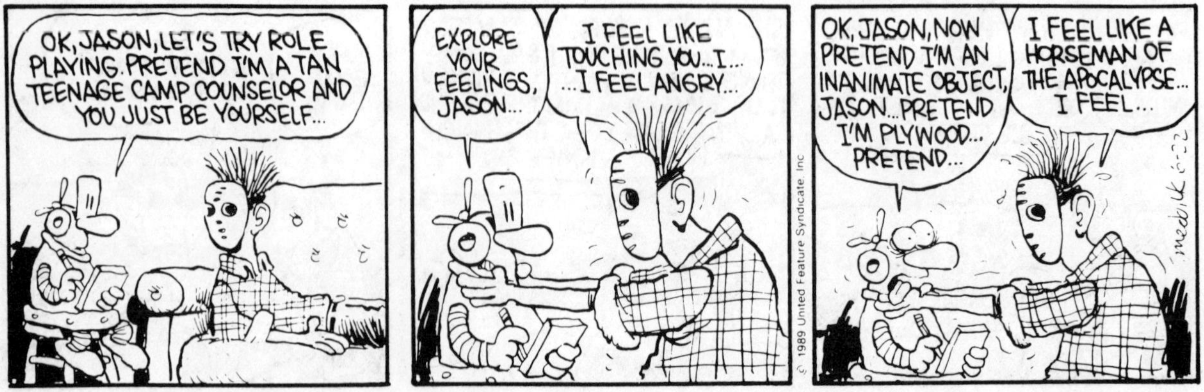
OK, JASON, LET'S TRY ROLE PLAYING. PRETEND I'M A TAN TEENAGE CAMP COUNSELOR AND YOU JUST BE YOURSELF...
EXPLORE YOUR FEELINGS, JASON...
I FEEL LIKE TOUCHING YOU... I... ...I FEEL ANGRY...
© 1989 United Feature Syndicate, Inc
OK, JASON, NOW PRETEND I'M AN INANIMATE OBJECT, JASON... PRETEND I'M PLYWOOD... PRETEND...
I FEEL LIKE A HORSEMAN OF THE APOCALYPSE... I FEEL...
Medrick 6-22

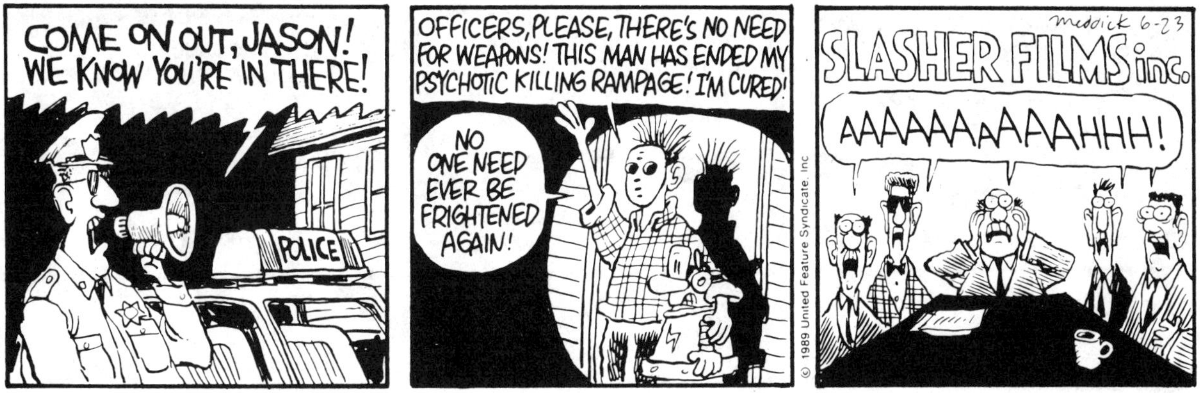
COME ON OUT, JASON! WE KNOW YOU'RE IN THERE!
POLICE
OFFICERS, PLEASE, THERE'S NO NEED FOR WEAPONS! THIS MAN HAS ENDED MY PSYCHOTIC KILLING RAMPAGE! I'M CURED!
NO ONE NEED EVER BE FRIGHTENED AGAIN!
© 1989 United Feature Syndicate, Inc.
meddick 6-23
SLASHER FILMS inc.
AAAAAAAAAAHHH!

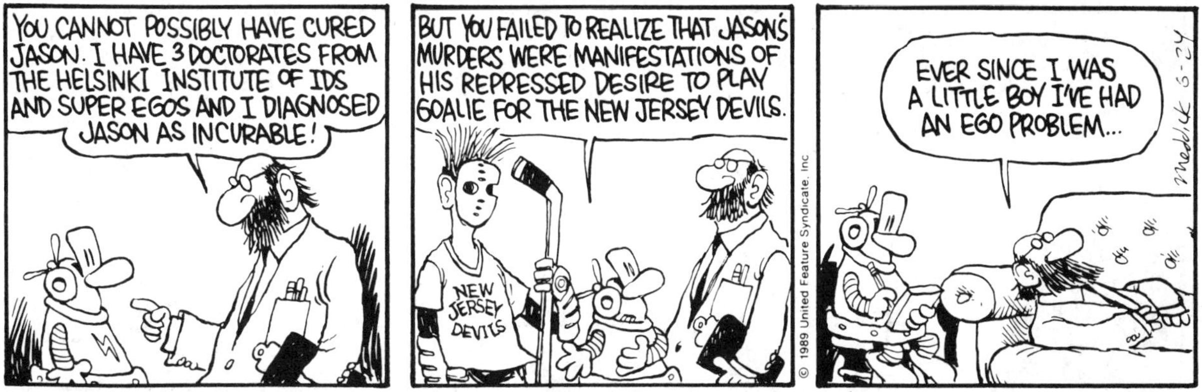
YOU CANNOT POSSIBLY HAVE CURED JASON. I HAVE 3 DOCTORATES FROM THE HELSINKI INSTITUTE OF IDS AND SUPER EGOS AND I DIAGNOSED JASON AS INCURABLE!
BUT YOU FAILED TO REALIZE THAT JASON'S MURDERS WERE MANIFESTATIONS OF HIS REPRESSED DESIRE TO PLAY GOALIE FOR THE NEW JERSEY DEVILS.
NEW JERSEY DEVILS
© 1989 United Feature Syndicate, Inc.
EVER SINCE I WAS A LITTLE BOY I'VE HAD AN EGO PROBLEM...
meddick 6-24

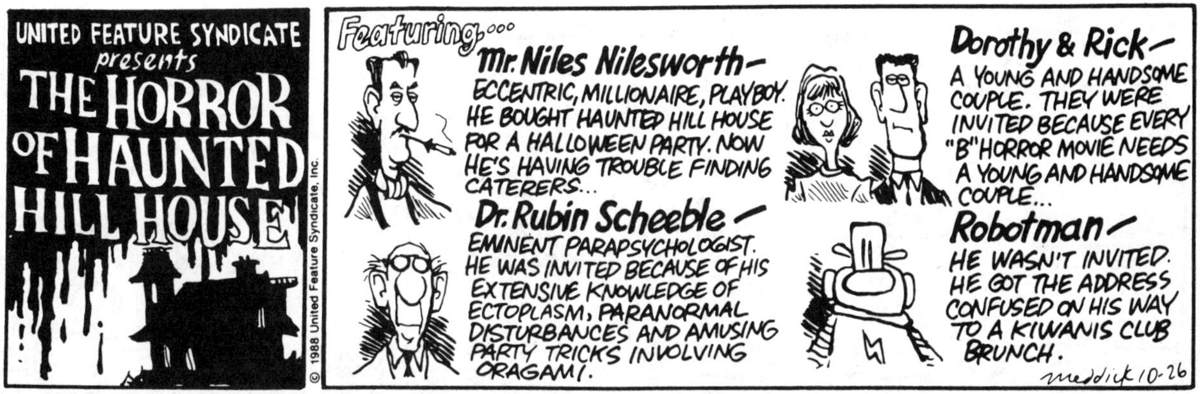
UNITED FEATURE SYNDICATE presents
THE HORROR OF HAUNTED HILL HOUSE
© 1988 United Feature Syndicate, Inc.
Featuring...
Mr. Niles Nilesworth—
ECCENTRIC, MILLIONAIRE, PLAYBOY. HE BOUGHT HAUNTED HILL HOUSE FOR A HALLOWEEN PARTY. NOW HE'S HAVING TROUBLE FINDING CATERERS...
Dorothy & Rick—
A YOUNG AND HANDSOME COUPLE. THEY WERE INVITED BECAUSE EVERY "B" HORROR MOVIE NEEDS A YOUNG AND HANDSOME COUPLE...
Dr. Rubin Scheeble—
EMINENT PARAPSYCHOLOGIST. HE WAS INVITED BECAUSE OF HIS EXTENSIVE KNOWLEDGE OF ECTOPLASM, PARANORMAL DISTURBANCES AND AMUSING PARTY TRICKS INVOLVING ORAGAMI.
Robotman—
HE WASN'T INVITED. HE GOT THE ADDRESS CONFUSED ON HIS WAY TO A KIWANIS CLUB BRUNCH.
meddick 10-26

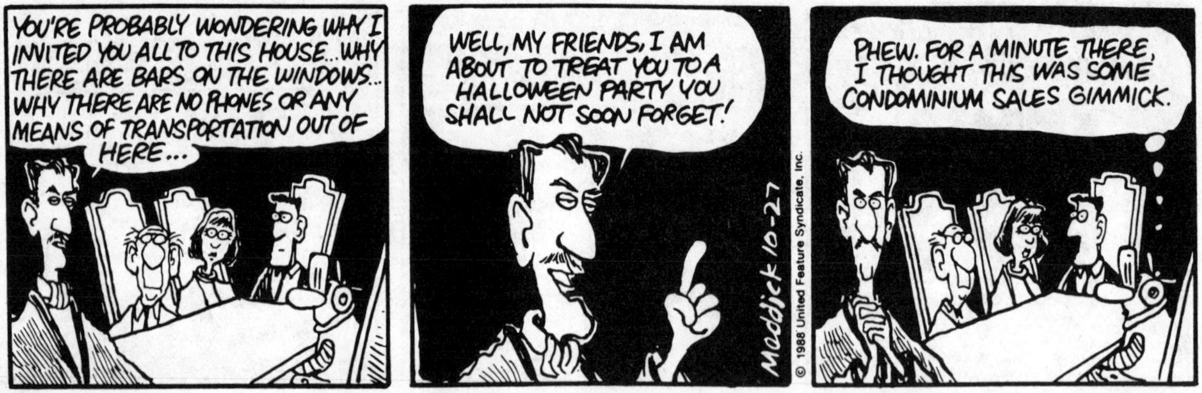
YOU'RE PROBABLY WONDERING WHY I INVITED YOU ALL TO THIS HOUSE...WHY THERE ARE BARS ON THE WINDOWS... WHY THERE ARE NO PHONES OR ANY MEANS OF TRANSPORTATION OUT OF HERE...
WELL, MY FRIENDS, I AM ABOUT TO TREAT YOU TO A HALLOWEEN PARTY YOU SHALL NOT SOON FORGET!
Meddick 10-27
PHEW. FOR A MINUTE THERE, I THOUGHT THIS WAS SOME CONDOMINIUM SALES GIMMICK.

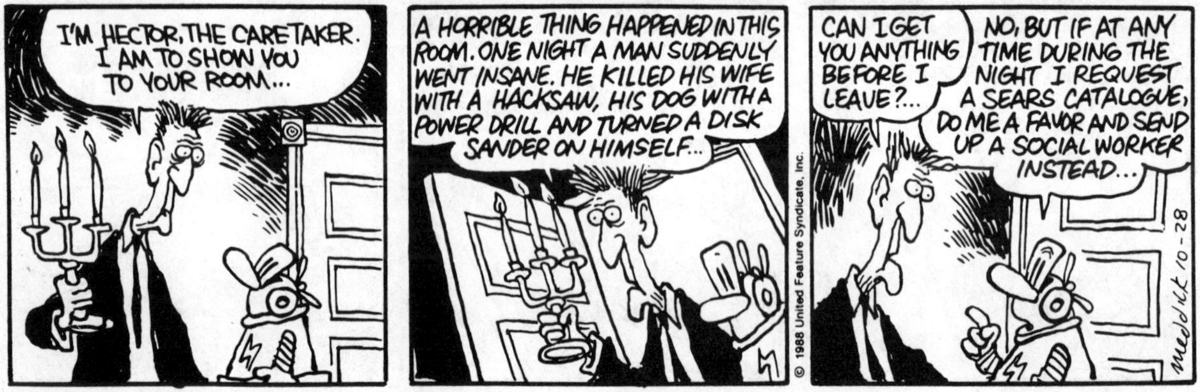
I'M HECTOR, THE CARETAKER. I AM TO SHOW YOU TO YOUR ROOM...
A HORRIBLE THING HAPPENED IN THIS ROOM. ONE NIGHT A MAN SUDDENLY WENT INSANE. HE KILLED HIS WIFE WITH A HACKSAW, HIS DOG WITH A POWER DRILL AND TURNED A DISK SANDER ON HIMSELF...
CAN I GET YOU ANYTHING BEFORE I LEAVE?...
NO, BUT IF AT ANY TIME DURING THE NIGHT I REQUEST A SEARS CATALOGUE, DO ME A FAVOR AND SEND UP A SOCIAL WORKER INSTEAD...
meddick 10-28

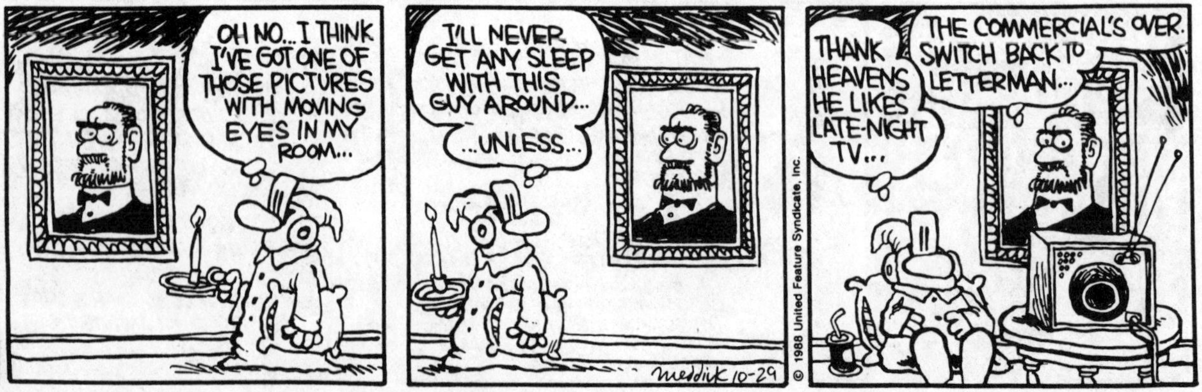
OH NO... I THINK I'VE GOT ONE OF THOSE PICTURES WITH MOVING EYES IN MY ROOM...
I'LL NEVER GET ANY SLEEP WITH THIS GUY AROUND...
...UNLESS...
meddick 10-29
THANK HEAVENS HE LIKES LATE-NIGHT TV...
THE COMMERCIAL'S OVER. SWITCH BACK TO LETTERMAN...

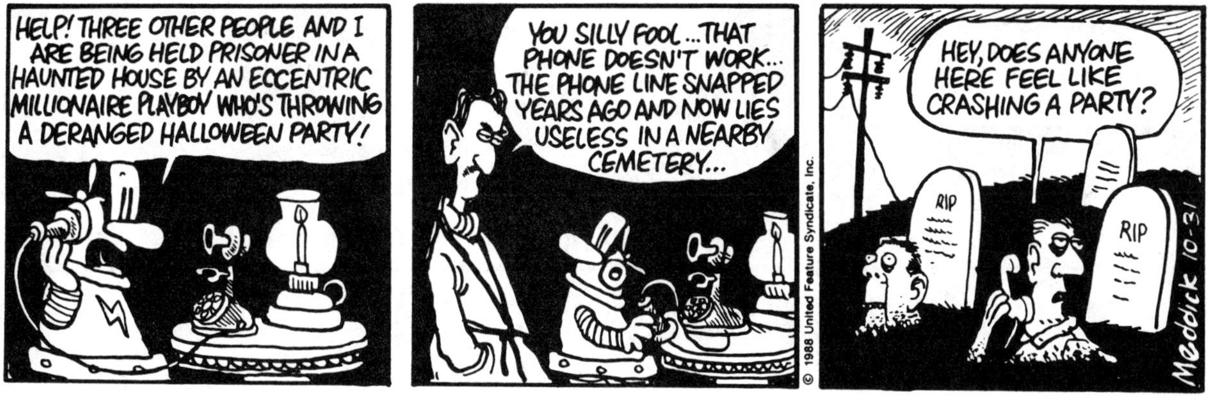
HELP! THREE OTHER PEOPLE AND I ARE BEING HELD PRISONER IN A HAUNTED HOUSE BY AN ECCENTRIC MILLIONAIRE PLAYBOY WHO'S THROWING A DERANGED HALLOWEEN PARTY!
YOU SILLY FOOL... THAT PHONE DOESN'T WORK... THE PHONE LINE SNAPPED YEARS AGO AND NOW LIES USELESS IN A NEARBY CEMETERY...
© 1988 United Feature Syndicate, Inc.
HEY, DOES ANYONE HERE FEEL LIKE CRASHING A PARTY?
RIP
RIP
Meddick 10-31

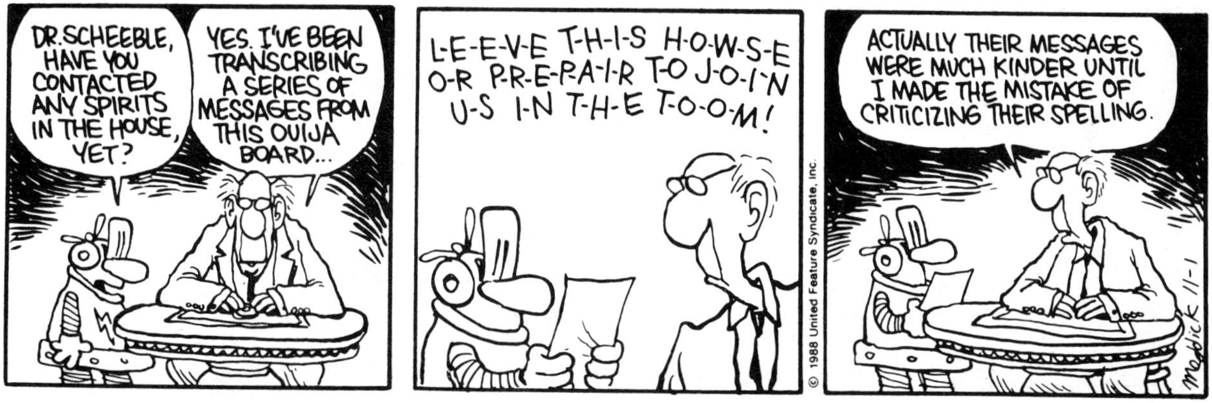
DR. SCHEEBLE, HAVE YOU CONTACTED ANY SPIRITS IN THE HOUSE, YET?
YES. I'VE BEEN TRANSCRIBING A SERIES OF MESSAGES FROM THIS OUIJA BOARD...
L-E-E-V-E T-H-I-S H-O-W-S-E O-R P-R-E-P-A-I-R T-O J-O-I-N U-S I-N T-H-E T-O-O-M!
© 1988 United Feature Syndicate, Inc.
ACTUALLY THEIR MESSAGES WERE MUCH KINDER UNTIL I MADE THE MISTAKE OF CRITICIZING THEIR SPELLING.
meddick 11-1

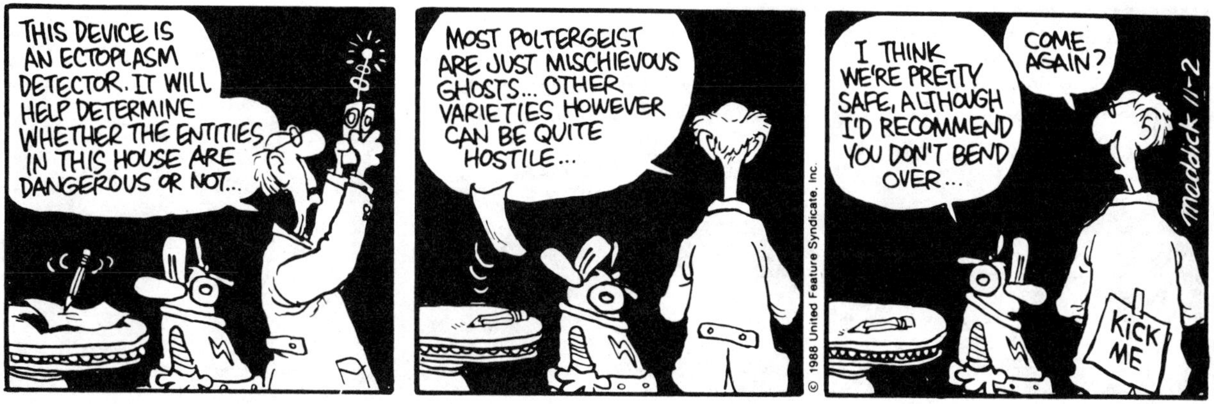
THIS DEVICE IS AN ECTOPLASM DETECTOR. IT WILL HELP DETERMINE WHETHER THE ENTITIES IN THIS HOUSE ARE DANGEROUS OR NOT...
MOST POLTERGEIST ARE JUST MISCHIEVOUS GHOSTS... OTHER VARIETIES HOWEVER CAN BE QUITE HOSTILE...
© 1988 United Feature Syndicate, Inc.
I THINK WE'RE PRETTY SAFE, ALTHOUGH I'D RECOMMEND YOU DON'T BEND OVER...
COME AGAIN?
KICK ME
meddick 11-2

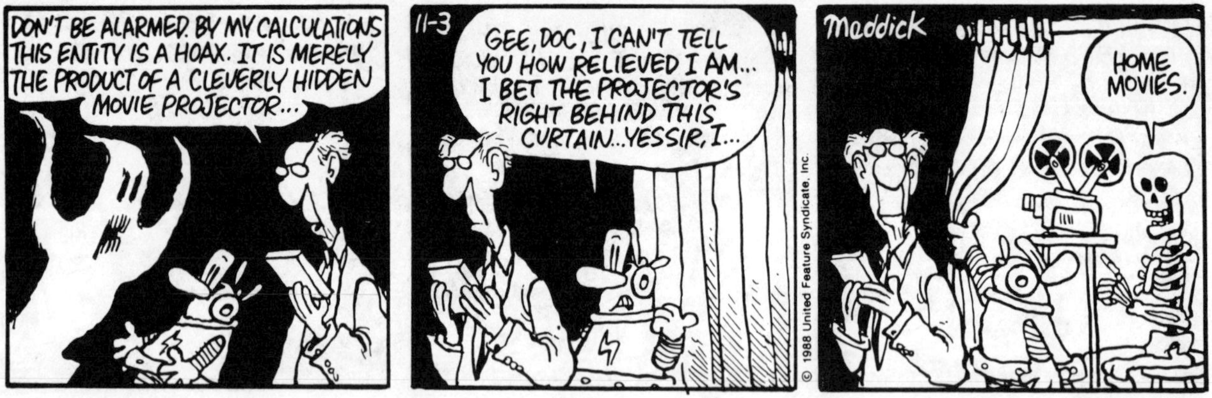
DON'T BE ALARMED. BY MY CALCULATIONS THIS ENTITY IS A HOAX. IT IS MERELY THE PRODUCT OF A CLEVERLY HIDDEN MOVIE PROJECTOR...
11-3
GEE, DOC, I CAN'T TELL YOU HOW RELIEVED I AM... I BET THE PROJECTOR'S RIGHT BEHIND THIS CURTAIN...YESSIR, I...
Maddick
HOME MOVIES.
© 1988 United Feature Syndicate, Inc.

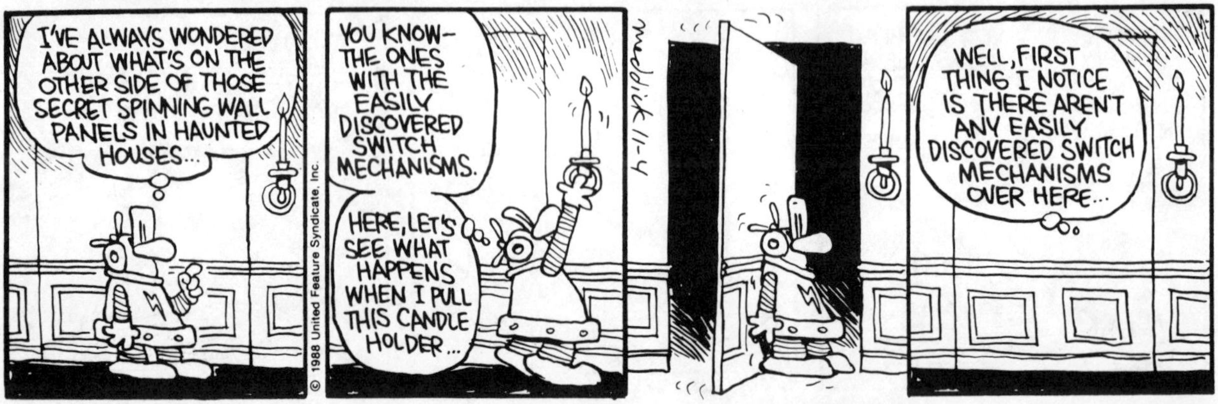
I'VE ALWAYS WONDERED ABOUT WHAT'S ON THE OTHER SIDE OF THOSE SECRET SPINNING WALL PANELS IN HAUNTED HOUSES...
© 1988 United Feature Syndicate, Inc.
YOU KNOW— THE ONES WITH THE EASILY DISCOVERED SWITCH MECHANISMS.
HERE, LET'S SEE WHAT HAPPENS WHEN I PULL THIS CANDLE HOLDER...
Maddick 11-4
WELL, FIRST THING I NOTICE IS THERE AREN'T ANY EASILY DISCOVERED SWITCH MECHANISMS OVER HERE...

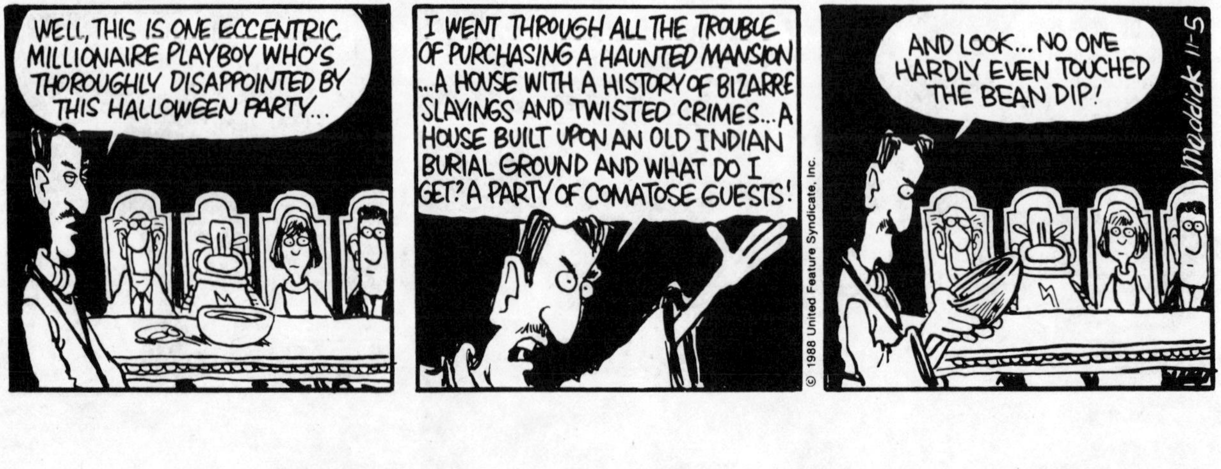
WELL, THIS IS ONE ECCENTRIC MILLIONAIRE PLAYBOY WHO'S THOROUGHLY DISAPPOINTED BY THIS HALLOWEEN PARTY...
I WENT THROUGH ALL THE TROUBLE OF PURCHASING A HAUNTED MANSION ...A HOUSE WITH A HISTORY OF BIZARRE SLAYINGS AND TWISTED CRIMES...A HOUSE BUILT UPON AN OLD INDIAN BURIAL GROUND AND WHAT DO I GET? A PARTY OF COMATOSE GUESTS!
© 1988 United Feature Syndicate, Inc.
AND LOOK... NO ONE HARDLY EVEN TOUCHED THE BEAN DIP!
Maddick 11-5

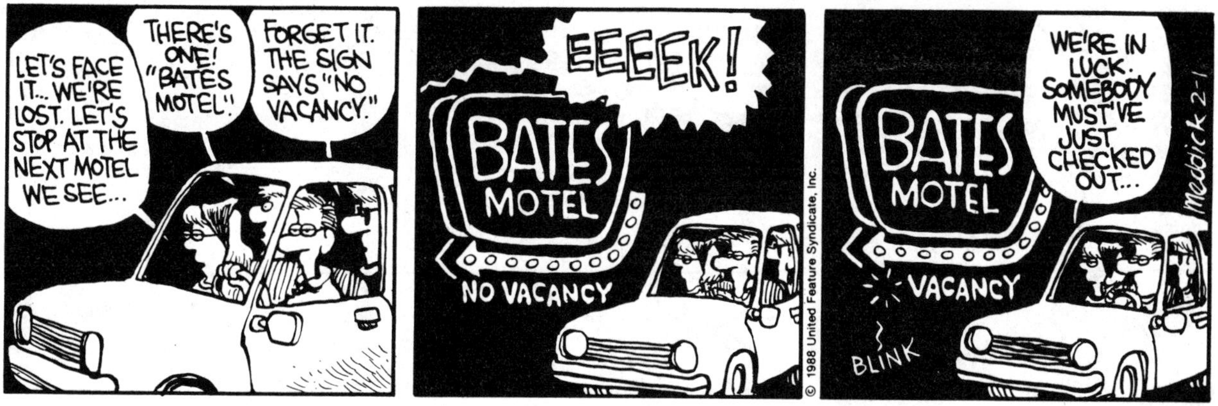
LET'S FACE IT... WE'RE LOST. LET'S STOP AT THE NEXT MOTEL WE SEE...
THERE'S ONE! "BATES MOTEL"!
FORGET IT. THE SIGN SAYS "NO VACANCY."
EEEEK!
BATES MOTEL
NO VACANCY
© 1988 United Feature Syndicate, Inc.
BATES MOTEL
VACANCY
BLINK
WE'RE IN LUCK. SOMEBODY MUST'VE JUST CHECKED OUT...
meddick 2-1

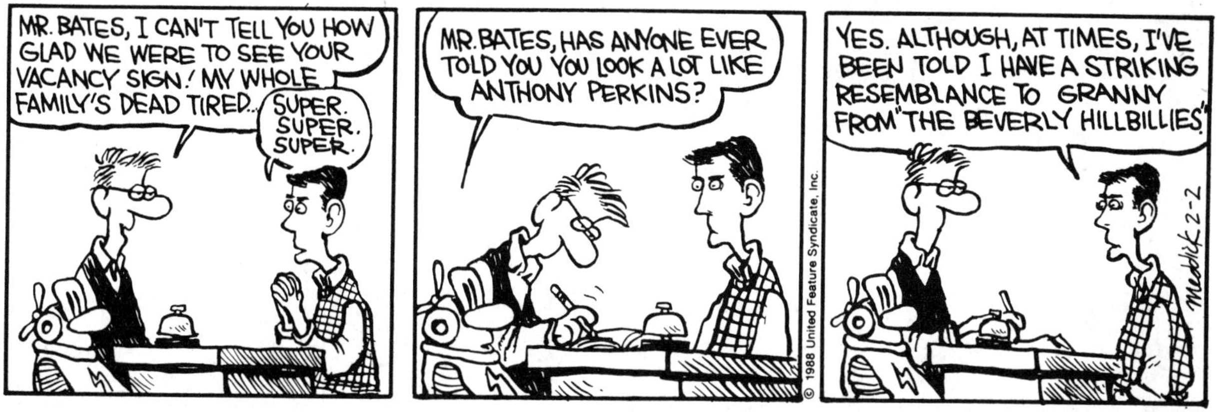
MR. BATES, I CAN'T TELL YOU HOW GLAD WE WERE TO SEE YOUR VACANCY SIGN! MY WHOLE FAMILY'S DEAD TIRED...
SUPER. SUPER. SUPER.
MR. BATES, HAS ANYONE EVER TOLD YOU YOU LOOK A LOT LIKE ANTHONY PERKINS?
© 1988 United Feature Syndicate, Inc.
YES. ALTHOUGH, AT TIMES, I'VE BEEN TOLD I HAVE A STRIKING RESEMBLANCE TO GRANNY FROM "THE BEVERLY HILLBILLIES."
meddick 2-2

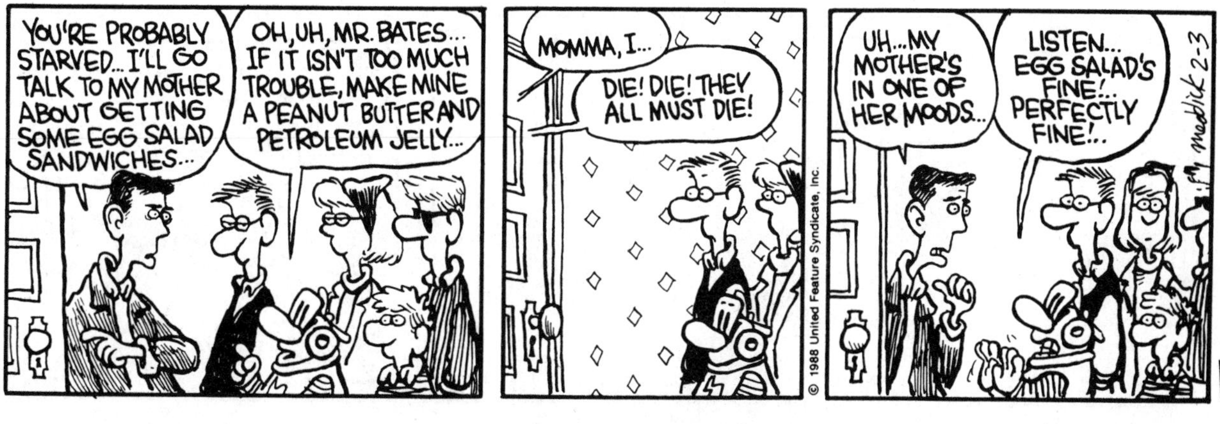
YOU'RE PROBABLY STARVED... I'LL GO TALK TO MY MOTHER ABOUT GETTING SOME EGG SALAD SANDWICHES...
OH, UH, MR. BATES... IF IT ISN'T TOO MUCH TROUBLE, MAKE MINE A PEANUT BUTTER AND PETROLEUM JELLY...
MOMMA, I...
DIE! DIE! THEY ALL MUST DIE!
© 1988 United Feature Syndicate, Inc.
UH... MY MOTHER'S IN ONE OF HER MOODS...
LISTEN... EGG SALAD'S FINE!... PERFECTLY FINE!...
meddick 2-3

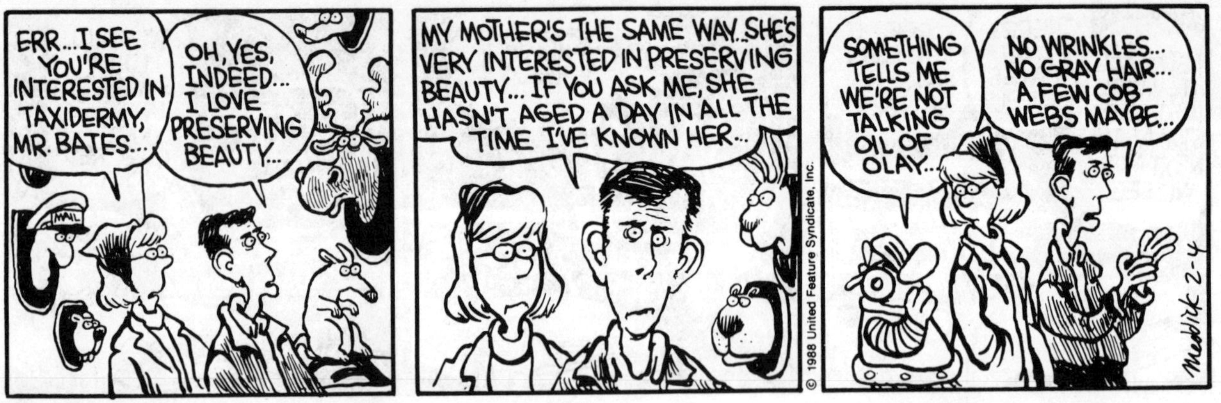
ERR... I SEE YOU'RE INTERESTED IN TAXIDERMY, MR. BATES...
OH, YES, INDEED... I LOVE PRESERVING BEAUTY...
MAIL
MY MOTHER'S THE SAME WAY.. SHE'S VERY INTERESTED IN PRESERVING BEAUTY... IF YOU ASK ME, SHE HASN'T AGED A DAY IN ALL THE TIME I'VE KNOWN HER...
© 1988 United Feature Syndicate, Inc.
SOMETHING TELLS ME WE'RE NOT TALKING OIL OF OLAY...
NO WRINKLES... NO GRAY HAIR... A FEW COB-WEBS MAYBE...
meddick 2-4

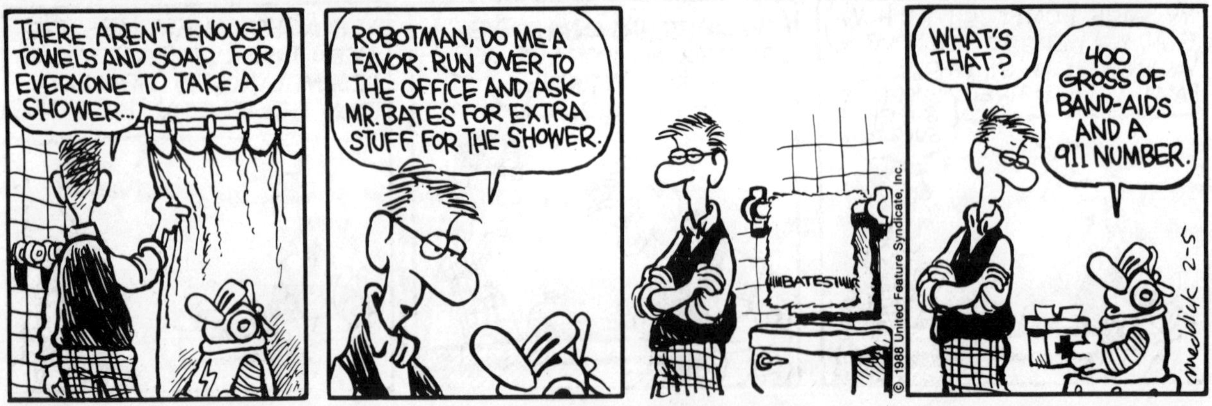
THERE AREN'T ENOUGH TOWELS AND SOAP FOR EVERYONE TO TAKE A SHOWER...
ROBOTMAN, DO ME A FAVOR. RUN OVER TO THE OFFICE AND ASK MR. BATES FOR EXTRA STUFF FOR THE SHOWER.
BATES
© 1988 United Feature Syndicate, Inc.
WHAT'S THAT?
400 GROSS OF BAND-AIDS AND A 911 NUMBER.
meddick 2-5

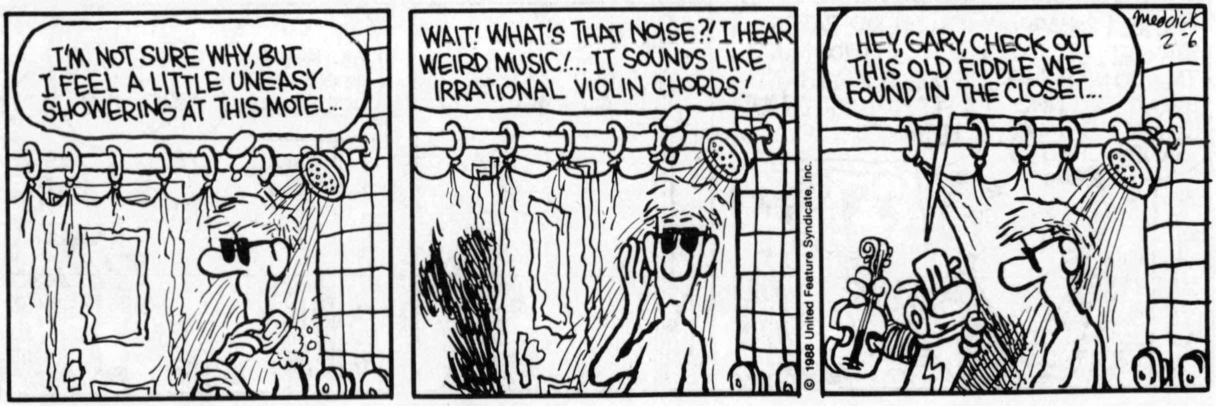
I'M NOT SURE WHY, BUT I FEEL A LITTLE UNEASY SHOWERING AT THIS MOTEL...
WAIT! WHAT'S THAT NOISE?! I HEAR WEIRD MUSIC!... IT SOUNDS LIKE IRRATIONAL VIOLIN CHORDS!
© 1988 United Feature Syndicate, Inc.
meddick 2-6
HEY, GARY, CHECK OUT THIS OLD FIDDLE WE FOUND IN THE CLOSET...

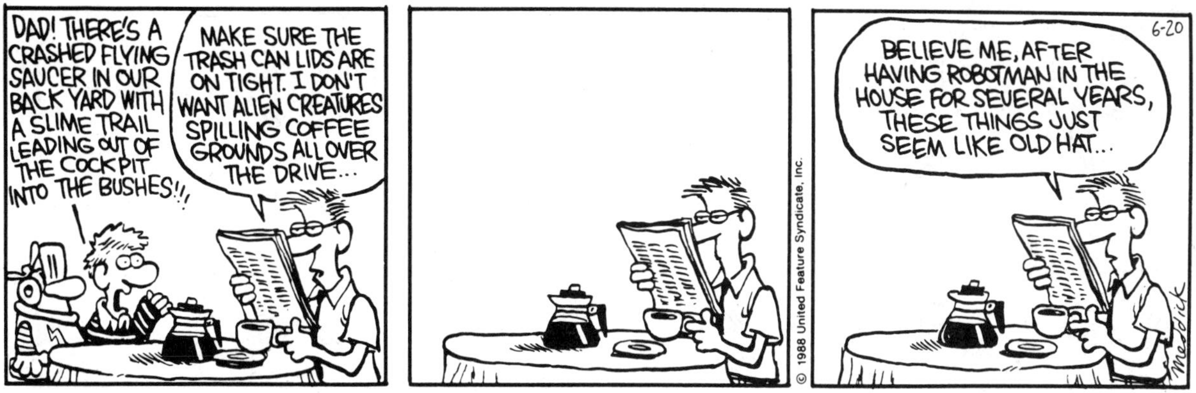
DAD! THERE'S A CRASHED FLYING SAUCER IN OUR BACK YARD WITH A SLIME TRAIL LEADING OUT OF THE COCKPIT INTO THE BUSHES!!,
MAKE SURE THE TRASH CAN LIDS ARE ON TIGHT. I DON'T WANT ALIEN CREATURES SPILLING COFFEE GROUNDS ALL OVER THE DRIVE...
6-20
BELIEVE ME, AFTER HAVING ROBOTMAN IN THE HOUSE FOR SEVERAL YEARS, THESE THINGS JUST SEEM LIKE OLD HAT...
meddick

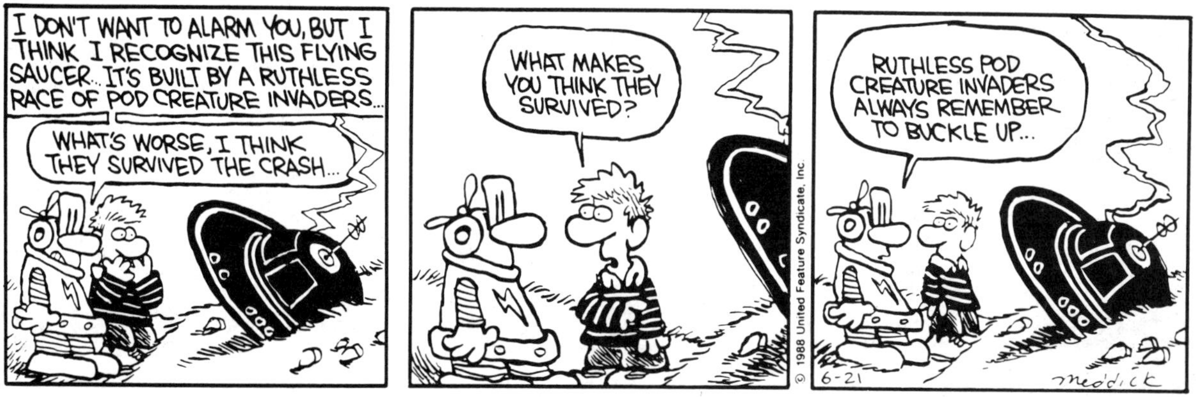
I DON'T WANT TO ALARM YOU, BUT I THINK I RECOGNIZE THIS FLYING SAUCER... IT'S BUILT BY A RUTHLESS RACE OF POD CREATURE INVADERS...
WHAT'S WORSE, I THINK THEY SURVIVED THE CRASH...
WHAT MAKES YOU THINK THEY SURVIVED?
RUTHLESS POD CREATURE INVADERS ALWAYS REMEMBER TO BUCKLE UP...
6-21
meddick

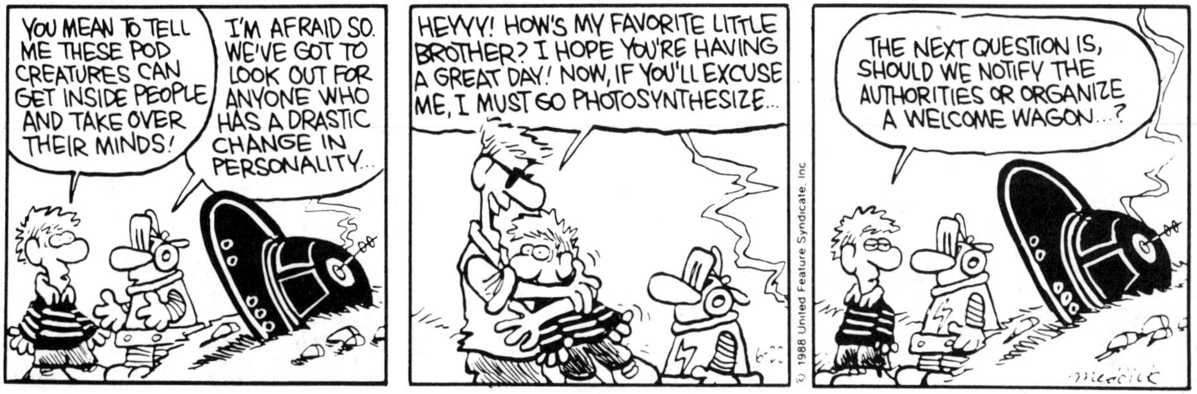
YOU MEAN TO TELL ME THESE POD CREATURES CAN GET INSIDE PEOPLE AND TAKE OVER THEIR MINDS!
I'M AFRAID SO. WE'VE GOT TO LOOK OUT FOR ANYONE WHO HAS A DRASTIC CHANGE IN PERSONALITY...
HEYYY! HOW'S MY FAVORITE LITTLE BROTHER? I HOPE YOU'RE HAVING A GREAT DAY! NOW, IF YOU'LL EXCUSE ME, I MUST GO PHOTOSYNTHESIZE...
THE NEXT QUESTION IS, SHOULD WE NOTIFY THE AUTHORITIES OR ORGANIZE A WELCOME WAGON...?
meddick

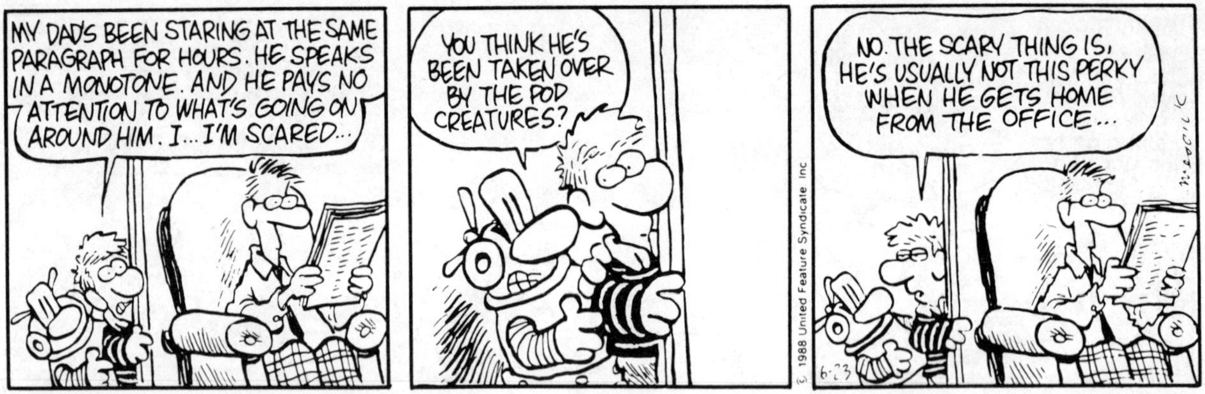
MY DAD'S BEEN STARING AT THE SAME PARAGRAPH FOR HOURS. HE SPEAKS IN A MONOTONE. AND HE PAYS NO ATTENTION TO WHAT'S GOING ON AROUND HIM. I... I'M SCARED...
YOU THINK HE'S BEEN TAKEN OVER BY THE POD CREATURES?
NO. THE SCARY THING IS, HE'S USUALLY NOT THIS PERKY WHEN HE GETS HOME FROM THE OFFICE...
© 1988 United Feature Syndicate, Inc.
6-23

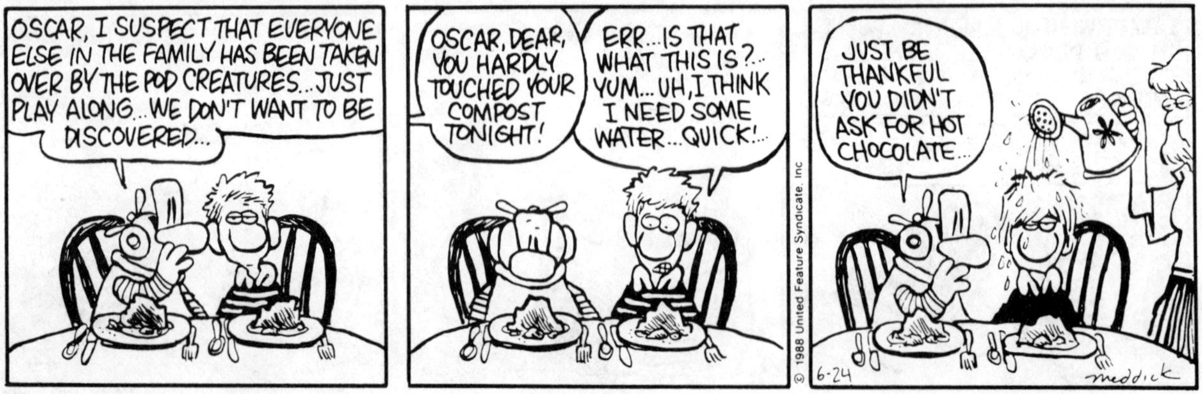
OSCAR, I SUSPECT THAT EVERYONE ELSE IN THE FAMILY HAS BEEN TAKEN OVER BY THE POD CREATURES... JUST PLAY ALONG... WE DON'T WANT TO BE DISCOVERED...
OSCAR, DEAR, YOU HARDLY TOUCHED YOUR COMPOST TONIGHT!
ERR... IS THAT WHAT THIS IS?... YUM... UH, I THINK I NEED SOME WATER... QUICK!...
JUST BE THANKFUL YOU DIDN'T ASK FOR HOT CHOCOLATE...
© 1988 United Feature Syndicate, Inc.
6-24
meddick

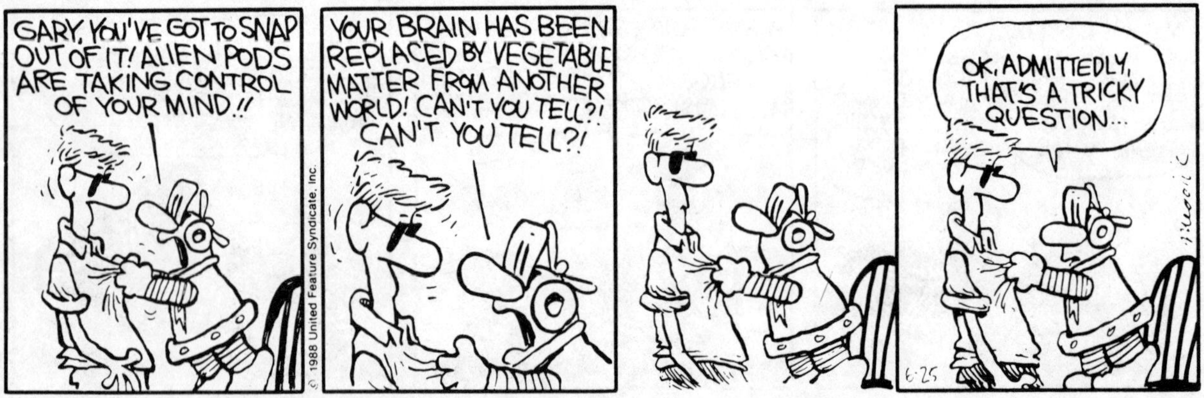
GARY, YOU'VE GOT TO SNAP OUT OF IT! ALIEN PODS ARE TAKING CONTROL OF YOUR MIND!!
YOUR BRAIN HAS BEEN REPLACED BY VEGETABLE MATTER FROM ANOTHER WORLD! CAN'T YOU TELL?! CAN'T YOU TELL?!
OK, ADMITTEDLY, THAT'S A TRICKY QUESTION...
© 1988 United Feature Syndicate, Inc.
6-25

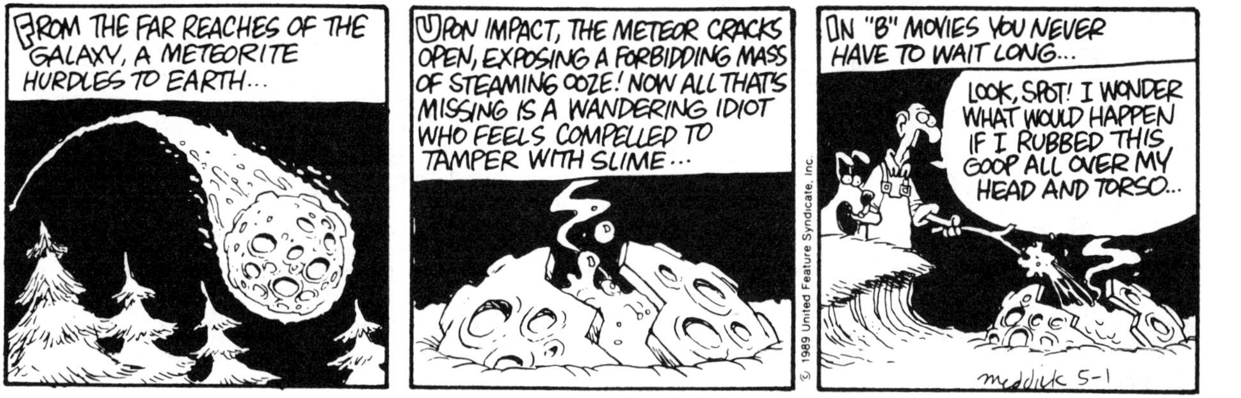
FROM THE FAR REACHES OF THE GALAXY, A METEORITE HURDLES TO EARTH...
UPON IMPACT, THE METEOR CRACKS OPEN, EXPOSING A FORBIDDING MASS OF STEAMING OOZE! NOW ALL THAT'S MISSING IS A WANDERING IDIOT WHO FEELS COMPELLED TO TAMPER WITH SLIME...
© 1989 United Feature Syndicate, Inc.
IN "B" MOVIES YOU NEVER HAVE TO WAIT LONG...
LOOK, SPOT! I WONDER WHAT WOULD HAPPEN IF I RUBBED THIS GOOP ALL OVER MY HEAD AND TORSO...
meddick 5-1

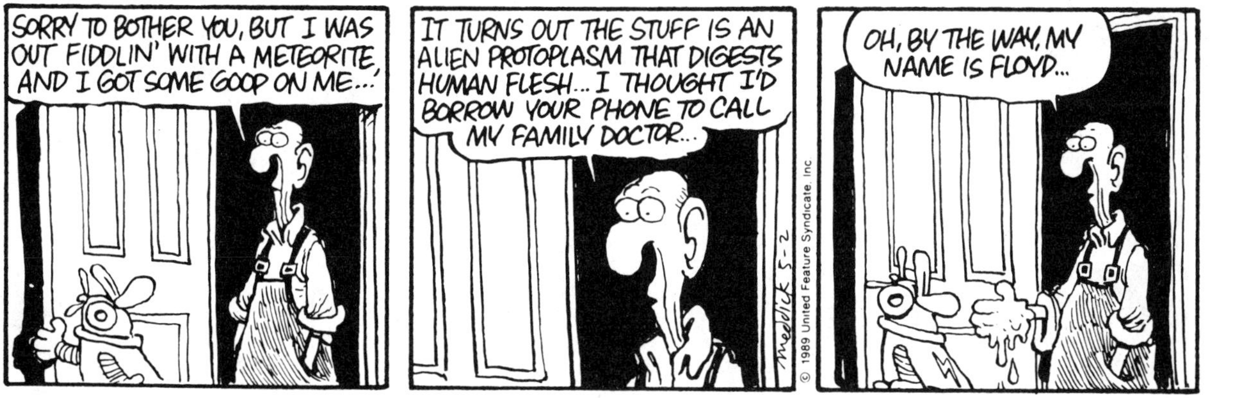
SORRY TO BOTHER YOU, BUT I WAS OUT FIDDLIN' WITH A METEORITE, AND I GOT SOME GOOP ON ME...
IT TURNS OUT THE STUFF IS AN ALIEN PROTOPLASM THAT DIGESTS HUMAN FLESH... I THOUGHT I'D BORROW YOUR PHONE TO CALL MY FAMILY DOCTOR...
meddick 5-2
© 1989 United Feature Syndicate, Inc.
OH, BY THE WAY, MY NAME IS FLOYD...

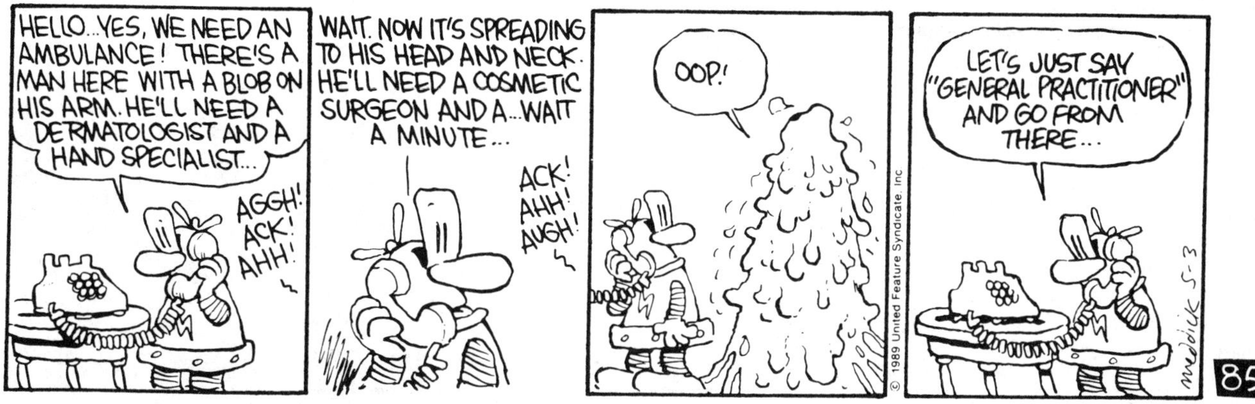
HELLO...YES, WE NEED AN AMBULANCE! THERE'S A MAN HERE WITH A BLOB ON HIS ARM. HE'LL NEED A DERMATOLOGIST AND A HAND SPECIALIST...
AGGH! ACK! AHH!
WAIT. NOW IT'S SPREADING TO HIS HEAD AND NECK. HE'LL NEED A COSMETIC SURGEON AND A...WAIT A MINUTE...
ACK! AHH! AUGH!
OOP!
© 1989 United Feature Syndicate, Inc.
LET'S JUST SAY "GENERAL PRACTITIONER" AND GO FROM THERE...
meddick 5-3

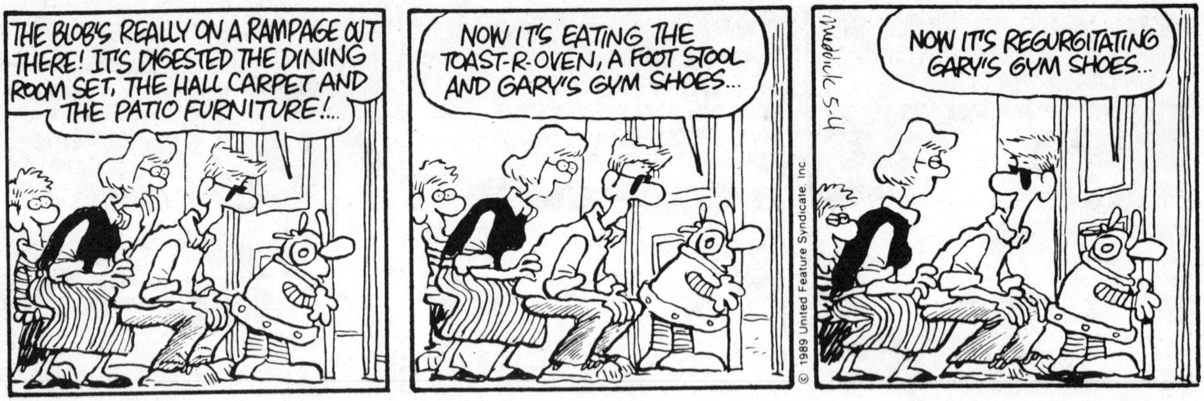
THE BLOB'S REALLY ON A RAMPAGE OUT THERE! IT'S DIGESTED THE DINING ROOM SET, THE HALL CARPET AND THE PATIO FURNITURE!...
NOW IT'S EATING THE TOAST-R-OVEN, A FOOT STOOL AND GARY'S GYM SHOES...
NOW IT'S REGURGITATING GARY'S GYM SHOES...
© 1989 United Feature Syndicate, Inc.

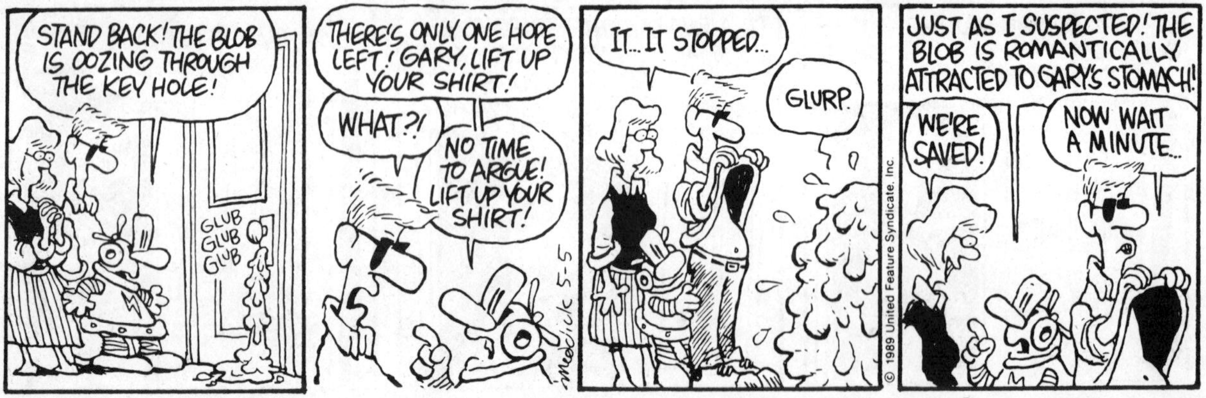
STAND BACK! THE BLOB IS OOZING THROUGH THE KEY HOLE!
GLUB GLUB GLUB
THERE'S ONLY ONE HOPE LEFT! GARY, LIFT UP YOUR SHIRT!
WHAT?!
NO TIME TO ARGUE! LIFT UP YOUR SHIRT!
IT... IT STOPPED...
GLURP.
JUST AS I SUSPECTED! THE BLOB IS ROMANTICALLY ATTRACTED TO GARY'S STOMACH!
WE'RE SAVED!
NOW WAIT A MINUTE...
© 1989 United Feature Syndicate, Inc.

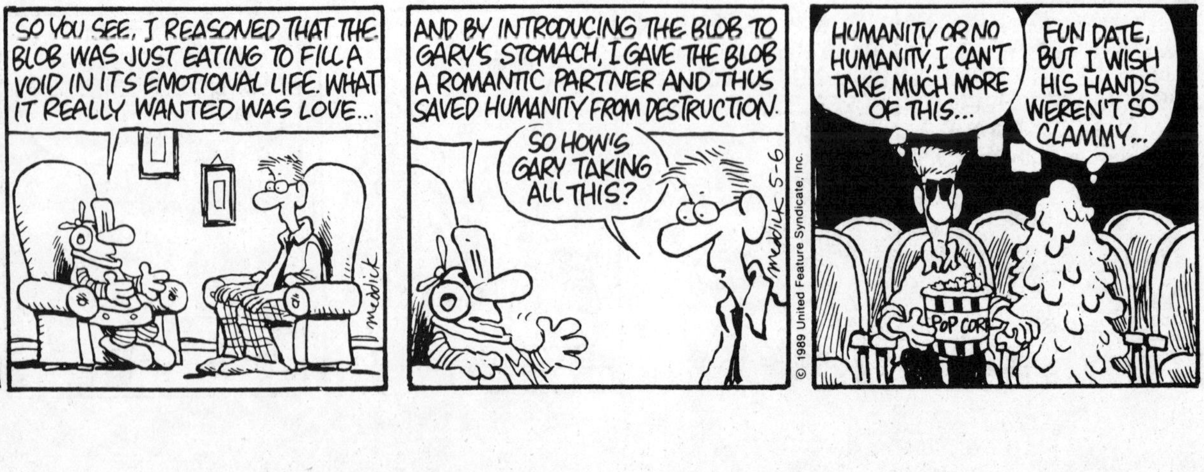
SO YOU SEE, I REASONED THAT THE BLOB WAS JUST EATING TO FILL A VOID IN ITS EMOTIONAL LIFE. WHAT IT REALLY WANTED WAS LOVE...
AND BY INTRODUCING THE BLOB TO GARY'S STOMACH, I GAVE THE BLOB A ROMANTIC PARTNER AND THUS SAVED HUMANITY FROM DESTRUCTION.
SO HOW'S GARY TAKING ALL THIS?
HUMANITY OR NO HUMANITY, I CAN'T TAKE MUCH MORE OF THIS...
FUN DATE, BUT I WISH HIS HANDS WEREN'T SO CLAMMY...
POP CORN
© 1989 United Feature Syndicate, Inc.

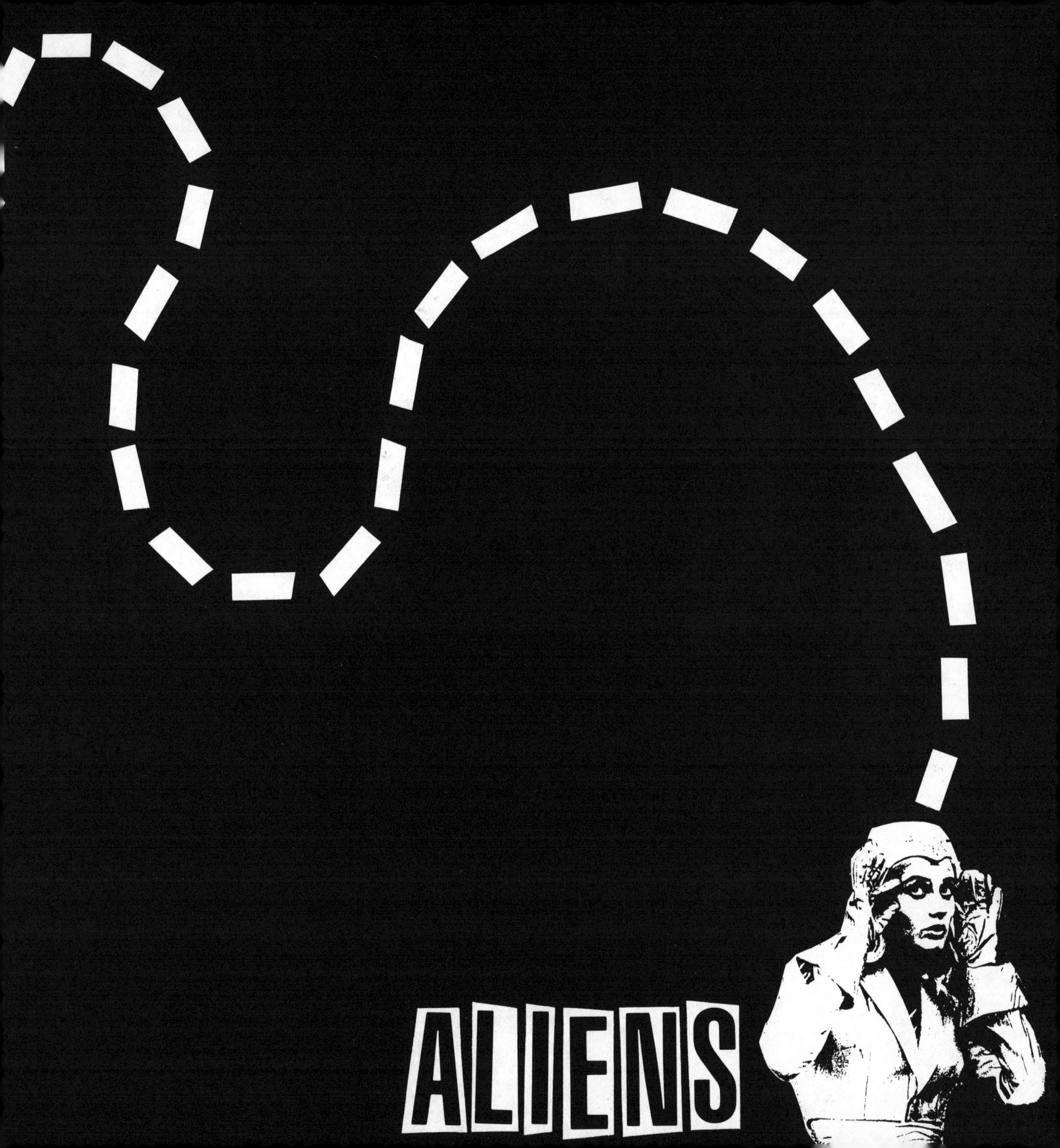
ALIENS

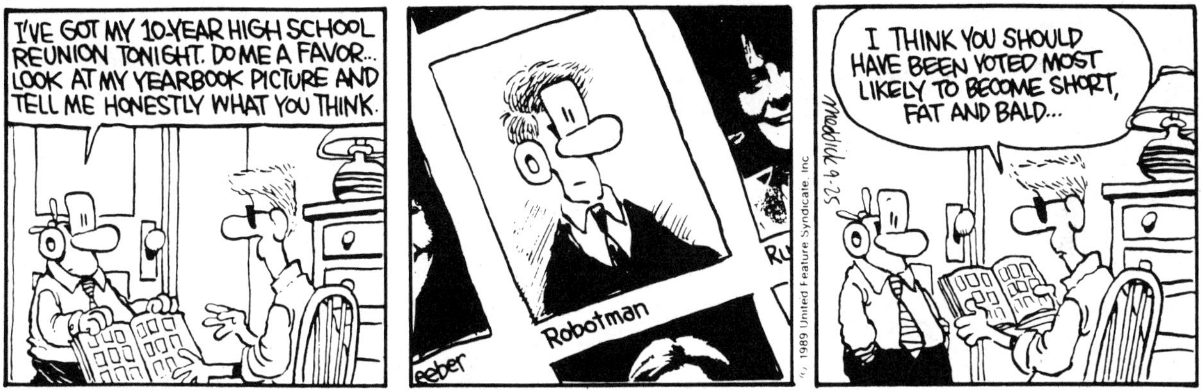
I'VE GOT MY 10-YEAR HIGH SCHOOL REUNION TONIGHT. DO ME A FAVOR... LOOK AT MY YEARBOOK PICTURE AND TELL ME HONESTLY WHAT YOU THINK.
Robotman
I THINK YOU SHOULD HAVE BEEN VOTED MOST LIKELY TO BECOME SHORT, FAT AND BALD...
© 1989 United Feature Syndicate, Inc.

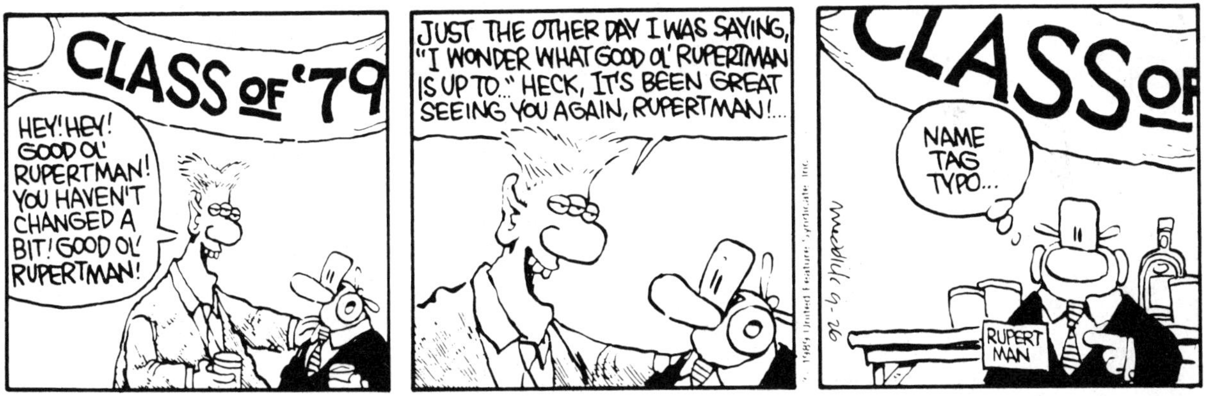
CLASS OF '79
HEY! HEY! GOOD OL' RUPERTMAN! YOU HAVEN'T CHANGED A BIT! GOOD OL' RUPERTMAN!
JUST THE OTHER DAY I WAS SAYING, "I WONDER WHAT GOOD OL' RUPERTMAN IS UP TO." HECK, IT'S BEEN GREAT SEEING YOU AGAIN, RUPERTMAN!...
CLASS OF
NAME TAG TYPO...
RUPERT MAN

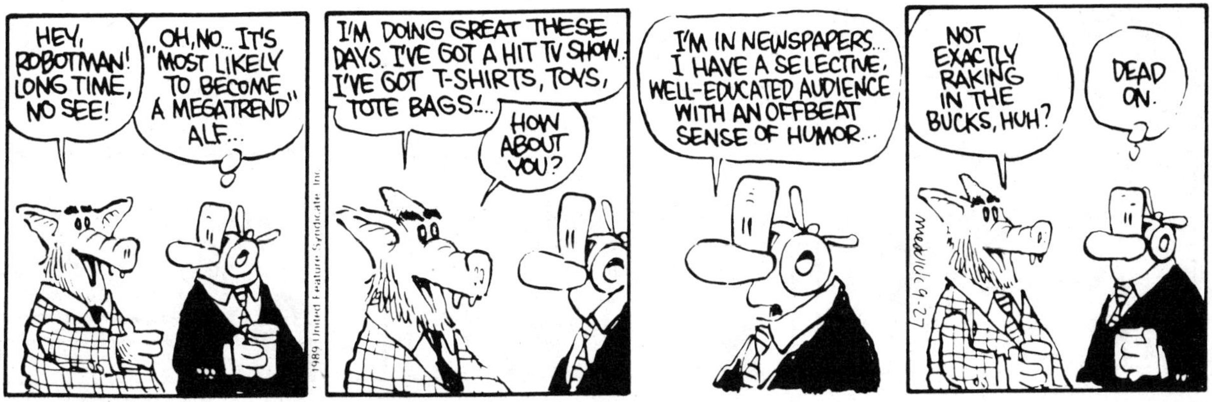
HEY, ROBOTMAN! LONG TIME, NO SEE!
OH, NO... IT'S "MOST LIKELY TO BECOME A MEGATREND" ALF...
I'M DOING GREAT THESE DAYS. I'VE GOT A HIT TV SHOW... I'VE GOT T-SHIRTS, TOYS, TOTE BAGS!...
HOW ABOUT YOU?
I'M IN NEWSPAPERS... I HAVE A SELECTIVE, WELL-EDUCATED AUDIENCE WITH AN OFFBEAT SENSE OF HUMOR...
NOT EXACTLY RAKING IN THE BUCKS, HUH?
DEAD ON.

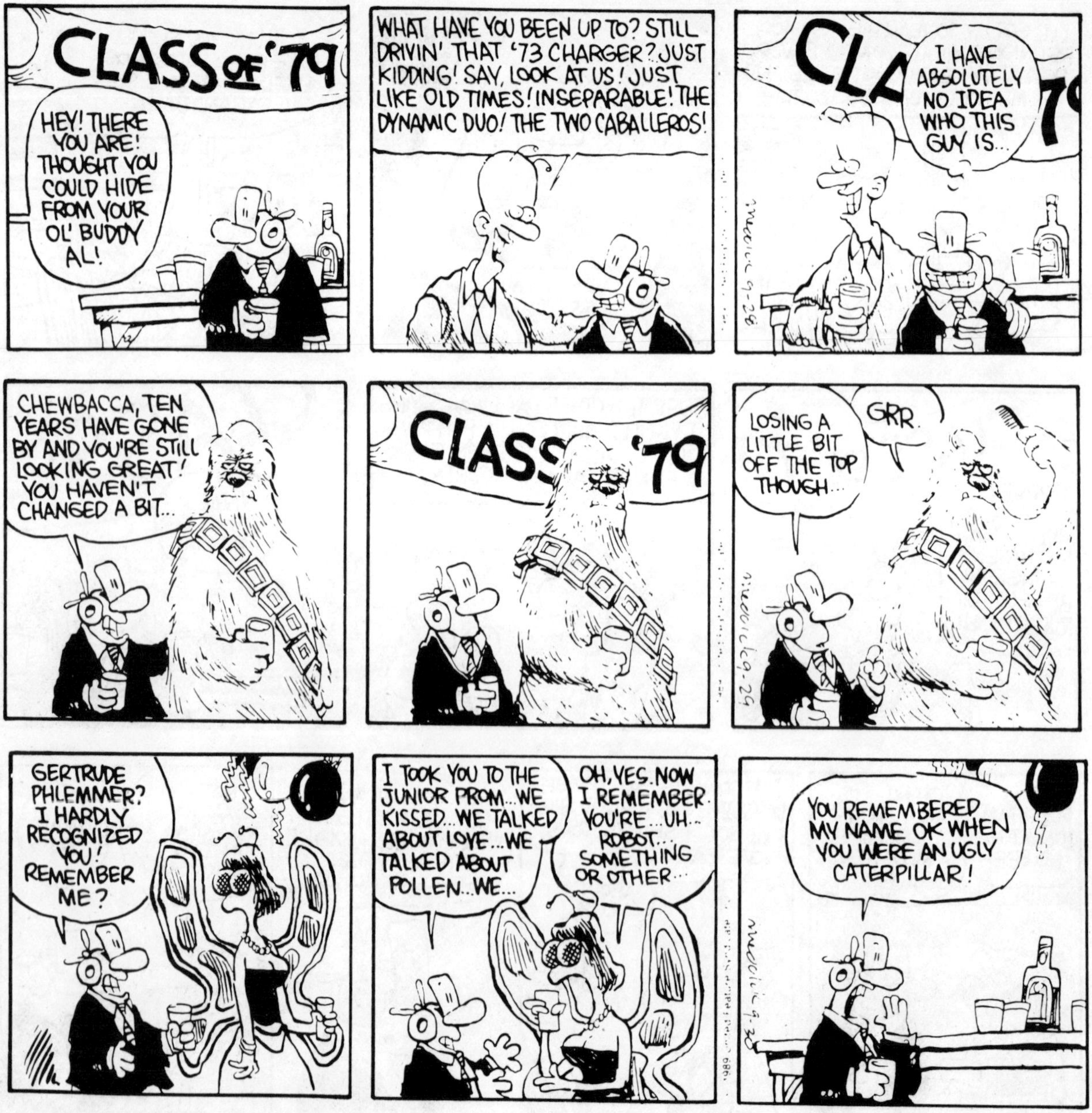
CLASS OF '79
HEY! THERE YOU ARE! THOUGHT YOU COULD HIDE FROM YOUR OL' BUDDY AL!
WHAT HAVE YOU BEEN UP TO? STILL DRIVIN' THAT '73 CHARGER? JUST KIDDING! SAY, LOOK AT US! JUST LIKE OLD TIMES! INSEPARABLE! THE DYNAMIC DUO! THE TWO CABALLEROS!
I HAVE ABSOLUTELY NO IDEA WHO THIS GUY IS...
CHEWBACCA, TEN YEARS HAVE GONE BY AND YOU'RE STILL LOOKING GREAT! YOU HAVEN'T CHANGED A BIT...
LOSING A LITTLE BIT OFF THE TOP THOUGH...
GRR.
GERTRUDE PHLEMMER? I HARDLY RECOGNIZED YOU! REMEMBER ME?
I TOOK YOU TO THE JUNIOR PROM... WE KISSED... WE TALKED ABOUT LOVE... WE TALKED ABOUT POLLEN... WE...
OH, YES. NOW I REMEMBER. YOU'RE... UH... ROBOT... SOMETHING OR OTHER...
YOU REMEMBERED MY NAME OK WHEN YOU WERE AN UGLY CATERPILLAR!

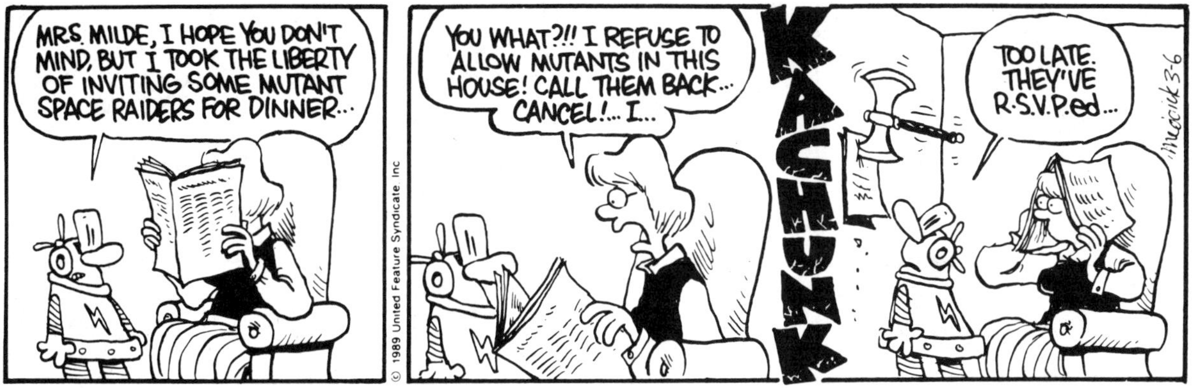
MRS. MILDE, I HOPE YOU DON'T MIND, BUT I TOOK THE LIBERTY OF INVITING SOME MUTANT SPACE RAIDERS FOR DINNER...
© 1989 United Feature Syndicate, Inc
YOU WHAT?!! I REFUSE TO ALLOW MUTANTS IN THIS HOUSE! CALL THEM BACK... CANCEL!... I...
KACHUNK
TOO LATE. THEY'VE R.S.V.P.ed...

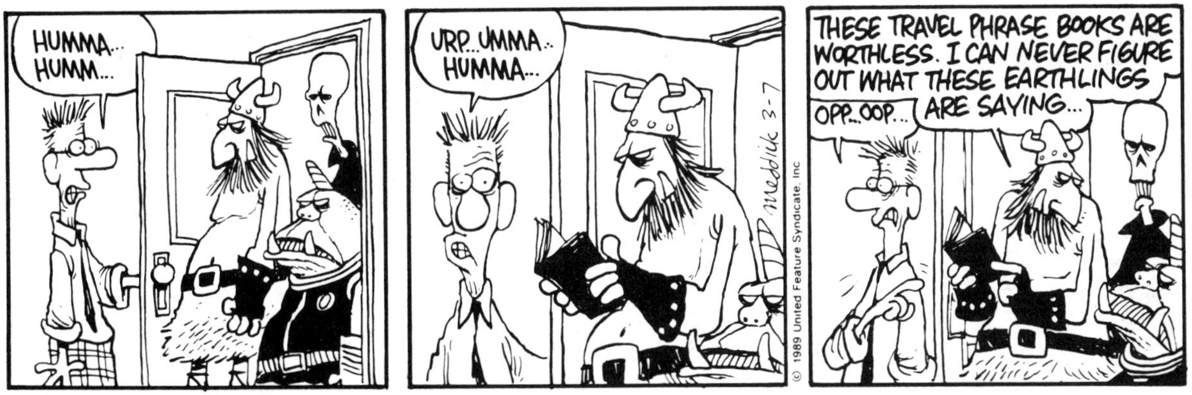
HUMMA... HUMM...
URP... UMMA... HUMMA...
© 1989 United Feature Syndicate, Inc
THESE TRAVEL PHRASE BOOKS ARE WORTHLESS. I CAN NEVER FIGURE OUT WHAT THESE EARTHLINGS ARE SAYING...
OPP... OOP...

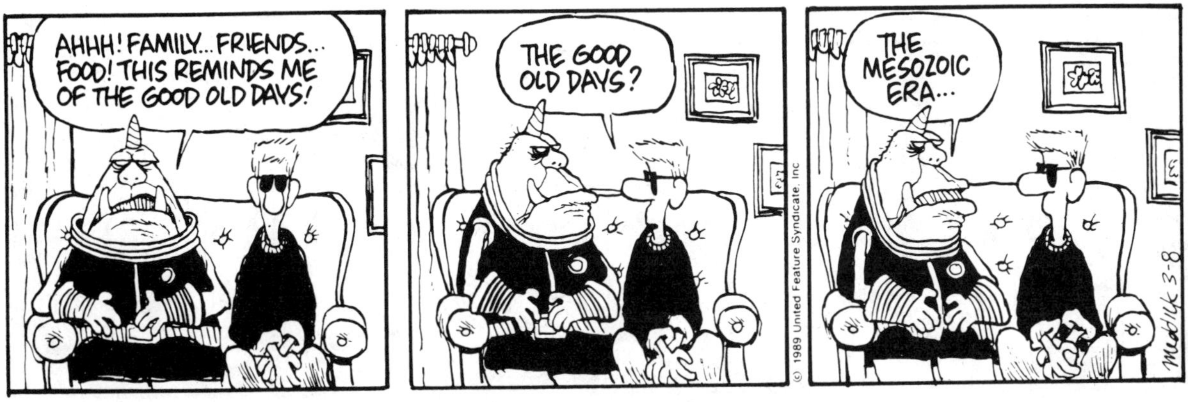
AHHH! FAMILY... FRIENDS... FOOD! THIS REMINDS ME OF THE GOOD OLD DAYS!
THE GOOD OLD DAYS?
© 1989 United Feature Syndicate, Inc
THE MESOZOIC ERA...

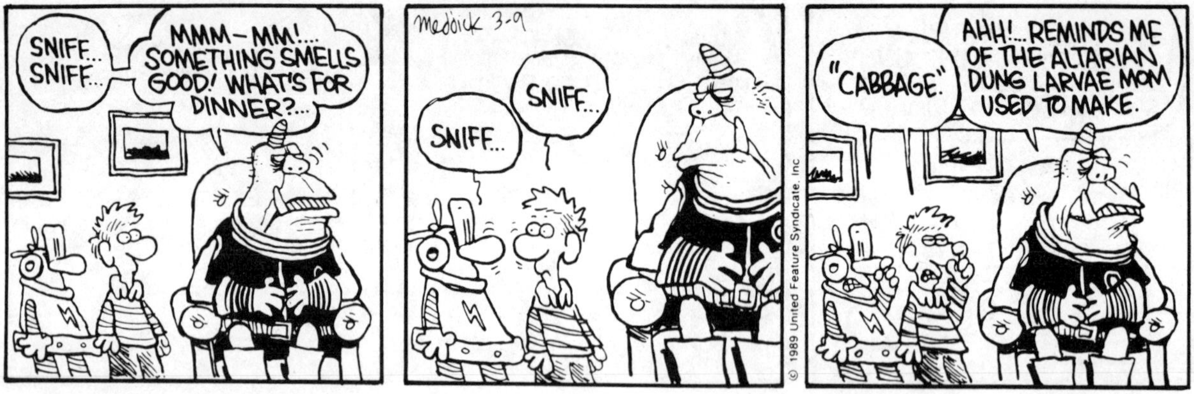
SNIFF... SNIFF...
MMM-MM!... SOMETHING SMELLS GOOD! WHAT'S FOR DINNER?...
Meddick 3-9
SNIFF...
SNIFF...
© 1989 United Feature Syndicate, Inc.
"CABBAGE."
AHH!... REMINDS ME OF THE ALTARIAN DUNG LARVAE MOM USED TO MAKE.

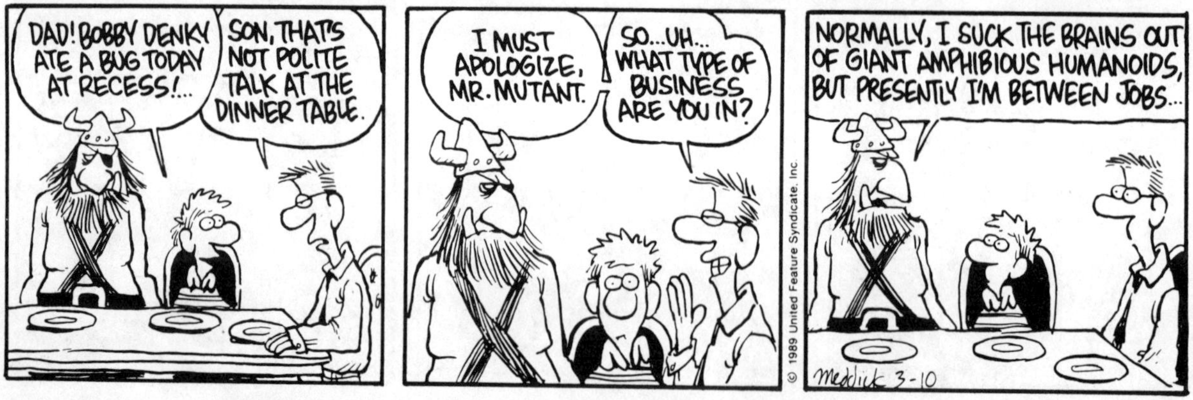
DAD! BOBBY DENKY ATE A BUG TODAY AT RECESS!...
SON, THAT'S NOT POLITE TALK AT THE DINNER TABLE.
I MUST APOLOGIZE, MR. MUTANT.
SO...UH... WHAT TYPE OF BUSINESS ARE YOU IN?
© 1989 United Feature Syndicate, Inc.
NORMALLY, I SUCK THE BRAINS OUT OF GIANT AMPHIBIOUS HUMANOIDS, BUT PRESENTLY I'M BETWEEN JOBS...
Meddick 3-10

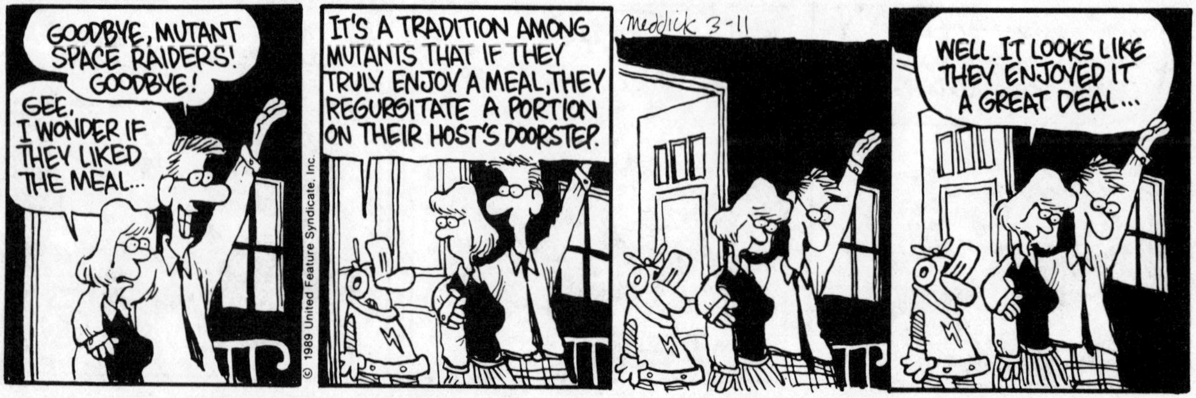
GOODBYE, MUTANT SPACE RAIDERS! GOODBYE!
GEE, I WONDER IF THEY LIKED THE MEAL...
© 1989 United Feature Syndicate, Inc.
IT'S A TRADITION AMONG MUTANTS THAT IF THEY TRULY ENJOY A MEAL, THEY REGURGITATE A PORTION ON THEIR HOST'S DOORSTEP.
Meddick 3-11
WELL. IT LOOKS LIKE THEY ENJOYED IT A GREAT DEAL...

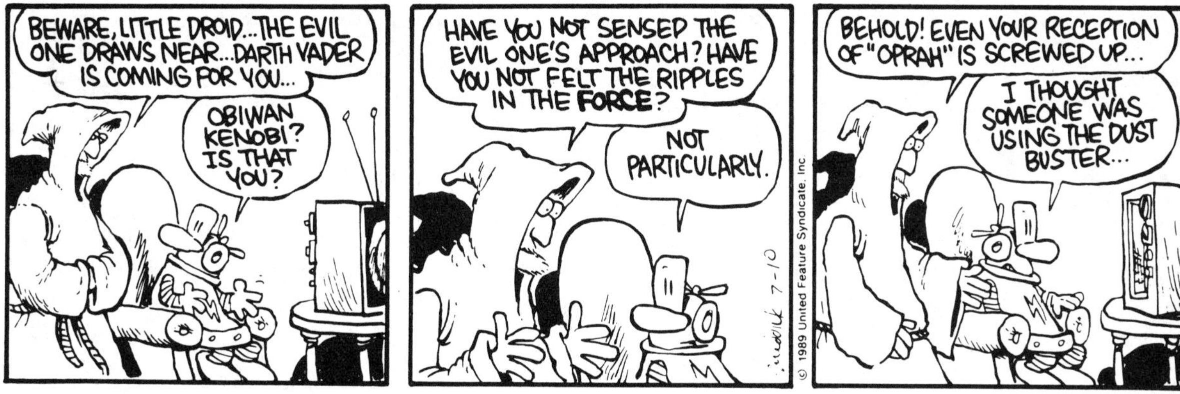

BEWARE, LITTLE DROID...THE EVIL ONE DRAWS NEAR...DARTH VADER IS COMING FOR YOU...
OBIWAN KENOBI? IS THAT YOU?
HAVE YOU NOT SENSED THE EVIL ONE'S APPROACH? HAVE YOU NOT FELT THE RIPPLES IN THE **FORCE**?
NOT PARTICULARLY.
BEHOLD! EVEN YOUR RECEPTION OF "OPRAH" IS SCREWED UP...
I THOUGHT SOMEONE WAS USING THE DUST BUSTER...
© 1989 United Feature Syndicate, Inc.

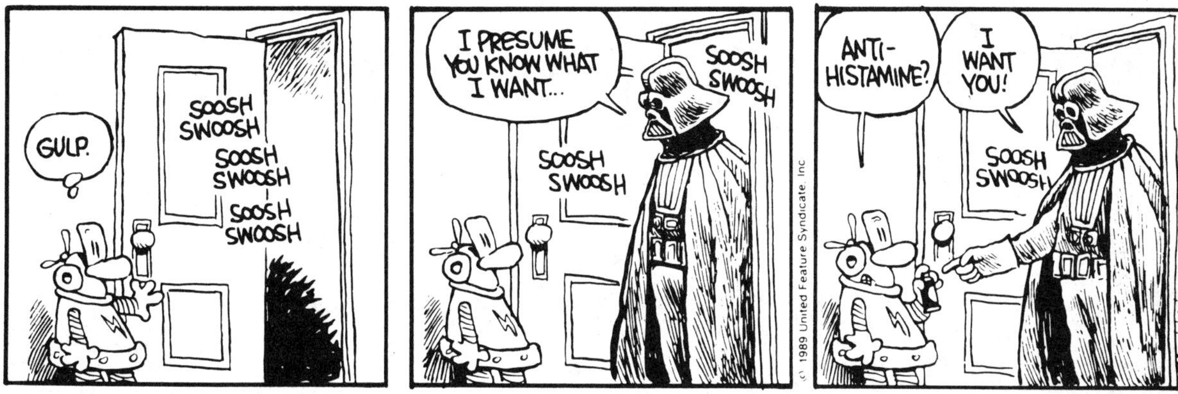

GULP.
SOOSH SWOOSH
SOOSH SWOOSH
SOOSH SWOOSH
I PRESUME YOU KNOW WHAT I WANT...
SOOSH SWOOSH
SOOSH SWOOSH
ANTI-HISTAMINE?
I WANT YOU!
SOOSH SWOOSH
© 1989 United Feature Syndicate, Inc.

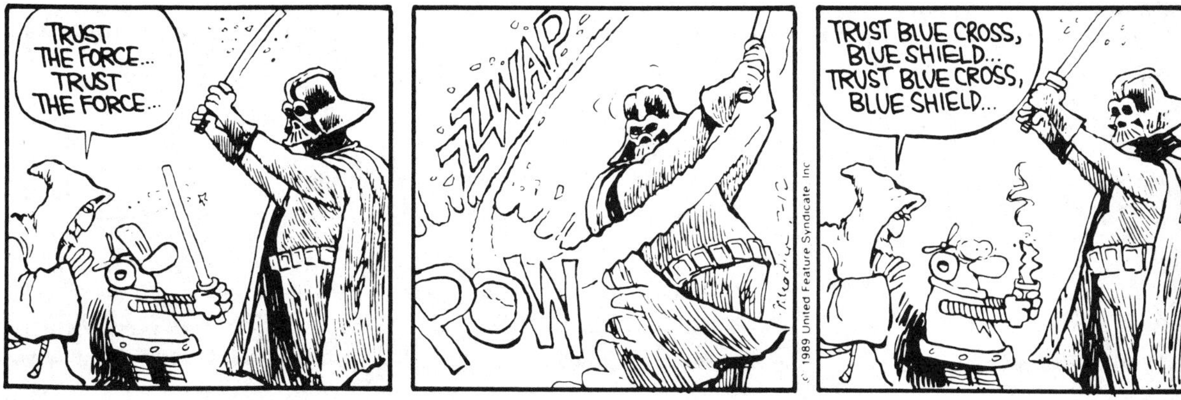

TRUST THE FORCE... TRUST THE FORCE...
ZZWAP
POW
TRUST BLUE CROSS, BLUE SHIELD... TRUST BLUE CROSS, BLUE SHIELD...
© 1989 United Feature Syndicate, Inc.

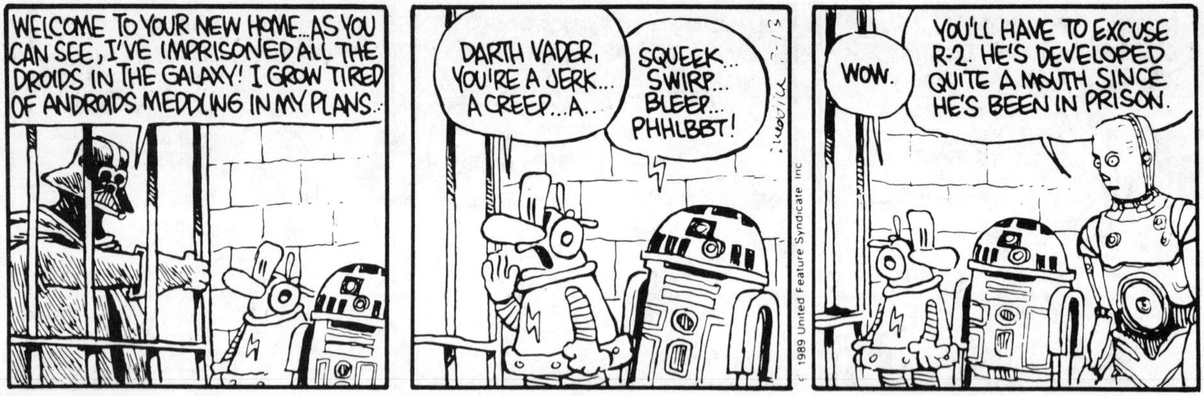
WELCOME TO YOUR NEW HOME... AS YOU CAN SEE, I'VE IMPRISONED ALL THE DROIDS IN THE GALAXY! I GROW TIRED OF ANDROIDS MEDDLING IN MY PLANS...
DARTH VADER, YOU'RE A JERK... A CREEP... A...
SQUEEK... SWIRP... BLEEP... PHHLBBT!
WOW.
YOU'LL HAVE TO EXCUSE R-2. HE'S DEVELOPED QUITE A MOUTH SINCE HE'S BEEN IN PRISON.
© 1989 United Feature Syndicate, Inc.

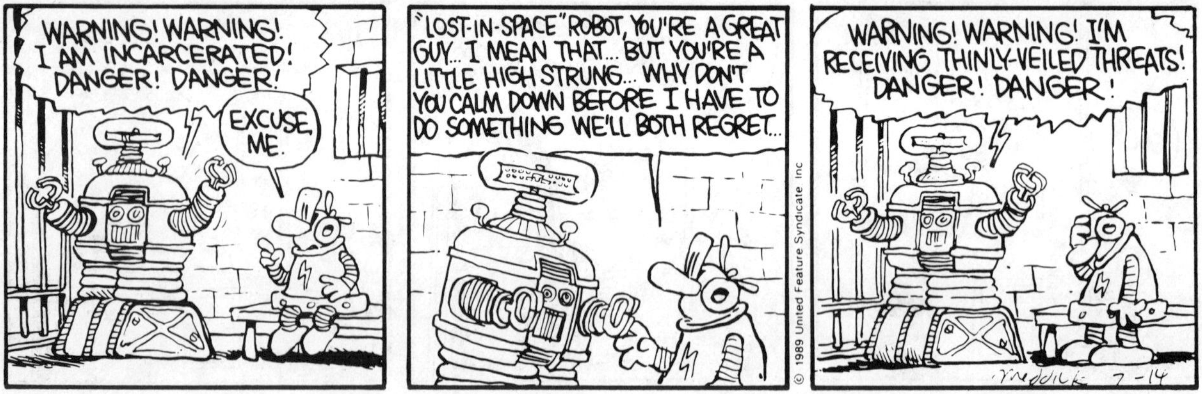
WARNING! WARNING! I AM INCARCERATED! DANGER! DANGER!
EXCUSE, ME.
"LOST-IN-SPACE" ROBOT, YOU'RE A GREAT GUY... I MEAN THAT... BUT YOU'RE A LITTLE HIGH STRUNG... WHY DON'T YOU CALM DOWN BEFORE I HAVE TO DO SOMETHING WE'LL BOTH REGRET...
WARNING! WARNING! I'M RECEIVING THINLY-VEILED THREATS! DANGER! DANGER!
© 1989 United Feature Syndicate, Inc.
Meddick 7-14

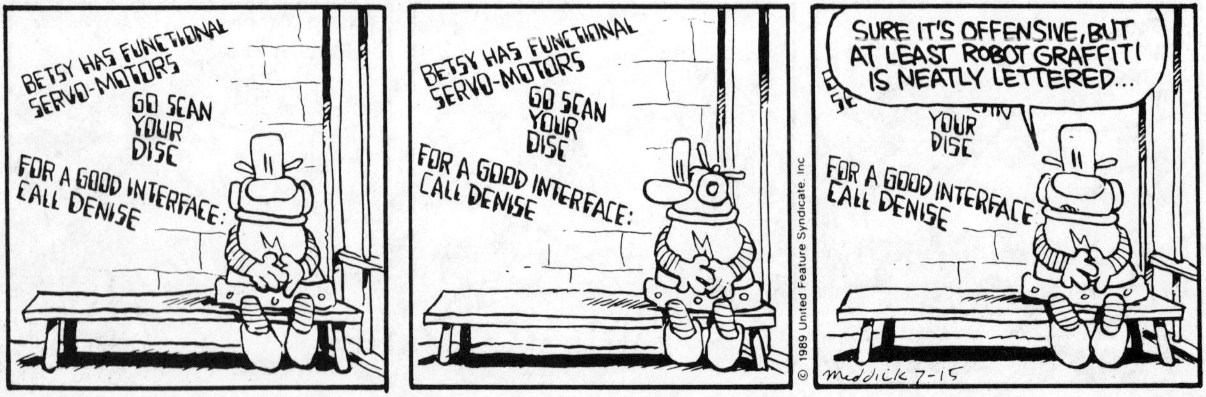
BETSY HAS FUNCTIONAL SERVO-MOTORS
GO SCAN YOUR DISC
FOR A GOOD INTERFACE: CALL DENISE
BETSY HAS FUNCTIONAL SERVO-MOTORS
GO SCAN YOUR DISC
FOR A GOOD INTERFACE: CALL DENISE
SURE IT'S OFFENSIVE, BUT AT LEAST ROBOT GRAFFITI IS NEATLY LETTERED...
YOUR DISC
FOR A GOOD INTERFACE CALL DENISE
© 1989 United Feature Syndicate, Inc.
Meddick 7-15

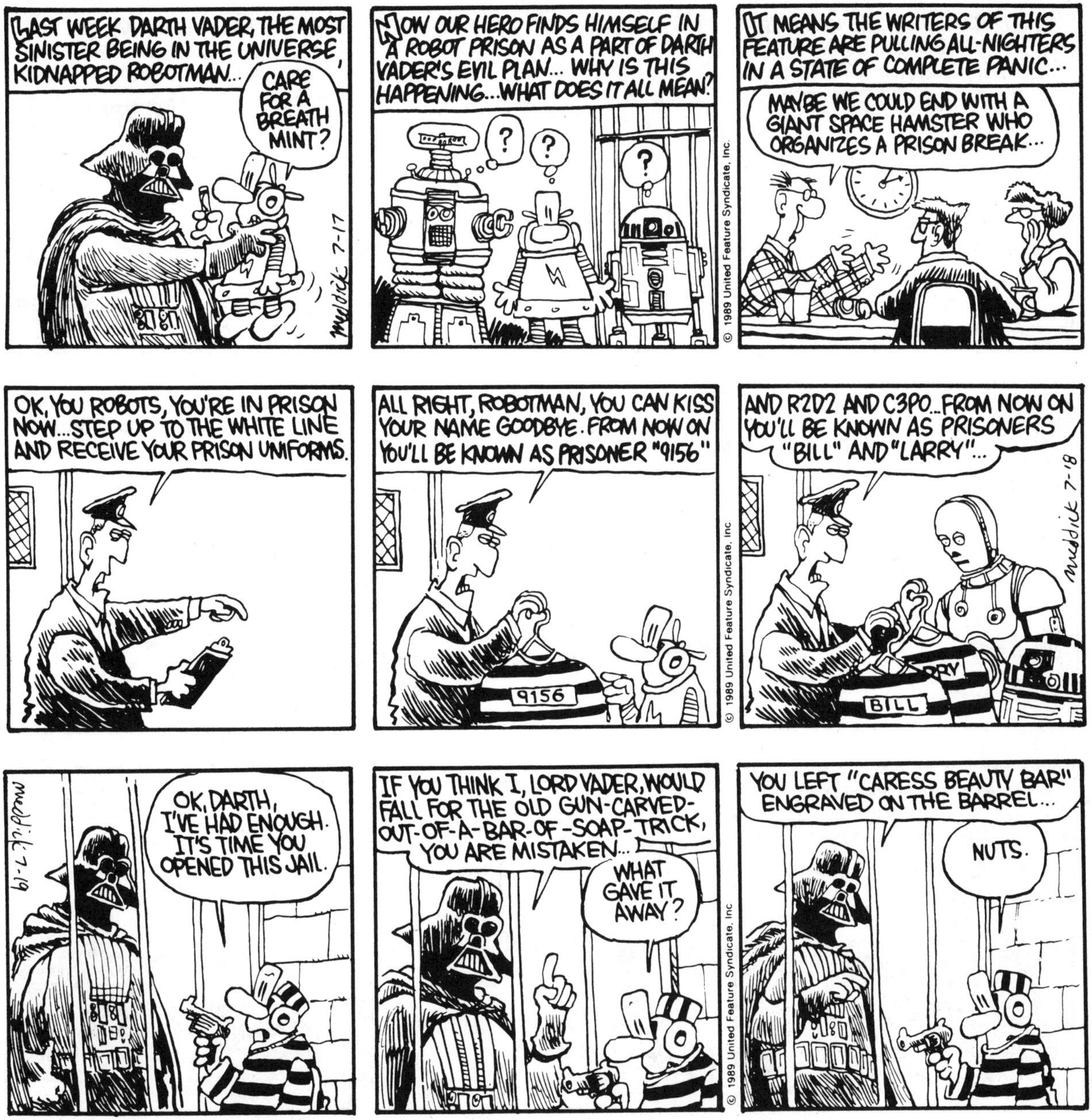
LAST WEEK DARTH VADER, THE MOST SINISTER BEING IN THE UNIVERSE, KIDNAPPED ROBOTMAN...
CARE FOR A BREATH MINT?
Muddick 7-17
NOW OUR HERO FINDS HIMSELF IN A ROBOT PRISON AS A PART OF DARTH VADER'S EVIL PLAN... WHY IS THIS HAPPENING...WHAT DOES IT ALL MEAN?
?
?
?
© 1989 United Feature Syndicate, Inc.
IT MEANS THE WRITERS OF THIS FEATURE ARE PULLING ALL-NIGHTERS IN A STATE OF COMPLETE PANIC...
MAYBE WE COULD END WITH A GIANT SPACE HAMSTER WHO ORGANIZES A PRISON BREAK...
OK, YOU ROBOTS, YOU'RE IN PRISON NOW...STEP UP TO THE WHITE LINE AND RECEIVE YOUR PRISON UNIFORMS.
ALL RIGHT, ROBOTMAN, YOU CAN KISS YOUR NAME GOODBYE. FROM NOW ON YOU'LL BE KNOWN AS PRISONER "9156"
9156
© 1989 United Feature Syndicate, Inc.
AND R2D2 AND C3PO...FROM NOW ON YOU'LL BE KNOWN AS PRISONERS "BILL" AND "LARRY"...
BILL
Muddick 7-18
Muddick 7-19
OK, DARTH, I'VE HAD ENOUGH. IT'S TIME YOU OPENED THIS JAIL.
IF YOU THINK I, LORD VADER, WOULD FALL FOR THE OLD GUN-CARVED-OUT-OF-A-BAR-OF-SOAP-TRICK, YOU ARE MISTAKEN...
WHAT GAVE IT AWAY?
© 1989 United Feature Syndicate, Inc.
YOU LEFT "CARESS BEAUTY BAR" ENGRAVED ON THE BARREL...
NUTS.

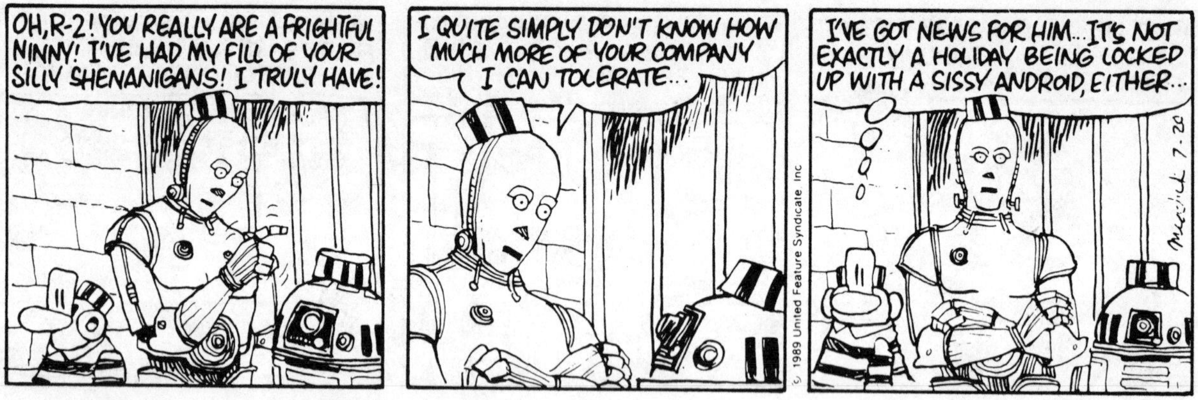
OH, R-2! YOU REALLY ARE A FRIGHTFUL NINNY! I'VE HAD MY FILL OF YOUR SILLY SHENANIGANS! I TRULY HAVE!
I QUITE SIMPLY DON'T KNOW HOW MUCH MORE OF YOUR COMPANY I CAN TOLERATE...
© 1989 United Feature Syndicate, Inc
I'VE GOT NEWS FOR HIM... IT'S NOT EXACTLY A HOLIDAY BEING LOCKED UP WITH A SISSY ANDROID, EITHER...

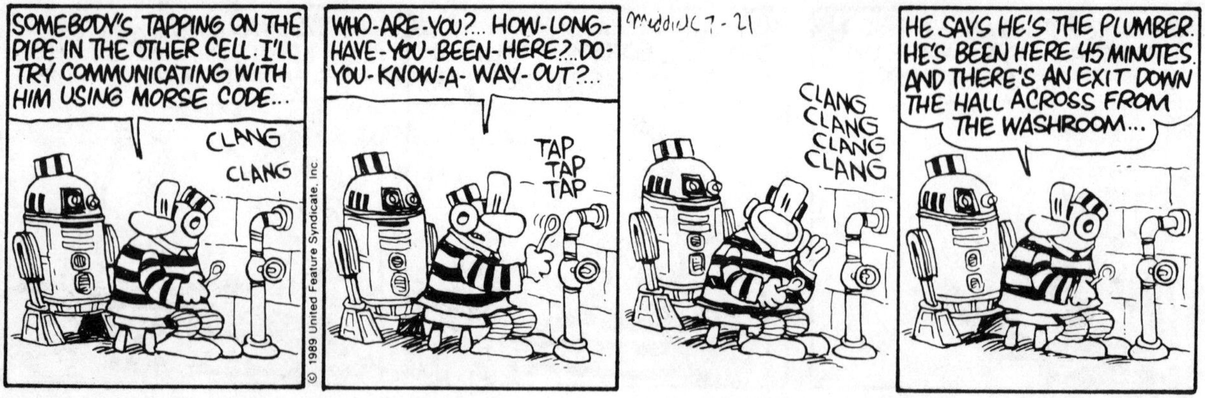
SOMEBODY'S TAPPING ON THE PIPE IN THE OTHER CELL. I'LL TRY COMMUNICATING WITH HIM USING MORSE CODE...
CLANG
CLANG
© 1989 United Feature Syndicate, Inc
WHO-ARE-YOU?... HOW-LONG-HAVE-YOU-BEEN-HERE?... DO-YOU-KNOW-A-WAY-OUT?...
TAP
TAP
TAP
CLANG
CLANG
CLANG
CLANG
HE SAYS HE'S THE PLUMBER. HE'S BEEN HERE 45 MINUTES. AND THERE'S AN EXIT DOWN THE HALL ACROSS FROM THE WASHROOM...

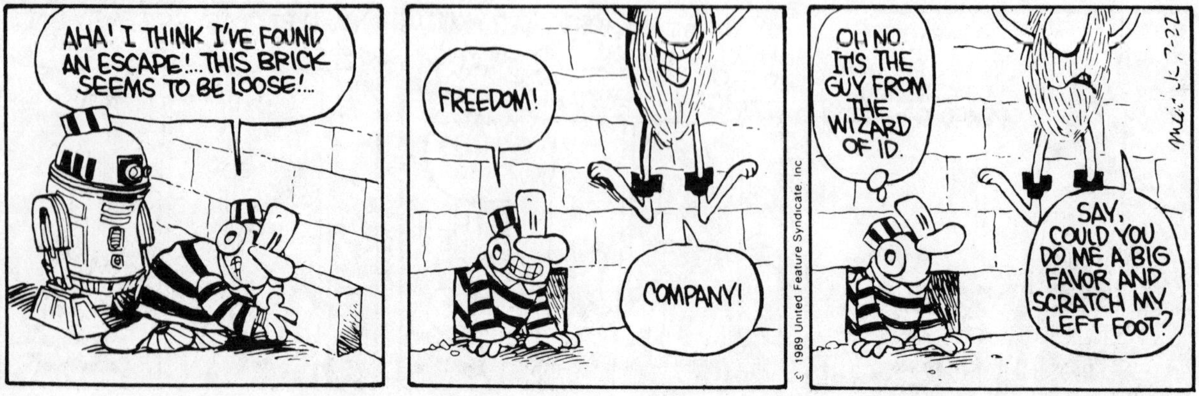
AHA! I THINK I'VE FOUND AN ESCAPE!... THIS BRICK SEEMS TO BE LOOSE!...
FREEDOM!
COMPANY!
© 1989 United Feature Syndicate, Inc
OH NO. IT'S THE GUY FROM THE WIZARD OF ID.
SAY, COULD YOU DO ME A BIG FAVOR AND SCRATCH MY LEFT FOOT?

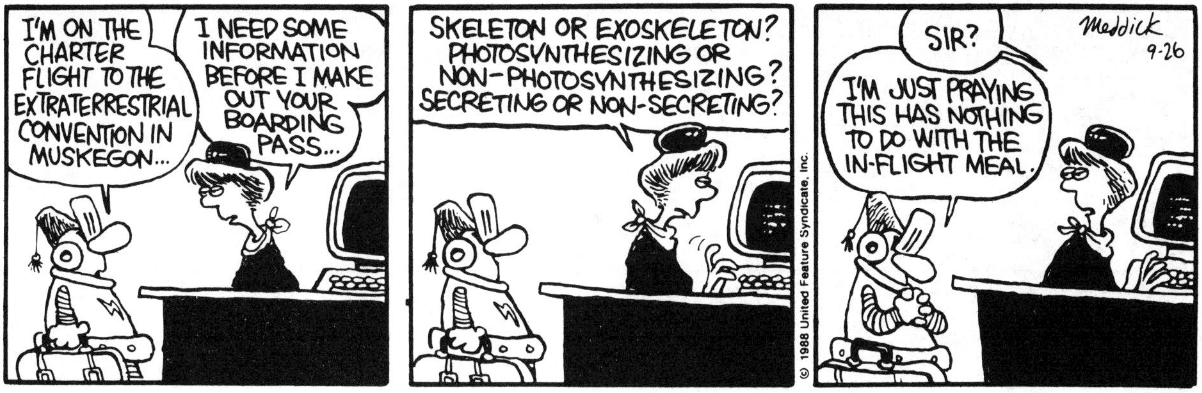
I'M ON THE CHARTER FLIGHT TO THE EXTRATERRESTRIAL CONVENTION IN MUSKEGON...
I NEED SOME INFORMATION BEFORE I MAKE OUT YOUR BOARDING PASS...
SKELETON OR EXOSKELETON? PHOTOSYNTHESIZING OR NON-PHOTOSYNTHESIZING? SECRETING OR NON-SECRETING?
© 1988 United Feature Syndicate, Inc.
Meddick 9-26
SIR?
I'M JUST PRAYING THIS HAS NOTHING TO DO WITH THE IN-FLIGHT MEAL.

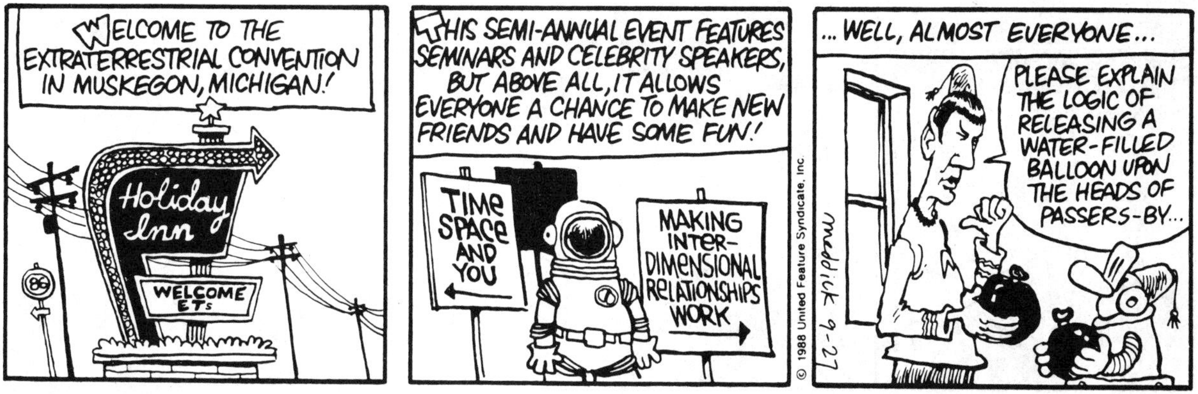
WELCOME TO THE EXTRATERRESTRIAL CONVENTION IN MUSKEGON, MICHIGAN!
Holiday Inn
WELCOME ETs
THIS SEMI-ANNUAL EVENT FEATURES SEMINARS AND CELEBRITY SPEAKERS, BUT ABOVE ALL, IT ALLOWS EVERYONE A CHANCE TO MAKE NEW FRIENDS AND HAVE SOME FUN!
TIME SPACE AND YOU
MAKING INTER-DIMENSIONAL RELATIONSHIPS WORK
© 1988 United Feature Syndicate, Inc.
meddick 9-27
... WELL, ALMOST EVERYONE...
PLEASE EXPLAIN THE LOGIC OF RELEASING A WATER-FILLED BALLOON UPON THE HEADS OF PASSERS-BY...

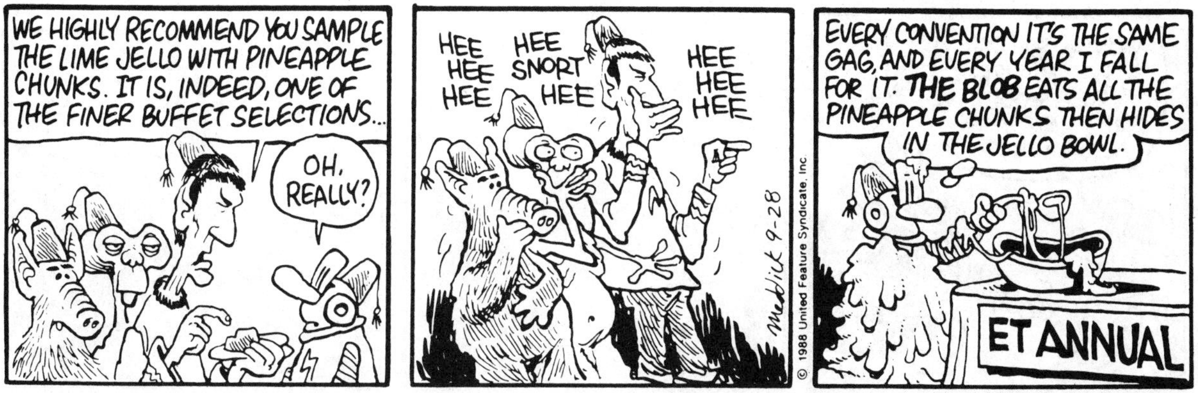
WE HIGHLY RECOMMEND YOU SAMPLE THE LIME JELLO WITH PINEAPPLE CHUNKS. IT IS, INDEED, ONE OF THE FINER BUFFET SELECTIONS...
OH, REALLY?
HEE HEE HEE
HEE SNORT HEE
HEE HEE HEE
meddick 9-28
© 1988 United Feature Syndicate, Inc.
EVERY CONVENTION IT'S THE SAME GAG, AND EVERY YEAR I FALL FOR IT. THE BLOB EATS ALL THE PINEAPPLE CHUNKS THEN HIDES IN THE JELLO BOWL.
ET ANNUAL

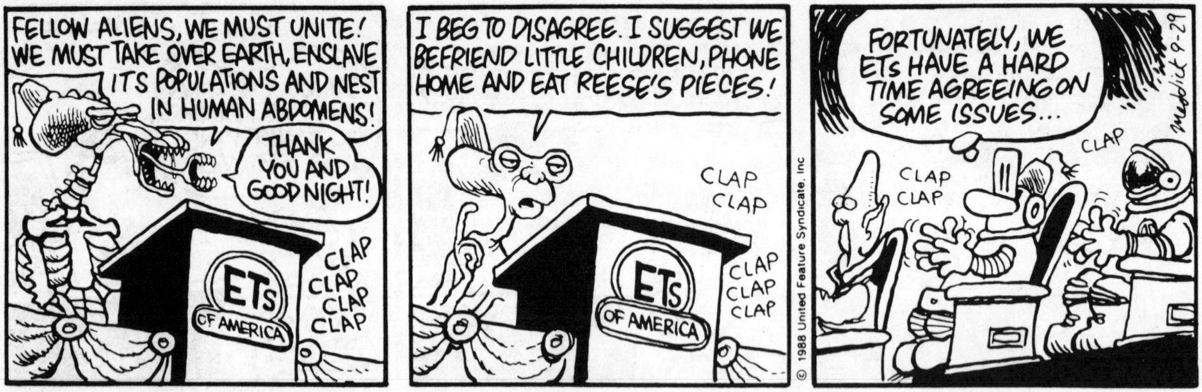
FELLOW ALIENS, WE MUST UNITE! WE MUST TAKE OVER EARTH, ENSLAVE ITS POPULATIONS AND NEST IN HUMAN ABDOMENS!
THANK YOU AND GOOD NIGHT!
ETs OF AMERICA
CLAP CLAP CLAP CLAP
I BEG TO DISAGREE. I SUGGEST WE BEFRIEND LITTLE CHILDREN, PHONE HOME AND EAT REESE'S PIECES!
CLAP CLAP
ETs OF AMERICA
CLAP CLAP CLAP
© 1988 United Feature Syndicate, Inc
FORTUNATELY, WE ETs HAVE A HARD TIME AGREEING ON SOME ISSUES...
CLAP
CLAP CLAP

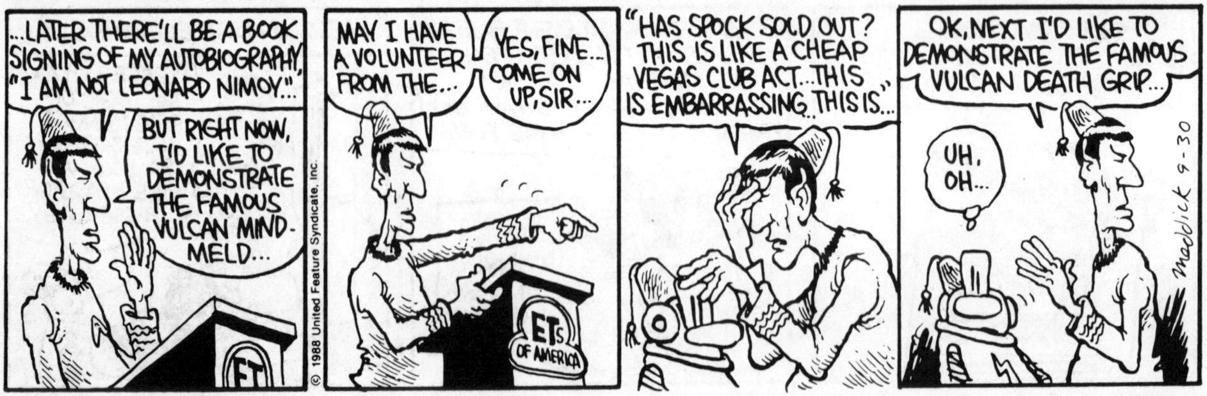
...LATER THERE'LL BE A BOOK SIGNING OF MY AUTOBIOGRAPHY, "I AM NOT LEONARD NIMOY."
BUT RIGHT NOW, I'D LIKE TO DEMONSTRATE THE FAMOUS VULCAN MIND-MELD...
© 1988 United Feature Syndicate, Inc.
MAY I HAVE A VOLUNTEER FROM THE...
YES, FINE... COME ON UP, SIR...
ETs OF AMERICA
"HAS SPOCK SOLD OUT? THIS IS LIKE A CHEAP VEGAS CLUB ACT...THIS IS EMBARRASSING...THIS IS."
OK, NEXT I'D LIKE TO DEMONSTRATE THE FAMOUS VULCAN DEATH GRIP...
UH, OH...

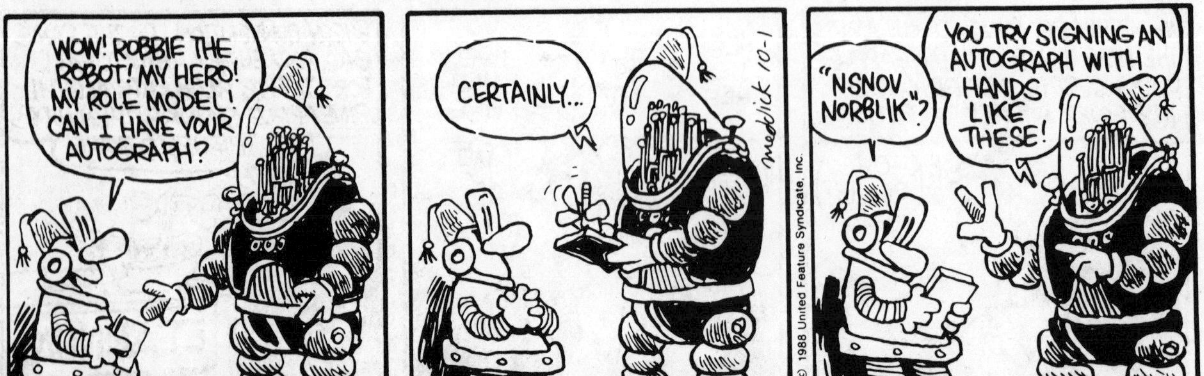
WOW! ROBBIE THE ROBOT! MY HERO! MY ROLE MODEL! CAN I HAVE YOUR AUTOGRAPH?
CERTAINLY...
© 1988 United Feature Syndicate, Inc.
"NSNOV NORBLIK"?
YOU TRY SIGNING AN AUTOGRAPH WITH HANDS LIKE THESE!

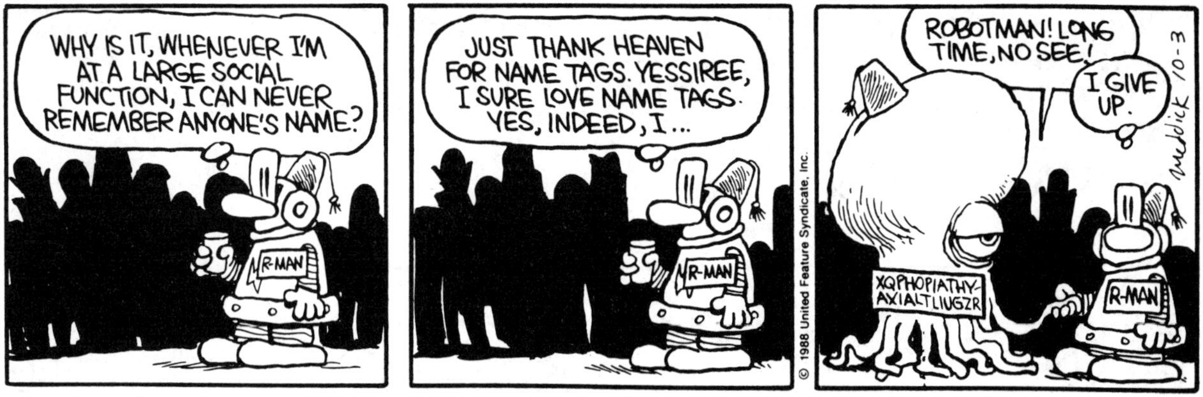
WHY IS IT, WHENEVER I'M AT A LARGE SOCIAL FUNCTION, I CAN NEVER REMEMBER ANYONE'S NAME?
R-MAN
JUST THANK HEAVEN FOR NAME TAGS. YESSIREE, I SURE LOVE NAME TAGS. YES, INDEED, I...
R-MAN
© 1988 United Feature Syndicate, Inc.
ROBOTMAN! LONG TIME, NO SEE!
I GIVE UP.
XQPHOPIATHY-AXIALTLIUGZR
R-MAN
meddick 10-3

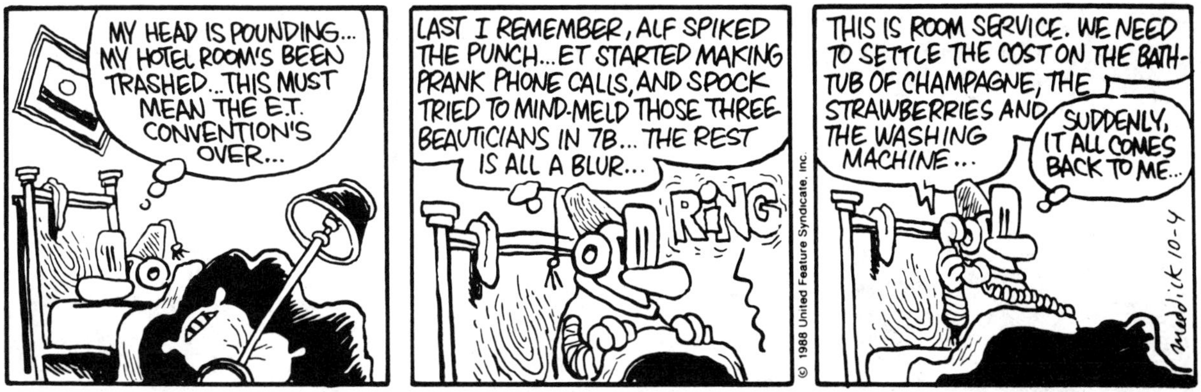
MY HEAD IS POUNDING... MY HOTEL ROOM'S BEEN TRASHED... THIS MUST MEAN THE E.T. CONVENTION'S OVER...
LAST I REMEMBER, ALF SPIKED THE PUNCH... ET STARTED MAKING PRANK PHONE CALLS, AND SPOCK TRIED TO MIND-MELD THOSE THREE BEAUTICIANS IN 7B... THE REST IS ALL A BLUR...
RING
© 1988 United Feature Syndicate, Inc.
THIS IS ROOM SERVICE. WE NEED TO SETTLE THE COST ON THE BATH-TUB OF CHAMPAGNE, THE STRAWBERRIES AND THE WASHING MACHINE...
SUDDENLY, IT ALL COMES BACK TO ME...
meddick 10-4

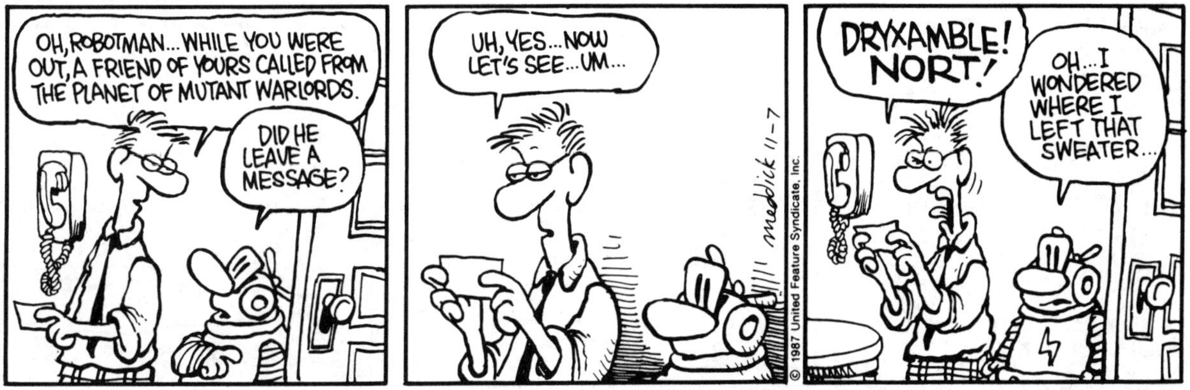
OH, ROBOTMAN... WHILE YOU WERE OUT, A FRIEND OF YOURS CALLED FROM THE PLANET OF MUTANT WARLORDS.
DID HE LEAVE A MESSAGE?
UH, YES... NOW LET'S SEE... UM...
meddick 11-7
© 1987 United Feature Syndicate, Inc.
DRYXAMBLE! NORT!
OH... I WONDERED WHERE I LEFT THAT SWEATER...

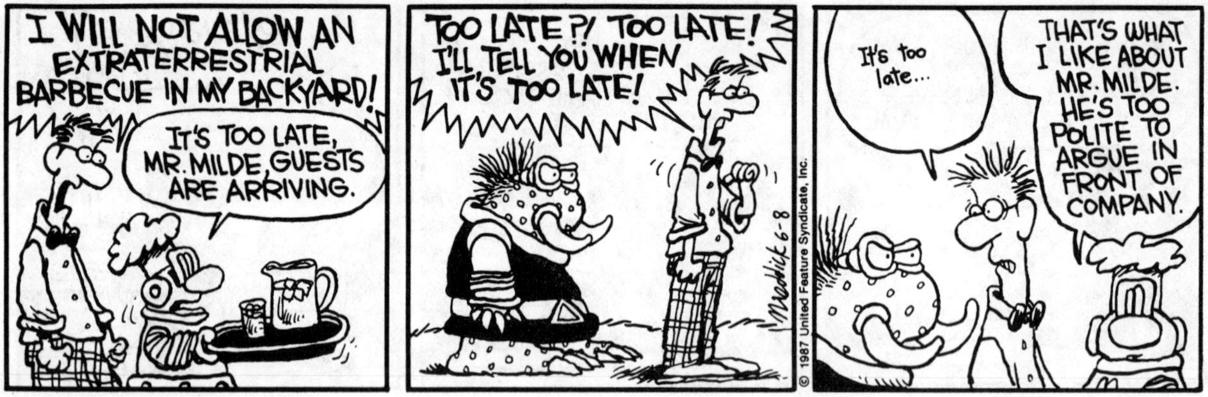
I WILL NOT ALLOW AN EXTRATERRESTRIAL BARBECUE IN MY BACKYARD!
IT'S TOO LATE, MR. MILDE, GUESTS ARE ARRIVING.
TOO LATE?! TOO LATE! I'LL TELL YOU WHEN IT'S TOO LATE!
It's too late...
THAT'S WHAT I LIKE ABOUT MR. MILDE. HE'S TOO POLITE TO ARGUE IN FRONT OF COMPANY.
Meddick 6-8
© 1987 United Feature Syndicate, Inc.

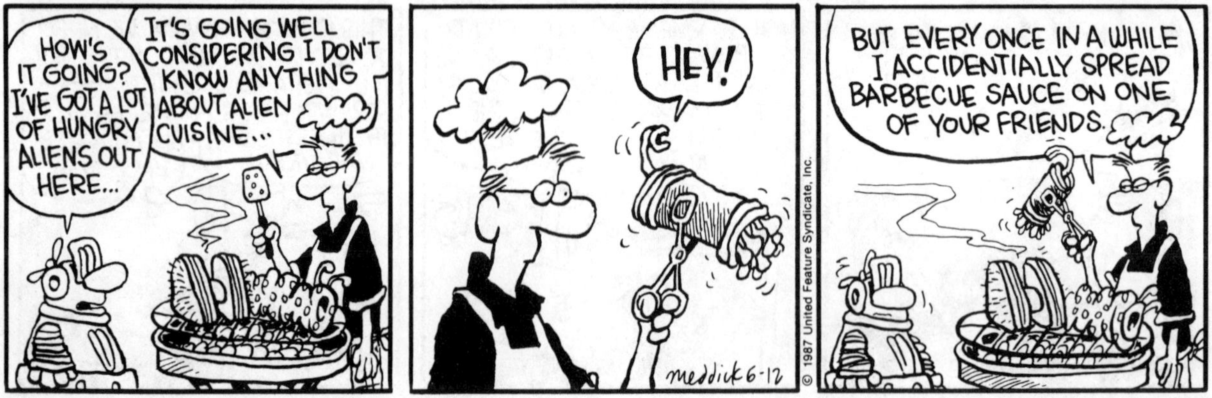
HOW'S IT GOING? I'VE GOT A LOT OF HUNGRY ALIENS OUT HERE...
IT'S GOING WELL CONSIDERING I DON'T KNOW ANYTHING ABOUT ALIEN CUISINE...
HEY!
meddick 6-12
© 1987 United Feature Syndicate, Inc.
BUT EVERY ONCE IN A WHILE I ACCIDENTIALLY SPREAD BARBECUE SAUCE ON ONE OF YOUR FRIENDS.

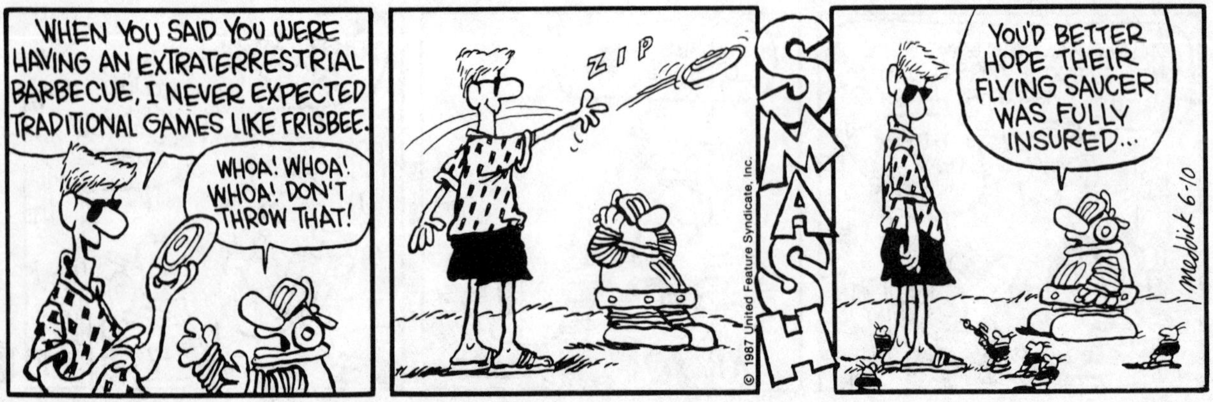
WHEN YOU SAID YOU WERE HAVING AN EXTRATERRESTRIAL BARBECUE, I NEVER EXPECTED TRADITIONAL GAMES LIKE FRISBEE.
WHOA! WHOA! WHOA! DON'T THROW THAT!
ZIP
© 1987 United Feature Syndicate, Inc.
SMASH
YOU'D BETTER HOPE THEIR FLYING SAUCER WAS FULLY INSURED...
meddick 6-10

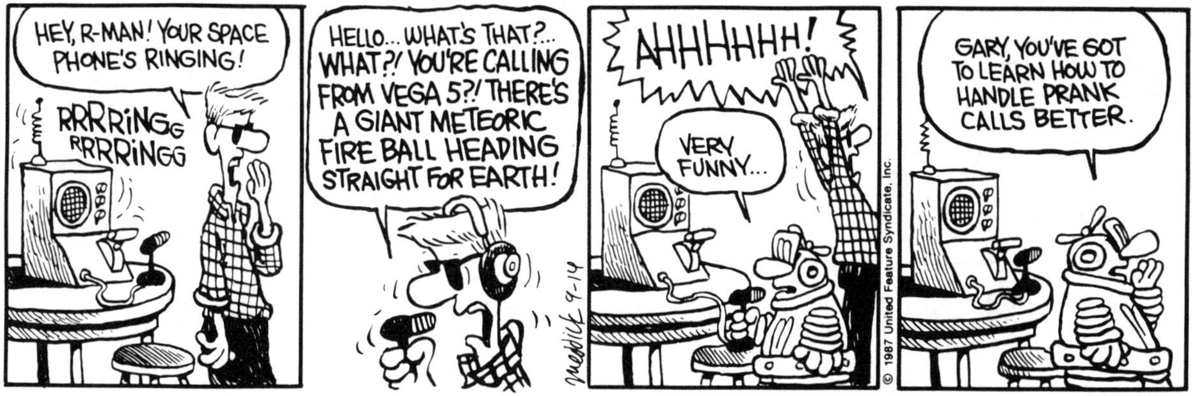
HEY, R-MAN! YOUR SPACE PHONE'S RINGING!
RRRRINGG RRRRINGG
HELLO... WHAT'S THAT?... WHAT?! YOU'RE CALLING FROM VEGA 5?! THERE'S A GIANT METEORIC FIRE BALL HEADING STRAIGHT FOR EARTH!
AHHHHHH!
VERY FUNNY...
GARY, YOU'VE GOT TO LEARN HOW TO HANDLE PRANK CALLS BETTER.
© 1987 United Feature Syndicate, Inc.

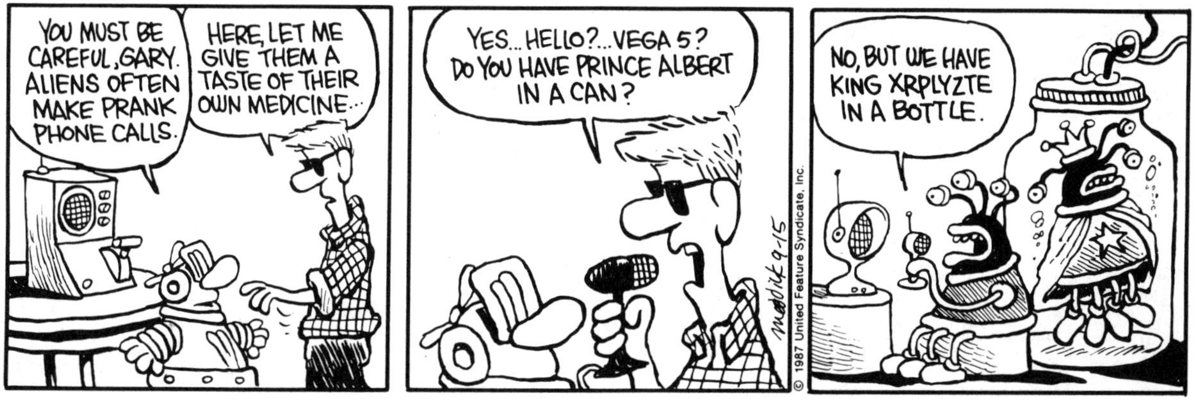
YOU MUST BE CAREFUL, GARY. ALIENS OFTEN MAKE PRANK PHONE CALLS.
HERE, LET ME GIVE THEM A TASTE OF THEIR OWN MEDICINE...
YES... HELLO?... VEGA 5? DO YOU HAVE PRINCE ALBERT IN A CAN?
NO, BUT WE HAVE KING XRPLYZTE IN A BOTTLE.
© 1987 United Feature Syndicate, Inc.

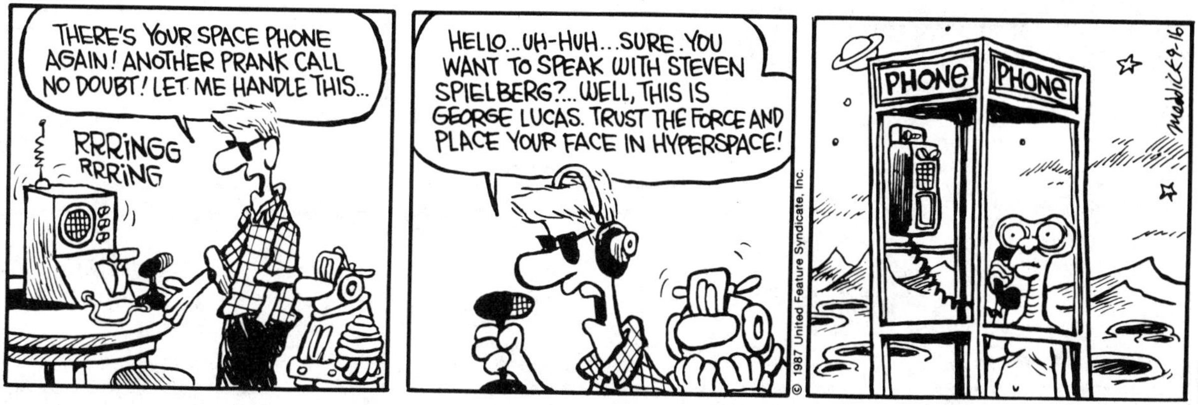
THERE'S YOUR SPACE PHONE AGAIN! ANOTHER PRANK CALL NO DOUBT! LET ME HANDLE THIS...
RRRINGG RRRING
HELLO... UH-HUH... SURE. YOU WANT TO SPEAK WITH STEVEN SPIELBERG?... WELL, THIS IS GEORGE LUCAS. TRUST THE FORCE AND PLACE YOUR FACE IN HYPERSPACE!
PHONE
PHONE
© 1987 United Feature Syndicate, Inc.

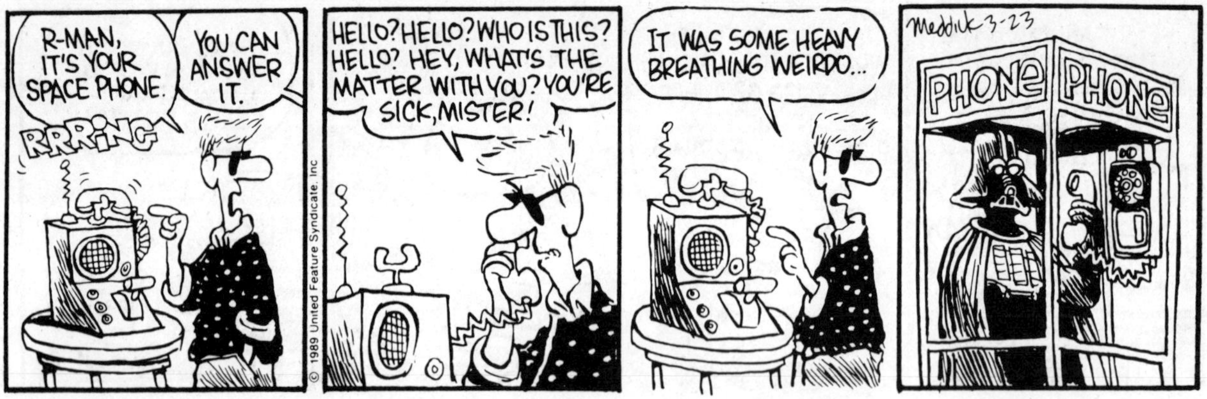
R-MAN, IT'S YOUR SPACE PHONE.
YOU CAN ANSWER IT.
RRRING
© 1989 United Feature Syndicate, Inc.
HELLO? HELLO? WHO IS THIS? HELLO? HEY, WHAT'S THE MATTER WITH YOU? YOU'RE SICK, MISTER!
IT WAS SOME HEAVY BREATHING WEIRDO...
Meddick 3-23
PHONE
PHONE

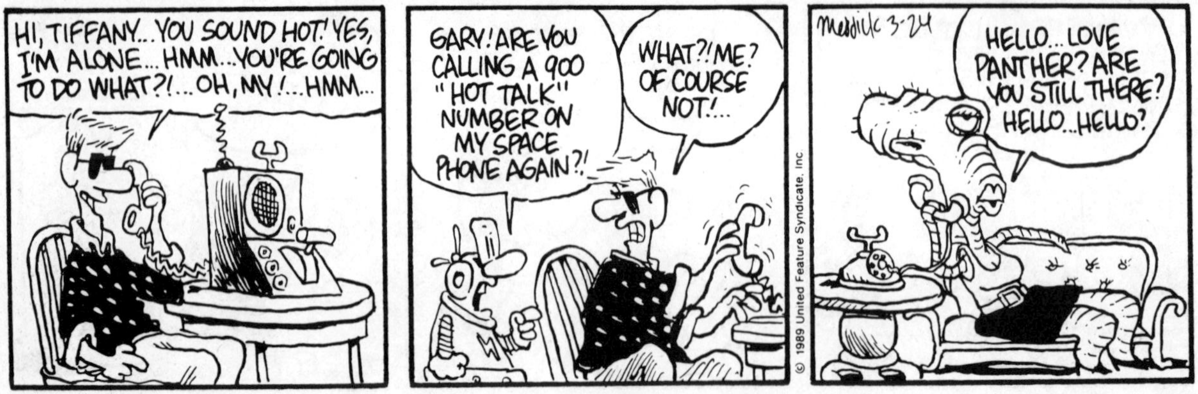
HI, TIFFANY... YOU SOUND HOT! YES, I'M ALONE... HMM... YOU'RE GOING TO DO WHAT?!... OH, MY!... HMM...
GARY! ARE YOU CALLING A 900 "HOT TALK" NUMBER ON MY SPACE PHONE AGAIN?!
WHAT?! ME? OF COURSE NOT!...
© 1989 United Feature Syndicate, Inc.
Meddick 3-24
HELLO... LOVE PANTHER? ARE YOU STILL THERE? HELLO... HELLO?

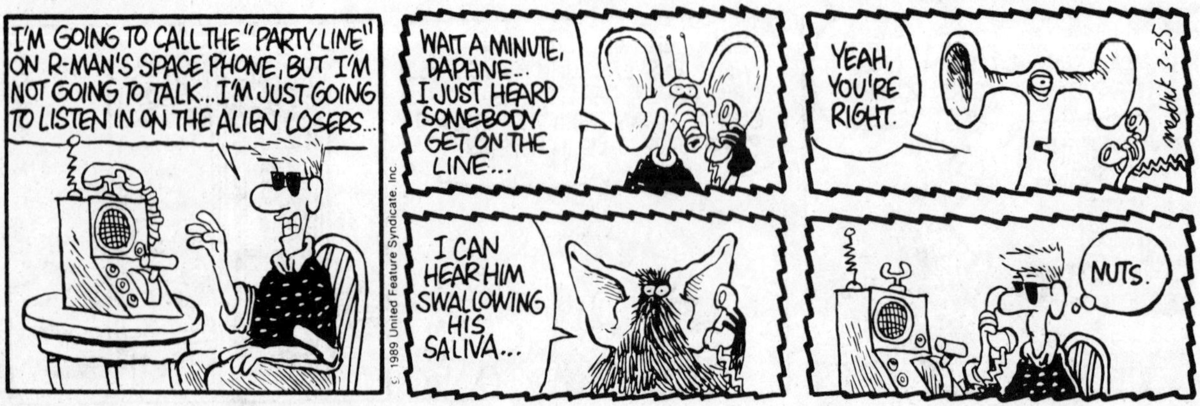
I'M GOING TO CALL THE "PARTY LINE" ON R-MAN'S SPACE PHONE, BUT I'M NOT GOING TO TALK... I'M JUST GOING TO LISTEN IN ON THE ALIEN LOSERS...
© 1989 United Feature Syndicate, Inc.
WAIT A MINUTE, DAPHNE... I JUST HEARD SOMEBODY GET ON THE LINE...
YEAH, YOU'RE RIGHT.
Meddick 3-25
I CAN HEAR HIM SWALLOWING HIS SALIVA...
NUTS.

ALTER EGOS

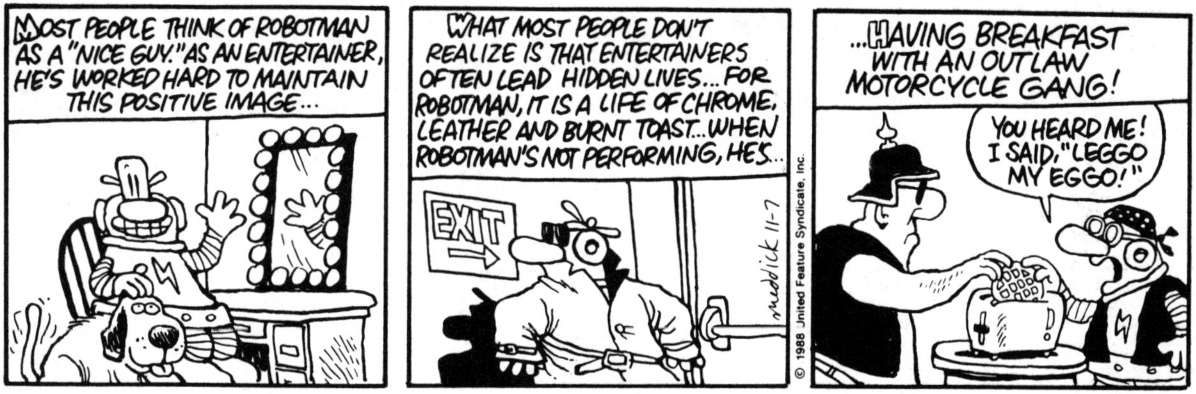
MOST PEOPLE THINK OF ROBOTMAN AS A "NICE GUY." AS AN ENTERTAINER, HE'S WORKED HARD TO MAINTAIN THIS POSITIVE IMAGE...
WHAT MOST PEOPLE DON'T REALIZE IS THAT ENTERTAINERS OFTEN LEAD HIDDEN LIVES... FOR ROBOTMAN, IT IS A LIFE OF CHROME, LEATHER AND BURNT TOAST... WHEN ROBOTMAN'S NOT PERFORMING, HE'S...
EXIT
meddick 11-7
...HAVING BREAKFAST WITH AN OUTLAW MOTORCYCLE GANG!
YOU HEARD ME! I SAID, "LEGGO MY EGGO!"

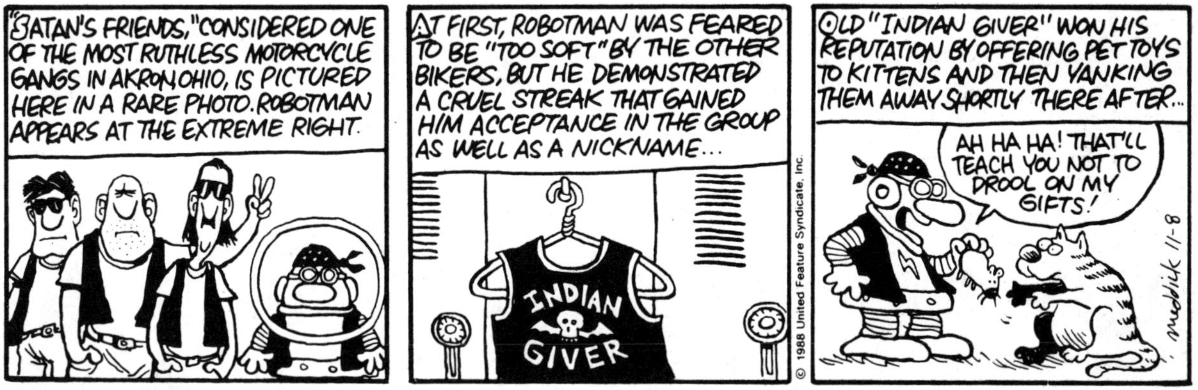
"SATAN'S FRIENDS," CONSIDERED ONE OF THE MOST RUTHLESS MOTORCYCLE GANGS IN AKRON OHIO, IS PICTURED HERE IN A RARE PHOTO. ROBOTMAN APPEARS AT THE EXTREME RIGHT.
AT FIRST, ROBOTMAN WAS FEARED TO BE "TOO SOFT" BY THE OTHER BIKERS, BUT HE DEMONSTRATED A CRUEL STREAK THAT GAINED HIM ACCEPTANCE IN THE GROUP AS WELL AS A NICKNAME...
INDIAN GIVER
OLD "INDIAN GIVER" WON HIS REPUTATION BY OFFERING PET TOYS TO KITTENS AND THEN YANKING THEM AWAY SHORTLY THERE AFTER...
AH HA HA! THAT'LL TEACH YOU NOT TO DROOL ON MY GIFTS!
meddick 11-8

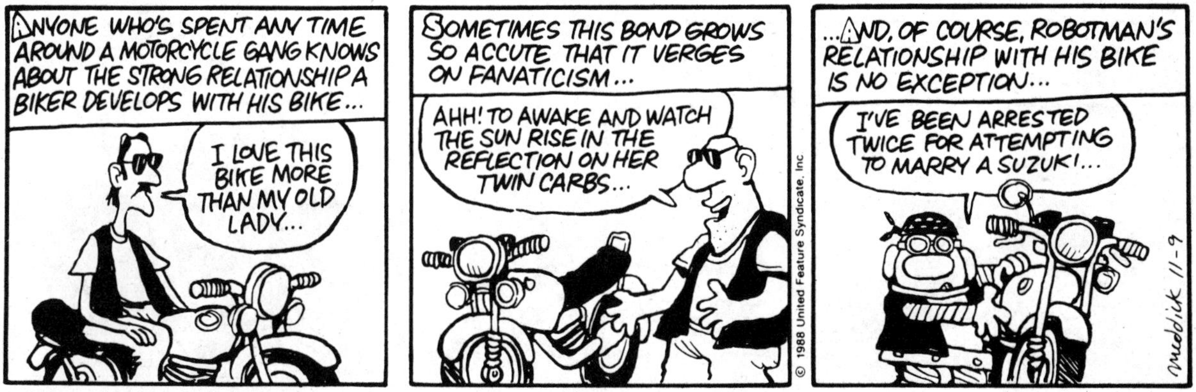
ANYONE WHO'S SPENT ANY TIME AROUND A MOTORCYCLE GANG KNOWS ABOUT THE STRONG RELATIONSHIP A BIKER DEVELOPS WITH HIS BIKE...
I LOVE THIS BIKE MORE THAN MY OLD LADY...
SOMETIMES THIS BOND GROWS SO ACCUTE THAT IT VERGES ON FANATICISM...
AHH! TO AWAKE AND WATCH THE SUN RISE IN THE REFLECTION ON HER TWIN CARBS...
...AND, OF COURSE, ROBOTMAN'S RELATIONSHIP WITH HIS BIKE IS NO EXCEPTION...
I'VE BEEN ARRESTED TWICE FOR ATTEMPTING TO MARRY A SUZUKI!...
meddick 11-9

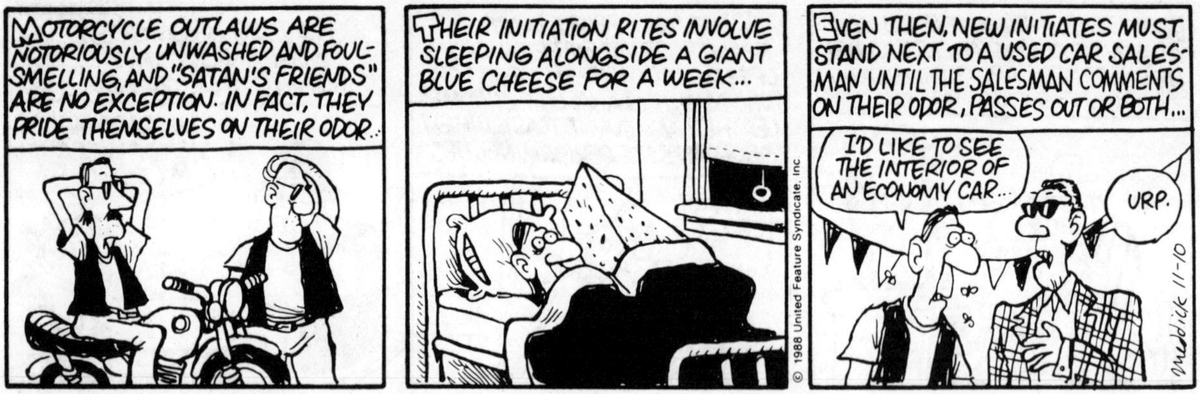
MOTORCYCLE OUTLAWS ARE NOTORIOUSLY UNWASHED AND FOUL-SMELLING, AND "SATAN'S FRIENDS" ARE NO EXCEPTION. IN FACT, THEY PRIDE THEMSELVES ON THEIR ODOR...
THEIR INITIATION RITES INVOLVE SLEEPING ALONGSIDE A GIANT BLUE CHEESE FOR A WEEK...
© 1988 United Feature Syndicate, Inc.
EVEN THEN, NEW INITIATES MUST STAND NEXT TO A USED CAR SALESMAN UNTIL THE SALESMAN COMMENTS ON THEIR ODOR, PASSES OUT OR BOTH...
I'D LIKE TO SEE THE INTERIOR OF AN ECONOMY CAR...
URP.
meddick 11-10

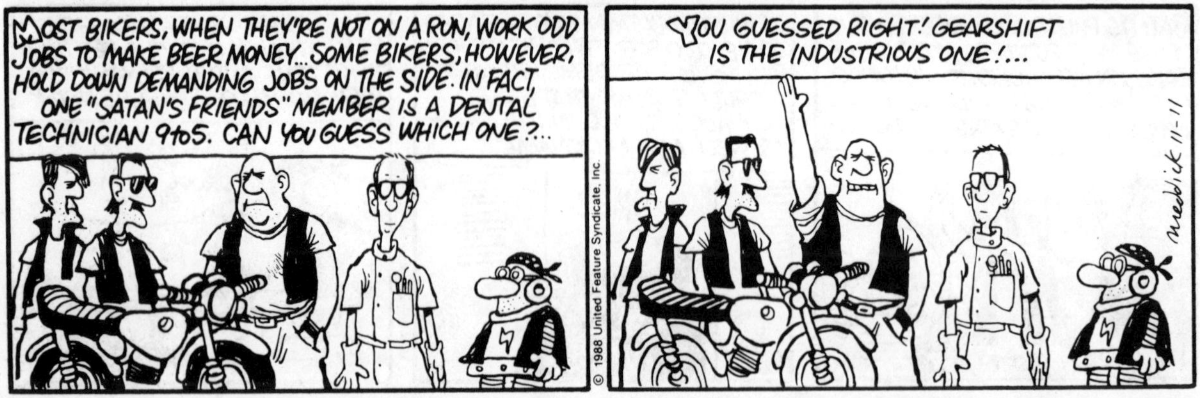
MOST BIKERS, WHEN THEY'RE NOT ON A RUN, WORK ODD JOBS TO MAKE BEER MONEY... SOME BIKERS, HOWEVER, HOLD DOWN DEMANDING JOBS ON THE SIDE. IN FACT, ONE "SATAN'S FRIENDS" MEMBER IS A DENTAL TECHNICIAN 9 to 5. CAN YOU GUESS WHICH ONE?...
© 1988 United Feature Syndicate, Inc.
YOU GUESSED RIGHT! GEARSHIFT IS THE INDUSTRIOUS ONE!...
meddick 11-11

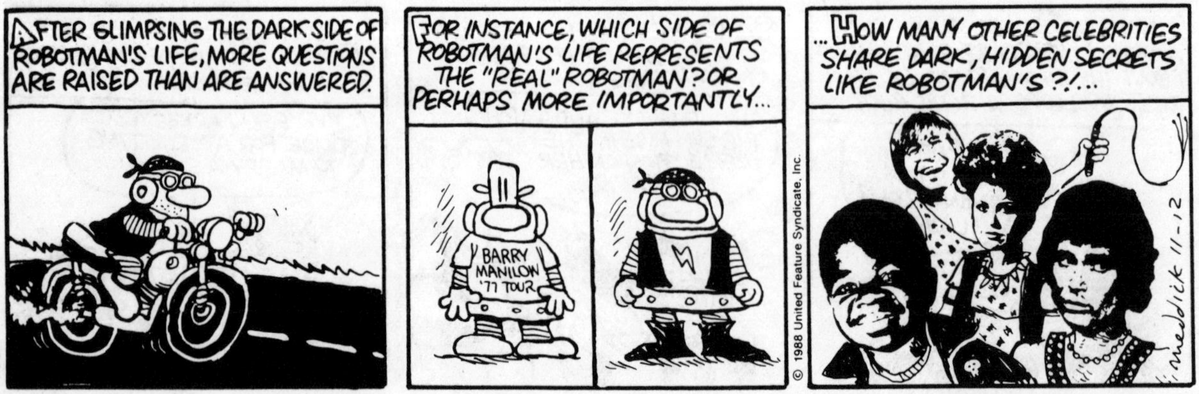
AFTER GLIMPSING THE DARK SIDE OF ROBOTMAN'S LIFE, MORE QUESTIONS ARE RAISED THAN ARE ANSWERED.
FOR INSTANCE, WHICH SIDE OF ROBOTMAN'S LIFE REPRESENTS THE "REAL" ROBOTMAN? OR PERHAPS MORE IMPORTANTLY...
BARRY MANILOW '77 TOUR
© 1988 United Feature Syndicate, Inc.
...HOW MANY OTHER CELEBRITIES SHARE DARK, HIDDEN SECRETS LIKE ROBOTMAN'S?!...
meddick 11-12

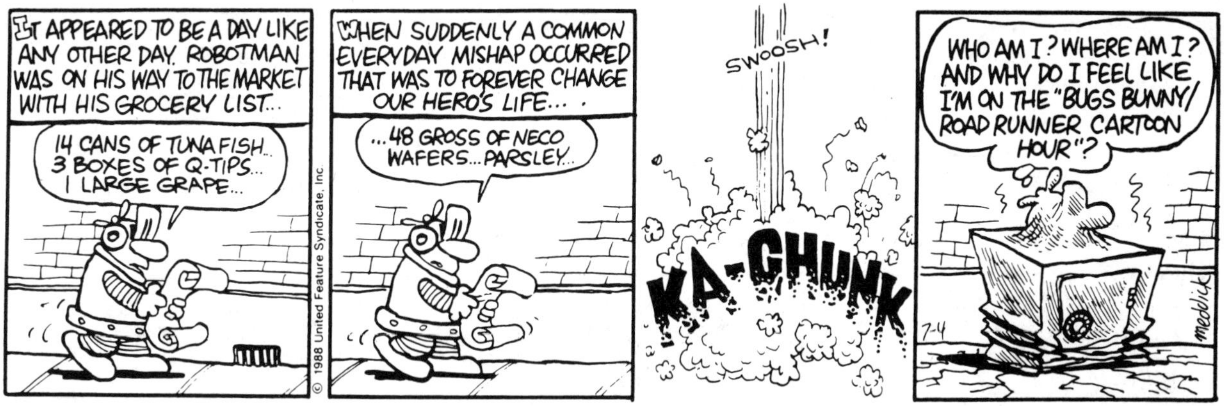
IT APPEARED TO BE A DAY LIKE ANY OTHER DAY. ROBOTMAN WAS ON HIS WAY TO THE MARKET WITH HIS GROCERY LIST...
14 CANS OF TUNA FISH... 3 BOXES OF Q-TIPS... 1 LARGE GRAPE...
© 1988 United Feature Syndicate, Inc.
WHEN SUDDENLY A COMMON EVERYDAY MISHAP OCCURRED THAT WAS TO FOREVER CHANGE OUR HERO'S LIFE... .
...48 GROSS OF NECO WAFERS... PARSLEY...
SWOOSH!
KA-CHUNK
WHO AM I? WHERE AM I? AND WHY DO I FEEL LIKE I'M ON THE "BUGS BUNNY/ ROAD RUNNER CARTOON HOUR"?
7-4
meddick

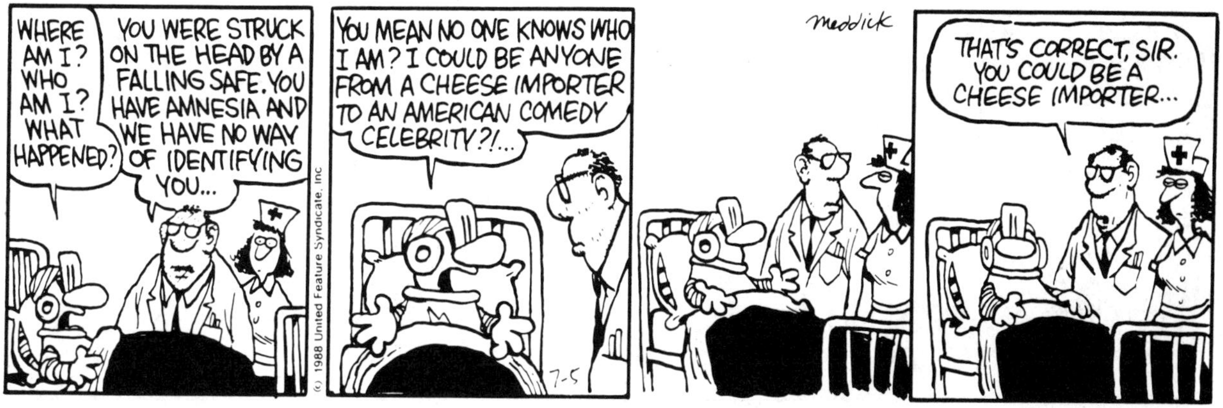
WHERE AM I? WHO AM I? WHAT HAPPENED?
YOU WERE STRUCK ON THE HEAD BY A FALLING SAFE. YOU HAVE AMNESIA AND WE HAVE NO WAY OF IDENTIFYING YOU...
© 1988 United Feature Syndicate, Inc.
YOU MEAN NO ONE KNOWS WHO I AM? I COULD BE ANYONE FROM A CHEESE IMPORTER TO AN AMERICAN COMEDY CELEBRITY?!...
7-5
meddick
THAT'S CORRECT, SIR. YOU COULD BE A CHEESE IMPORTER...

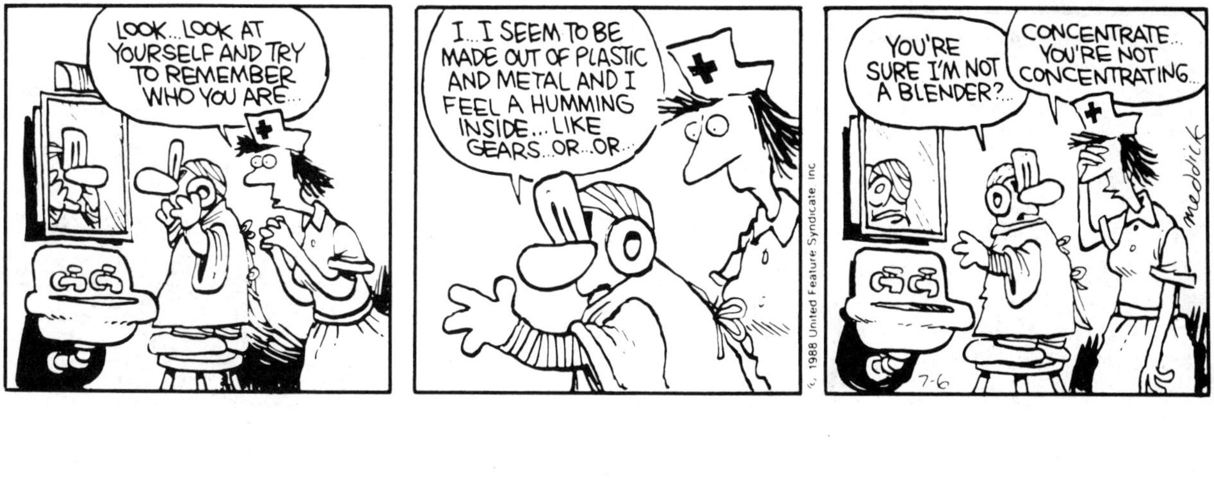
LOOK... LOOK AT YOURSELF AND TRY TO REMEMBER WHO YOU ARE...
I... I SEEM TO BE MADE OUT OF PLASTIC AND METAL AND I FEEL A HUMMING INSIDE... LIKE GEARS...OR...OR...
© 1988 United Feature Syndicate, Inc.
YOU'RE SURE I'M NOT A BLENDER?...
CONCENTRATE... YOU'RE NOT CONCENTRATING...
7-6
meddick

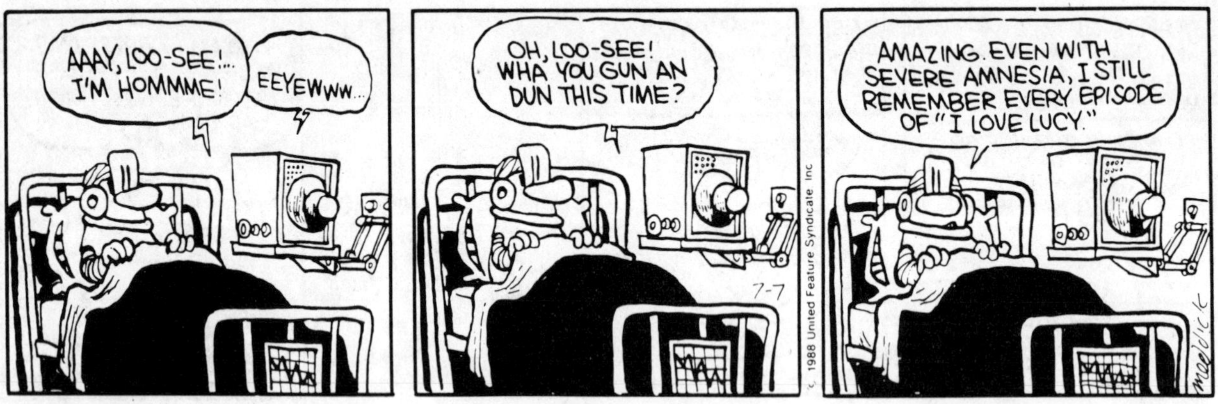
AAAY, LOO-SEE!... I'M HOMMME!
EEYEWWW...
OH, LOO-SEE! WHA' YOU GUN AN DUN THIS TIME?
7-7
© 1988 United Feature Syndicate Inc
AMAZING. EVEN WITH SEVERE AMNESIA, I STILL REMEMBER EVERY EPISODE OF "I LOVE LUCY."

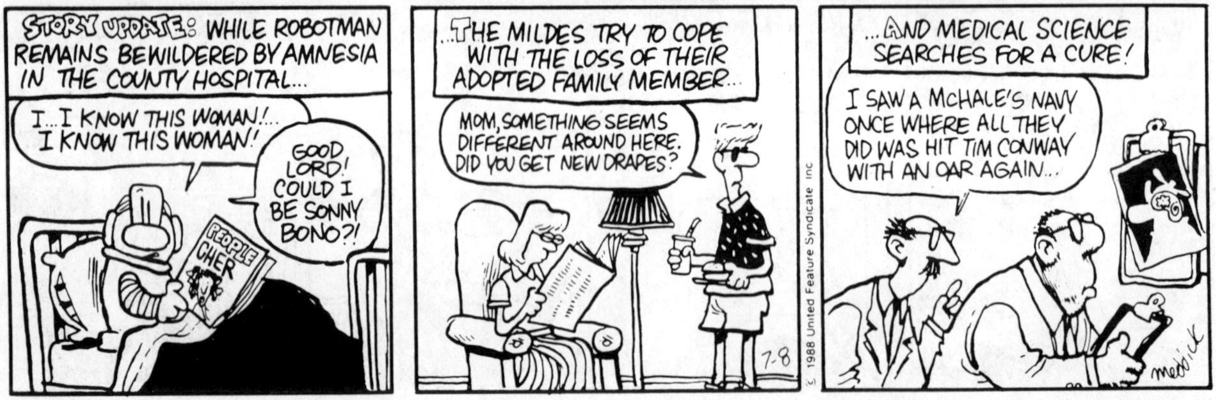
STORY UPDATE: WHILE ROBOTMAN REMAINS BEWILDERED BY AMNESIA IN THE COUNTY HOSPITAL...
I... I KNOW THIS WOMAN!... I KNOW THIS WOMAN!
PEOPLE
CHER
GOOD LORD! COULD I BE SONNY BONO?!
...THE MILDES TRY TO COPE WITH THE LOSS OF THEIR ADOPTED FAMILY MEMBER...
MOM, SOMETHING SEEMS DIFFERENT AROUND HERE. DID YOU GET NEW DRAPES?
7-8
© 1988 United Feature Syndicate Inc
...AND MEDICAL SCIENCE SEARCHES FOR A CURE!
I SAW A MCHALE'S NAVY ONCE WHERE ALL THEY DID WAS HIT TIM CONWAY WITH AN OAR AGAIN...

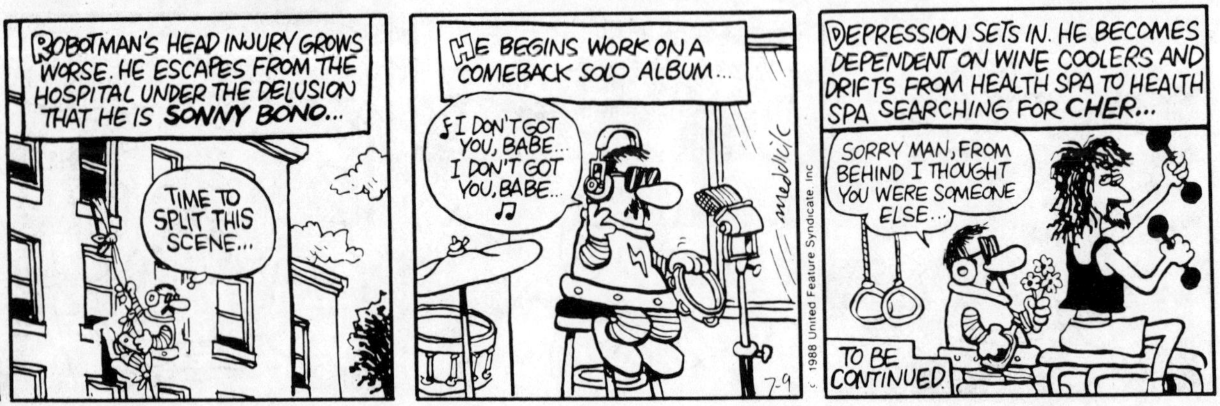
ROBOTMAN'S HEAD INJURY GROWS WORSE. HE ESCAPES FROM THE HOSPITAL UNDER THE DELUSION THAT HE IS SONNY BONO...
TIME TO SPLIT THIS SCENE...
HE BEGINS WORK ON A COMEBACK SOLO ALBUM...
I DON'T GOT YOU, BABE... I DON'T GOT YOU, BABE...
7-9
© 1988 United Feature Syndicate Inc
DEPRESSION SETS IN. HE BECOMES DEPENDENT ON WINE COOLERS AND DRIFTS FROM HEALTH SPA TO HEALTH SPA SEARCHING FOR CHER...
SORRY MAN, FROM BEHIND I THOUGHT YOU WERE SOMEONE ELSE...
TO BE CONTINUED.

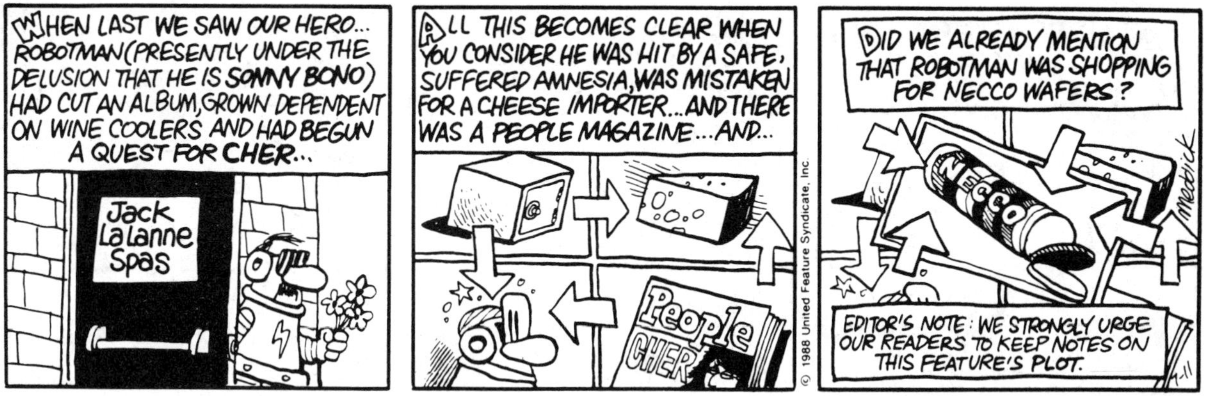
WHEN LAST WE SAW OUR HERO... ROBOTMAN (PRESENTLY UNDER THE DELUSION THAT HE IS SONNY BONO) HAD CUT AN ALBUM, GROWN DEPENDENT ON WINE COOLERS AND HAD BEGUN A QUEST FOR CHER...
Jack LaLanne Spas
ALL THIS BECOMES CLEAR WHEN YOU CONSIDER HE WAS HIT BY A SAFE, SUFFERED AMNESIA, WAS MISTAKEN FOR A CHEESE IMPORTER... AND THERE WAS A PEOPLE MAGAZINE... AND...
People
CHER
© 1988 United Feature Syndicate, Inc.
DID WE ALREADY MENTION THAT ROBOTMAN WAS SHOPPING FOR NECCO WAFERS?
NECCO
EDITOR'S NOTE: WE STRONGLY URGE OUR READERS TO KEEP NOTES ON THIS FEATURE'S PLOT.
Meddick

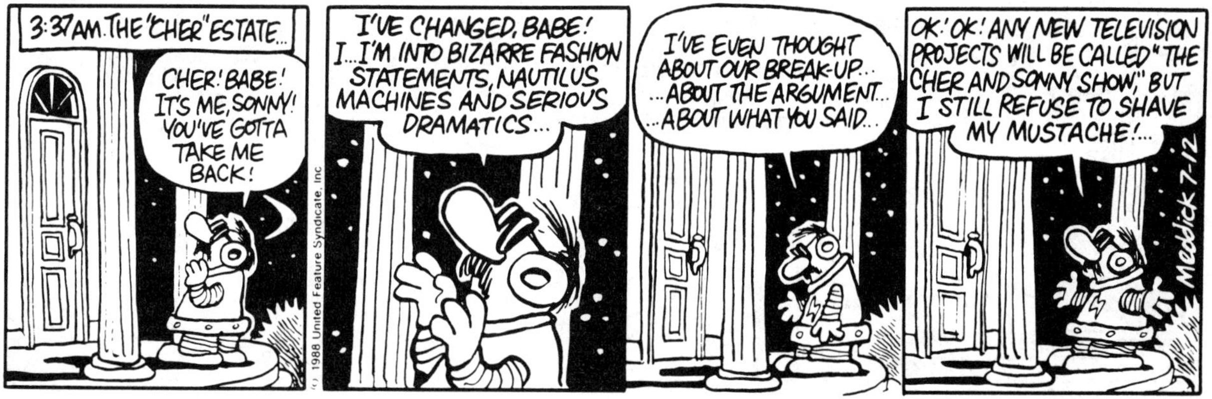
3:37 AM. THE "CHER" ESTATE...
CHER! BABE! IT'S ME, SONNY! YOU'VE GOTTA TAKE ME BACK!
© 1988 United Feature Syndicate, Inc.
I'VE CHANGED, BABE! I...I'M INTO BIZARRE FASHION STATEMENTS, NAUTILUS MACHINES AND SERIOUS DRAMATICS...
I'VE EVEN THOUGHT ABOUT OUR BREAK-UP... ...ABOUT THE ARGUMENT... ...ABOUT WHAT YOU SAID...
OK! OK! ANY NEW TELEVISION PROJECTS WILL BE CALLED "THE CHER AND SONNY SHOW," BUT I STILL REFUSE TO SHAVE MY MUSTACHE!...
Meddick 7-12

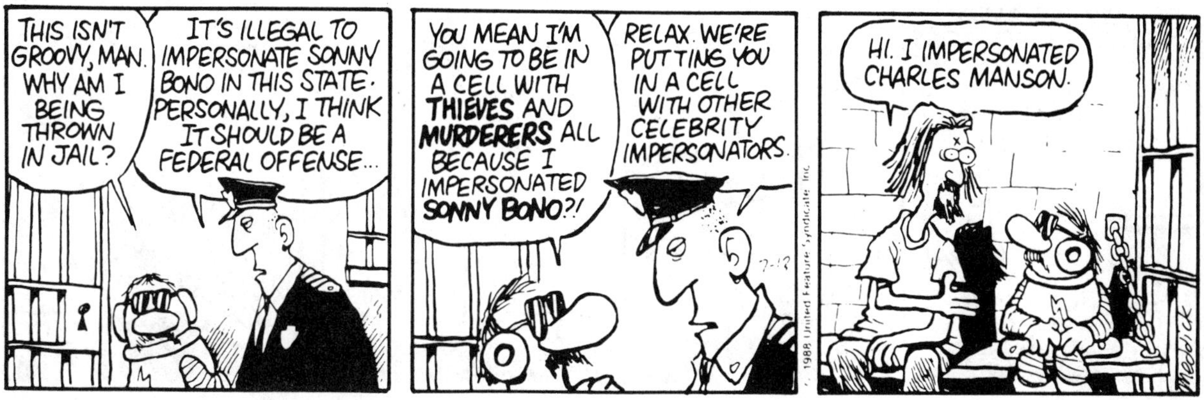
THIS ISN'T GROOVY, MAN. WHY AM I BEING THROWN IN JAIL?
IT'S ILLEGAL TO IMPERSONATE SONNY BONO IN THIS STATE. PERSONALLY, I THINK IT SHOULD BE A FEDERAL OFFENSE...
YOU MEAN I'M GOING TO BE IN A CELL WITH THIEVES AND MURDERERS ALL BECAUSE I IMPERSONATED SONNY BONO?!
RELAX. WE'RE PUTTING YOU IN A CELL WITH OTHER CELEBRITY IMPERSONATORS.
© 1988 United Feature Syndicate, Inc.
HI. I IMPERSONATED CHARLES MANSON.
Meddick

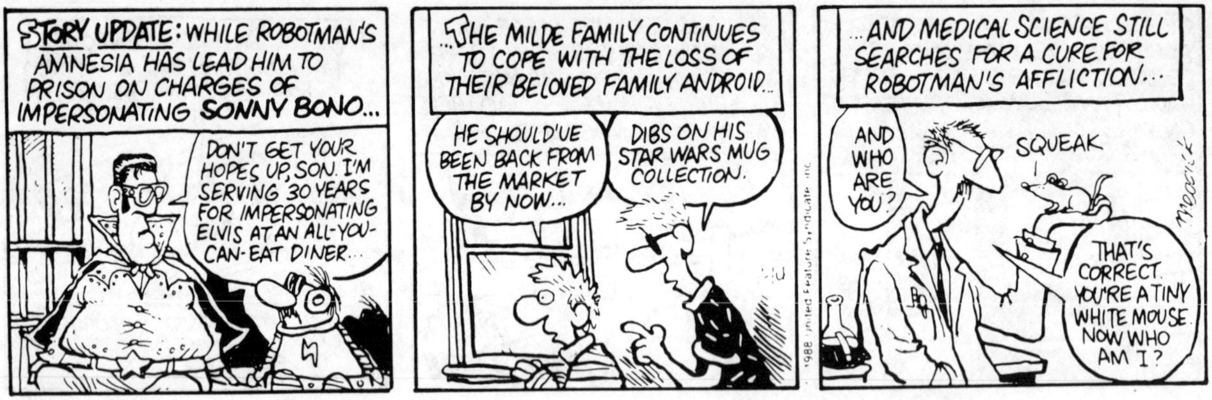
STORY UPDATE: WHILE ROBOTMAN'S AMNESIA HAS LEAD HIM TO PRISON ON CHARGES OF IMPERSONATING SONNY BONO...
DON'T GET YOUR HOPES UP, SON. I'M SERVING 30 YEARS FOR IMPERSONATING ELVIS AT AN ALL-YOU-CAN-EAT DINER...
...THE MILDE FAMILY CONTINUES TO COPE WITH THE LOSS OF THEIR BELOVED FAMILY ANDROID...
HE SHOULD'VE BEEN BACK FROM THE MARKET BY NOW...
DIBS ON HIS STAR WARS MUG COLLECTION.
© 1988 United Feature Syndicate, Inc.
...AND MEDICAL SCIENCE STILL SEARCHES FOR A CURE FOR ROBOTMAN'S AFFLICTION...
AND WHO ARE YOU?
SQUEAK
THAT'S CORRECT. YOU'RE A TINY WHITE MOUSE. NOW WHO AM I?
MEGLICK

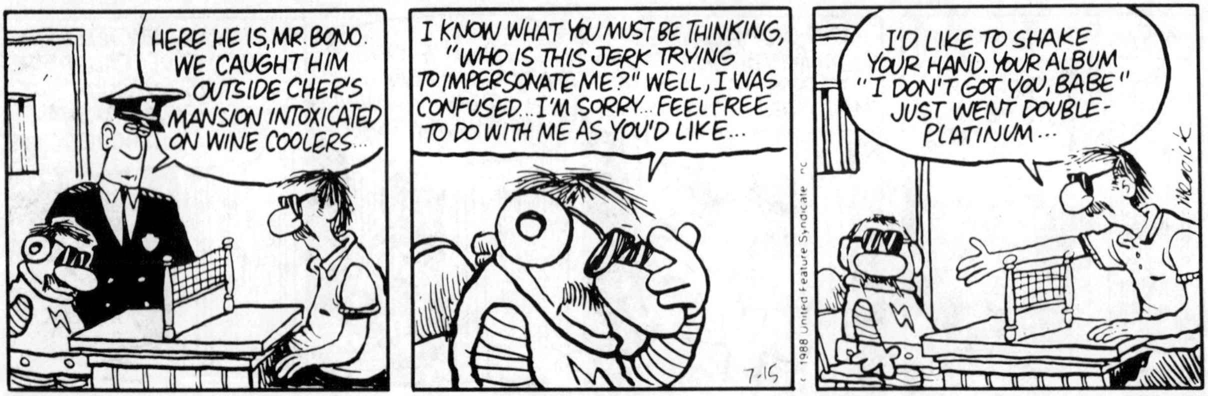
HERE HE IS, MR. BONO. WE CAUGHT HIM OUTSIDE CHER'S MANSION INTOXICATED ON WINE COOLERS...
I KNOW WHAT YOU MUST BE THINKING, "WHO IS THIS JERK TRYING TO IMPERSONATE ME?" WELL, I WAS CONFUSED... I'M SORRY... FEEL FREE TO DO WITH ME AS YOU'D LIKE...
7-15
© 1988 United Feature Syndicate, Inc.
I'D LIKE TO SHAKE YOUR HAND. YOUR ALBUM "I DON'T GOT YOU, BABE" JUST WENT DOUBLE-PLATINUM...
MEGLICK

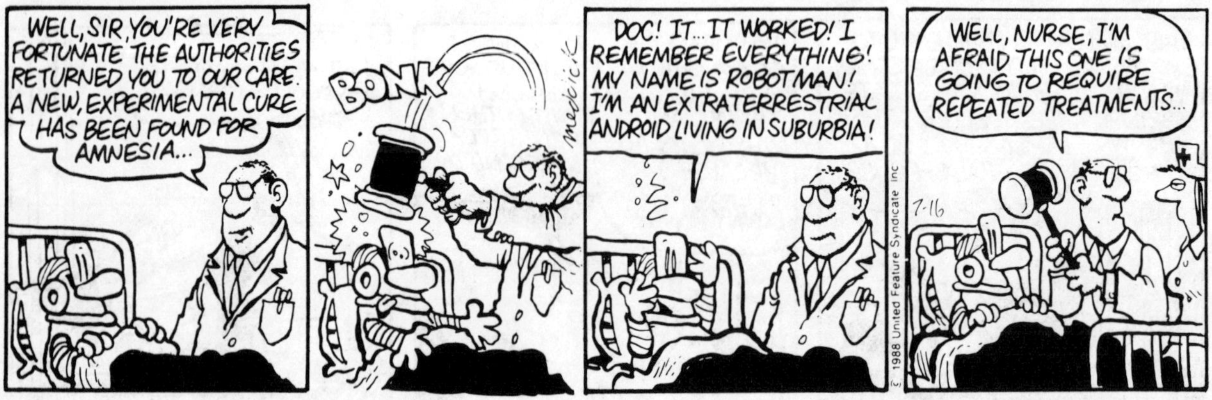
WELL, SIR, YOU'RE VERY FORTUNATE THE AUTHORITIES RETURNED YOU TO OUR CARE. A NEW, EXPERIMENTAL CURE HAS BEEN FOUND FOR AMNESIA...
BONK
MEGLICK
DOC! IT... IT WORKED! I REMEMBER EVERYTHING! MY NAME IS ROBOTMAN! I'M AN EXTRATERRESTRIAL ANDROID LIVING IN SUBURBIA!
© 1988 United Feature Syndicate, Inc.
7-16
WELL, NURSE, I'M AFRAID THIS ONE IS GOING TO REQUIRE REPEATED TREATMENTS...

THE COMPLETE ROBOTMAN®

DON'T SETTLE FOR LESS!
SIGN UP NOW!

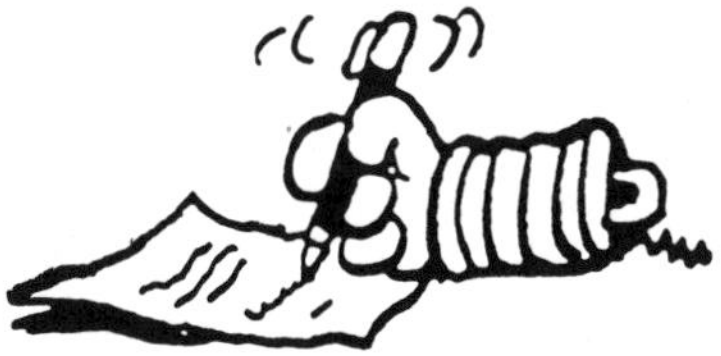

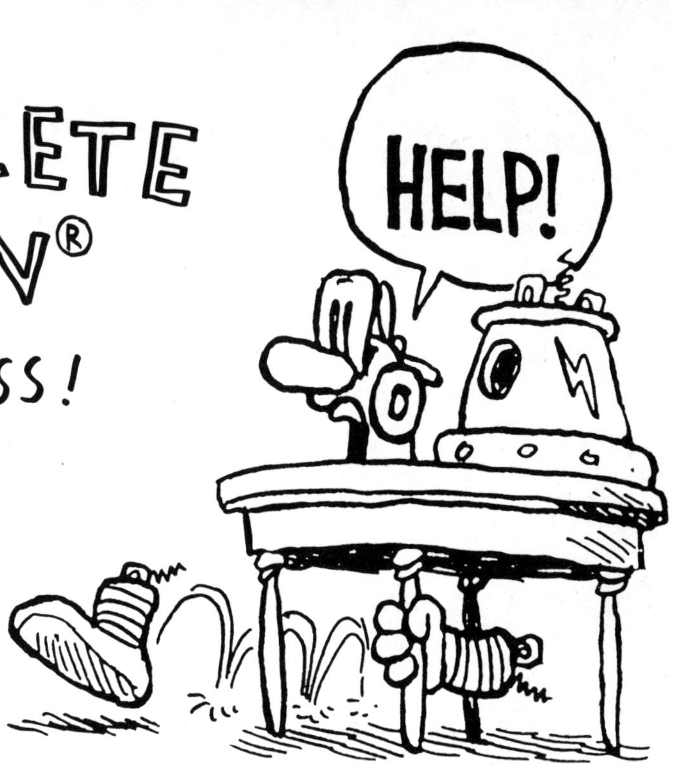
HELP!

- ☐ **Robotman Takes Off** $5.95
- ☐ **Robotman: the Untold Story** $5.95
- ☐ **Cyberpunktrek** $6.95

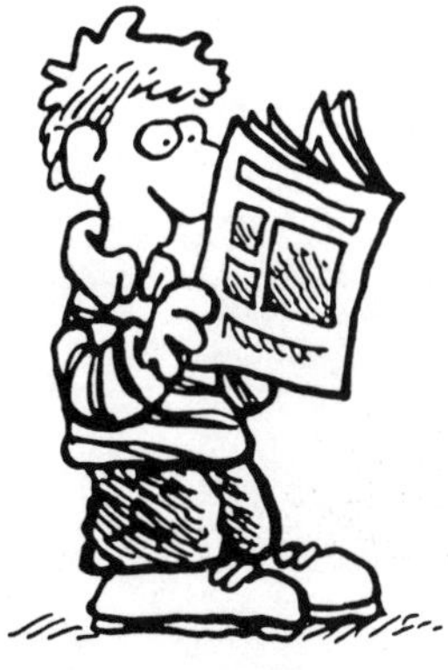

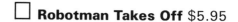

My check for $ __________ is enclosed. Please add .50 per book for postage and handling. Make check or money order payable to Pharos Books.

NAME ______________________________

ADDRESS ______________________________

CITY ______________ STATE ______________ ZIP ________

Return to: Pharos Books, Sales Department, 200 Park Avenue, New York, NY 10166